ALASKA
BEAR
TALES

ALASKA BEAR TALES

LARRY KANIUT

ALASKA NORTHWEST PUBLISHING COMPANY
Anchorage, Alaska

First printing: 1983
Eighth printing: 1988

Library of Congress cataloging in publication data:
Kaniut, Larry.
  Alaska bear tales.
  Bibliography: p.
  Includes index.
  1. Bears.   2. Bear hunting — Alaska.
3. Dangerous animals — Alaska.   4. Mammals — Alaska.
I. Title.
QL737.C27K36   1983   559.74′446′09798   83-5974
ISBN 0-88240-232-3

Design and Illustration by Barbara Swanson

Alaska Northwest Publishing Company
137 E. 7th, Anchorage, Alaska 99501

Printed in U.S.A.

Contents

DEDICATION

With all my love I dedicate my "bear book" to my wife Pamela and our three children, Ginger, Jill, and Benny.

ACKNOWLEDGMENTS

Without the help, willingness and work of dozens of people *Alaska Bear Tales* would not exist. My thanks go to those individuals whose stories fill these pages, those who steered me to stories and information, and those representatives of various departments and organizations who willingly gave me their time and information.

INTRODUCTION

In many ways it seems as if I was destined early in life to compile this book. My stepfather, Chuck Jenkins, introduced me to the out-of-doors. An insatiable hunger for adventure stories, primarily those involving bears developed. While I was in junior high school my Sunday school teacher, Wayne Soper, of Clarkston, Washington, whetted my appetite with his Alaskan hunting stories, and he took me to view a James Bond movie on Alaska.

In 1966 Principal Ray Hanes of A.J. Dimond High School, in Anchorage, Alaska, employed me to teach English, and later Literature of the North for the same department.

This spurred me to approach Alaska Northwest Publishing Company about the possibility of a book of North "adventures." The publisher suggested a book of man-bear encounters.

We hope this is not only a factual book but also one the reader will find both entertaining and educational.

Our search for Alaskan bear encounters began in January 1975 with research in *ALASKA*® magazine, and its original title, *The ALASKA SPORTSMAN*®, which began publication in 1935. The search widened as more and more reports came to me by word of mouth. The list of contacts grew from a few friends and acquaintances to more than 200 individuals who had had experiences with bears that seemed worth recounting. There were hundreds of letters, more than a hundred telephone contacts, and interviews with hundreds of people.

I cannot attest to the veracity of all the stories contained herein, but I have tried to present them as they came to me. Stories that have been "stretched" should be obvious, and are not to be found in any serious section.

We're sorry we could not locate *all* of the best bear stories in Alaska. Many people and sources would not comply with requests for stories. Many stories, for instance, abound along the Alaska Railroad, but many unfortunately were unavailable.

It would have been nice if we had gotten more stories about Native-bear (that is, Indian, Eskimo, and Aleut) experiences and traditions, but these are difficult to uncover. There are undoubtedly super bear stories "out there." One of the most extraordinary tales, the mauling and death of trapper King Thurmond, was discovered just prior to typing the final manuscript.

Many people were reluctant to share bear experiences for different reasons: they were too close to the victim, didn't want their names associated with the story, were on the fringes of illegality (game regulations), did not want to appear boastful, felt their stories would be disbelieved, and so on.

There is no attempt herein to create a grisly compilation of horrors, but the fact is, when bears attack, blood usually flows.

I hope that my descriptions of various bear maulings are sufficiently graphic to motivate the reader to study and choose a reasonable course of action, and to use every precaution, when in the proximity of bears. They are, like the heading of one of the chapters to follow, unpredictable.

Larry Kaniut
Anchorage, Alaska

THE BROWNIE (GRIZZLY) IS BIG AND TOUGH

"I must confess that after 30 years of hunting these animals it would be impossible for me to distinguish between a grizzly and brown bear of the same size if I saw them walking side by side." *(The late Andy Simons, famed Alaskan guide.* Sam Langford, "Bears I Have Met," Alaska Hunting Annual, *1970-71)*

"You cannot judge a bear by his track. I've seen some 6-foot brown bear that would have a mammoth big foot; and then you get another bear that's 10-foot, and it's got a small foot." *(Joe Beaty, former Kodiak cattle rancher, in an interview with author, November 1977)*

"A grizzly can lick anything alive, and I mean anything too. He'll spot a lion or a tiger two blows, then flatten him with one swing of his paw. A grizzly can crack a steer's neck with one swing . . . Match two tons of grizzlies against two tons of elephant — then dig a hole to bury your elephant in." *(Fred Mansell as told to Ed Green, "The Unknown Quantity,"* The ALASKA SPORTSMAN®, *August 1938)*

"Alders the size of a man's legs were broken and scattered about and the ground was torn up as if by a huge machine. The bear and Pete were lying a few feet apart, both covered with blood and gore. Pete's rifle was broken in half. . . ." *(The late Alf Madsen, Master*

Guide, "What Caliber for the Kodiak?", The ALASKA SPORTS-MAN®, September 1957)

Over the past several years more than one bear-wise Alaskan has poked fun at the experts who have stamped and labeled the Great Land's ursine inhabitants. Generally speaking, there are four bears in Alaska ranging in size from the smallest to the largest — black, grizzly, polar and brown. In the early 1900s Dr. C. Hart Merriam, Chief of the U.S. Biological Survey, U.S. Department of Agriculture, devoted monumental efforts to the study and classification of grizzlies in North America. He came up with 84 subspecies of grizzly.

There are two schools of thought in classifying animals — the *splitters* and the *lumpers*. Those who attempt to classify under a myriad of classifications are *splitters* while those who lump the Alaskan groups into one category are *lumpers*.

There *are* differences in these bears, however; the major assumption nowadays is that brown bears inhabit the coastal areas of Alaska and the grizzlies dwell inland. Because the trophy conscious people representing the Boone and Crockett Club (riflemen's big game record club) and the Pope and Young Club (archers' division of big game records) wanted accurate records kept on bears, it was arbitrarily established that any bear of the grizzly clan taken within 75 miles of tidewater was a brown bear; others of the tribe were grizzlies.

More recently, however, the Boone and Crockett Club has designated the Alaska Range as the physical boundary. Animals to the north and west of the Alaska Range are called grizzlies, while animals on the eastern slopes of the Alaska Range and southward are called brown bears.

Most guides and knowledgeable bear persons in Alaska consider the brown and the grizzly the same animal, with varying shades of difference. In this book the term *brown* refers to the coastal bruin (including the islands of Admiralty, Baranof, Chichagof and Kodiak); *grizzly* denotes Interior grizzlies; and *brown/grizzly* designates these animals in general.

The brown/grizzly bear is an awesome creature — a magnificent animal worthy of the praise given him by such experts as the late Frank Dufresne and the late William H. Chase. Frank Dufresne was once Director of the Alaska Game Commission and wrote *No Room For Bears* (Holt, Rinehart and Winston, 1965). Will Chase was a noted physician and mayor of Cordova. His *Alaska's*

Mammoth Brown Bears (Burton Publishing Co., 1947), which analyzes brown bears, is now a collector's item.

At birth the brown/grizzly is hairless and blind, and weighs but a pound or two. But during the many years he roams the wilds, he grows to immense proportions (evidence indicates some brown/ grizzlies reach almost 30 years of age). Alf Madsen, Master Guide, made an interesting observation in the October 1955 issue of *The ALASKA SPORTSMAN®*: "One fall, late in November, we shot an exceptionally large bear. In skinning his left hind quarter we found an old Russian musket ball. It was in the heavy muscle of the leg where it had flattened from the impact. It was covered by a heavy coat of sinew and skin which adhered to it. This bear was minus his tail and ear and had no teeth.

"Long scar tissues on his hind quarters and neck indicated that he was a veteran of many battles. His claws were extremely heavy and white and very long. From these indications one could easily believe that a bear of this size could reach the age of 70. The only definite proof of a bear's age, however, can be estimated by its residence in a zoo." [Biologists determine bear age by analyzing cross sections of teeth, counting annual rings like those of a tree.]

Gust Jensen is an Athabascan Indian who now lives in Anchorage. About 1938, Gust, his brother and a cousin were hunting bears for food for their Iliamna Lake village. They had just killed a bear. Gust, alert, vigorous, white-haired little man that he is, told me, "We were out hunting. We had the biggest bear that has ever been shot over there in Iniskin Bay. And I got shot, and then they rushed me back to the village, and we lost the hide (the tide got it). That bear must have been a 14-footer. I couldn't lift his head, and I was 18 years old and I could lift pretty good."

From the *ALASKA SPORTSMAN®*, October 1966, in "Gunshot" by Bill Vaudrin: ". . . as they worked over it, they remarked again and again about the unbelievable size of the brute. The head alone was half and again as broad as a man's shoulders. To this day Gust remembers having great difficulty in trying to lift it by himself, even though he was enjoying the strength of youth.

"When they finally rolled the giant carcass aside and straightened out the hide, it measured just over fourteen feet in length without stretching."

In those days people weren't much interested in the size of a bear's skull. It was common for hunters and guides to leave 27- and 28-inch skulls in the field prior to Boone and Crockett's keeping records on skull size.

One of Alaska's great guides, Hal Waugh, was in on some

monster bear kills. In 1951 a client of Hal's shot a bear that had just left hibernation, with a hide that squared 10'8" (average of the greatest length from tip of nose to tip of tail and the greatest width — usually from claw tip to claw tip across the shoulders), had a skull score of 29$^{11}\!/_{16}$" (length plus width) and the fleshed pelt weighed 191 pounds. The bear weighed an estimated 1,600 pounds, alive.

The largest bodied bear ever taken by a hunter guided by Hal Waugh was shot in 1969 by Herman Gibson of Seagoville, Texas, and Hal estimated its weight at close to 2,000 pounds. Its hide weighed 212 pounds on the hunting camp scales at Karluk Lake on Kodiak Island.

Kodiak was the site of another hunt Hal booked in the 1950s with Grancel Fritz of New York City, New York, who shot a brownie. The measurement around its skinned neck was 45½". The bear measured 57" from the top of the front shoulder to mid-pad on the foreleg. The hide squared 10' 3½", rear pad was 13¾"x9", and its longest claw was six inches long.

Several men who have faced the all-out charge of a brown bear have commented that the animal's eyes were level with their own. Calvin H. Barkdull described just such a bear in the June 1954 issue of *The ALASKA SPORTSMAN®*. He had heard about a huge bear in Pybus Bay, Admiralty Island, had shot another large brown and was returning the next day to retrieve its hide when he spotted a huge bear. "This was without a doubt the freak monster of Pybus Bay.

"I had a fairly good view of him. He looked to be five feet tall standing on all fours, and 11 feet long . . . I was satisfied with a look at what I believe was undoubtedly the biggest bear in Alaska, and probably in the world."

A few days later Barkdull measured the monster's track. "I had seen his tracks in the hard mud. With my elbow in the heel of his hind foot track, the ends of my fingers came to the imprint of the long claw marks. It was at least four inches longer than any other bear track I had ever seen."

While working as a trail foreman for the U.S. Forest Service Robert McCully was run up a tree near Juneau by an angry sow with a cub. She stood on her hind legs and tried to reach him, shedding bark and limbs with her razor sharp claws. Unable to connect, she left. McCully's colleagues returned later and measured her claw marks—exactly 11 feet, 6 inches above the ground.

Fred Mansell related to *The ALASKA SPORTSMAN®* in August 1938 that "I've seen claw marks on trees as high as 13 feet from the ground. No, I don't know why bears leave their marks on trees and I doubt if anyone else does.

"I killed the biggest bear ever taken in Canadian territory at Toba and he was five feet from his pads to his shoulders. His hide measured 11' 2" from his buttocks to his nose when it was hung up.

In May 1948 the late Bob Reeve, famed bush pilot of Anchorage, killed an Alaska Peninsula brown bear with a hide that squared 11' 4". Its skull measured 19%16"x11½". The bear's live weight was 1,800 pounds, and the estimated fall weight was 2,200 pounds. The bear measured 5' 4" at the shoulder and stood over 12 feet on its hind legs.

Hind legs were about all Bob Brown saw one fall while hunting deer on the Joe Beaty ranch on Kodiak. Bob, currently a sergeant with the Alaska Department of Public Safety in Anchorage, was sitting in his vehicle scanning a field in the predawn when he spotted an enormous brownie on the beach. He started the vehicle's engine in an attempt to drive closer, but Mr. Ursus would have none of that. The bear hightailed it for cover, leaving behind tracks that Bob and Joe measured with a steel tape. The running strides were nearly 20 feet between tracks. Bob, wearing size 15 rubber hip waders, stood in the hind print with both boots. His boots were side by side, and the bear's print extended on either side as well as beyond the tips and heels of his boots.

Big bears are not as plentiful as they used to be, and different reasons are given for the lack of monster bears today. Judge George Folta, a famous Alaskan judge, believed that in the early 1900s brown bears grew larger because of a greater abundance of salmon. When he arrived in Kodiak in 1913, there was a bear hide hanging from a dock that measured 13' 6" in length.

Others feel that the lack of large bears is due to hunting pressure which has eliminated the big bears, thus reducing the breeding stock for producing huge offspring.

Lee Miller, game technician for the Alaska Department of Fish & Game, shared his thoughts on bear size with me. "I feel the bears today are just as big as they ever were. I have probably measured more bear hides than anyone in the world and you have to be very careful when you talk about a 10-, 11- or 12-foot bear.

"A bear's hide size just depends on what condition the hide is in and how you stretch it — that's why Boone and Crockett uses the skull measurement instead of measuring the hide, it's pretty hard to stretch a skull. The hide measurement will certainly give you an indication of a huge bear.

"In the spring of 1980, four record book bears were killed in Game Management Unit 8 (Kodiak Island) and three were taken in GMU 9 (the Alaska Peninsula). A skull was found in 1979 that measured 30¼ inches (total of length plus width)."

The brown/grizzly's physical size is more than matched by his strength. Guide Bernd A. Gaedeke of Fairbanks told about three men hunting in Southeastern Alaska when a young assistant guide accompanying them went ashore to pick blueberries. He began picking in a patch where a brown bear and her cub were eating berries. The bear made a few false charges toward the man who ultimately threw his berry pail at the sow. She charged him; he ran for the skiff. (A brown/grizzly can cover nearly 50 feet a second. Captain Bob Penman of the Alaska Department of Public Safety told me he'd heard of bears being clocked at 35 miles per hour and outrunning a horse in rough terrain. Veteran Alaskan guide, Ralph Young of Petersburg, claimed a brownie in full possession of its faculties could cover 100 feet in two seconds!)

As the men watched helplessly from their boat at anchor, "The sow took one swipe at the luckless man and his head went flying through the air. He took about 10 or 15 more steps, and the sow, after knocking his head off with one clean sweep, went after the head and batted it around several more times." (Charles J. Keim, *Alaska Game Trails with a Master Guide*, Alaska Northwest Publishing Company, 1977)

Many instances exist of brown/grizzlies killing black bears with a single blow of the paw. One such case was recorded by Fred Mansell in *The ALASKA SPORTSMAN®* in August 1938: "The grizzly had lain near a big log and when the black bear came by he'd reached over the log and knocked the black bear flat with one swing. He'd picked him up, then, and smashed him down over the log. There wasn't a whole bone left in that black bear's body."

An old trapper named Sherrett once watched an aged brownie digging under a fallen spruce on a mountainside opposite him. It was obvious the starving bear had bruin chops on his mind as he dug a black bear from its den. A battle royal ensued, and the brownie won. Sherrett shot the victor and examined both animals. The brown was nearly toothless (from age), and the black's skull was crushed and beaten to a pulp by the hammer-like blows of the brown bear. (*The ALASKA SPORTSMAN®*, January 1939)

The brown/grizzly is known for the battering power his paws possess when in contention for a mate. Few male bears grow to adulthood without some body damage. More than one bear has paid the price for a mate with broken jaw, teeth or sightless eyes.

A battle between two boars for a sow's attention was related by Frank Dufresne in the December 1963 *The ALASKA SPORTS-MAN®*: "Survivors of these sanguinary contests sometimes plod around the tundra like punch-drunk prize-fighters, their massive heads covered with scar tissue. Teeth are shattered against the skulls of their opponents. Cavities develop, raw nerves are exposed and toothaches plague them for the rest of their days. Grouchy? Who wouldn't be?"

A bear that can break another's jaw can do considerable damage to other creatures. Joe Beaty, former Kodiak rancher, told me, "I've never seen a bear walk up and knock a critter down, but by the evidence of the carcass, you could tell they had their neck broken with one swat of the paw, a grown steer. The bulk of the animals that I've seen killed, the bear will bite the bone in the neck and almost immediately, kinda crush clear through it. It had to be before the animal's heart stopped because you could tell by the hemorrhaging. I pretty near always opened 'em up and took the hide off."

One of the most amazing incidents regarding a brown/grizzly's power was related in F.M. Young's *Man Meets Grizzly* (pages 183-186, Houghton, Mifflin Company, 1980). When traveling down Anchorage to Mabel Mine early in the 20th century at the age of 12, Young experienced a bear-moose confrontation. He and his father watched from horseback while a brown bear stalked a bull and two cows. For eight hours the humans watched the two beasts struggle. Finally the bear moved to one side and looked back at the battered bull. The bull made a final charge, heaving the bear against a rock ledge, pinning him there until the agonizing moans of the bear died away, upon which the moose retreated. The Youngs measured the bear's body which was 13' 6" from nose to tail. On their return trip a week later they found the skeleton of the moose, which may have succumbed later to wolves.

Gust Jensen told me about a bear-moose confrontation: "Bull moose can get best of a bear because the bull's got that horn; but the bear, if he gets the bull's horns, then he can break that bull's neck. My brother-in-law seen 'em fightin' one time, a bear and a moose. They fought for hours. He said the bear is powerful, caught ahold of the moose somewheres along the side. He put his claws in there and pulled the ribs right out, the whole side, broke his neck."

Another bull moose with a broken neck was observed by guide Clark Engle, of Anchorage. In the fall of 1974 he flew over a recent moose kill, dropped down for a closer look and noticed a large grizzly on the moose. Clark said, "You could see the bull's neck had been broken because it was twisted back, and the antlers were laying across the backbone. The bear had actually twisted the moose's neck and killed the moose this way. I'm talking about a high mountain bear that has never seen a fish in his life other than a small fish like a grayling. Such a bear will go 800 pounds maximum. I'm sure the moose outweighed him; a big bull moose will weigh well over a thousand pounds."

From bending necks to bending barrels, the bear can do it all. Many hunters have had their rifles swatted from their hands and have witnessed various states of destruction which include bent barrels (on heavy bore rifles), splintered stocks and chewed floor plates. In the fall of 1912 or 1913 a prospector from Nome had a run-in with a sow grizzly. When she attacked him roaring like a runaway freight train, he automatically jammed his double-barrel into her mouth and touched off both triggers. She died instantly, but in her death throes she clamped her jaws onto the shotgun, crushing the barrels. (*The ALASKA SPORTSMAN*®, January 1939)

Several rifles have been found at the scenes of maulings with barrels bent. One such weapon was discovered with a half-inch bend in the barrel, and it was surmised that the bear accomplished this with a shake of the head while biting onto the barrel.

In September 1962, while moose hunting near Puritan Creek at Mile 90 of the Glenn Highway, Harold Tuttle of Anchorage was mauled by a grizzly which left his .30-'06 in the shape of a boomerang.

Other phenomenal examples of raw power include bears moving carcasses of large animals like steers or moose. John Graybill of Peters Creek, Alaska, saw a bear drag a moose up a mountain at Gold Hill Lake. They had killed a big moose and gutted it prior to darkness. "Next day we were going back for the moose, and the bear had gotten hold of that moose and dragged it uphill through the alders (I can't even drag a piece of moose *down*hill in the alders). Where the moose would hang up, it would tear alders out roots and all; you could see where he uprooted 'em just like you took a plow through there for several hundred yards up that hill, right through the alders."

Brown/grizzlies are powerful alive, but they are also tenacious in death. An astonishing account of a bear's refusal to die involved three British Columbia Indians who were hunting bears for their hides prior to 1938. They were hunting the slopes of Groundhog Mountain in the Cassiar District by the light of the moon one night near their tent. Two were on the ground while the third sat on a horse nearby. They began firing their .45-90s at a grizzly which charged them. The horseman rode to a nearby camp and summoned help while his companions stood their ground and fired their last three shots into the bear's chest as he reached them.

When the rescue party arrived, they found a mass of blood and bone — what had been the two Indians. The bear had departed. The rescuers followed the bear and found it dead. They opened it up and found his heart was shot almost clean out; but he had gone 400 yards after killing and mutilating both men.

Fred Mansell was with the party that examined the bear. He also examined another bear carcass which he told about in *The ALASKA SPORTSMAN®* in August 1938. A fisherman and his wife had spotted a bear on the Marka River in Southeastern Alaska, and the man shot it. He allowed some time for the animal to die, then approached it. When he bent over the animal, the bear reared with slashing fury. Its first blow smashed the man's head while the second ripped all the flesh from his shoulders and ribs. The bear cuffed him a few times then wandered into the brush.

While the bear mauled her husband, the woman screamed, attracting the attention of Mansell. Fred was aghast at the sight of the dead husband, his ribs stuck out through his shirt and his broken Martin-Henry rifle lay nearby. Fred followed the beast into the brush 200 yards distant and found it dead. He cut the bear open and found that the bullet that the dead man had fired had split the heart completely in half.

A grizzly's ability to pack lead is an age-old subject. One reads about mammoth bears being killed with one shot from a .22 rifle and yet others having been shot several times with .375 Magnums and still going. Some hunters tell of shooting out the heart of a bear and watching it continue on its path of destruction, but they draw any number of cynics.

An incredible account of a brownie killed with a .22 was related in the January 1946 issue of *The ALASKA SPORTSMAN®*. Two men were in the bear's path with but a .22 for a weapon. Norman Rinehart fired from 75 yards.

The bear sat down and slapped himself in the face with both paws (the bullet had struck an inch from his right eye). Rinehart awakened his partner who handed him the tiny shells one at a time. The next shot hit bruin in the jaw causing him to paw the air and turn around. The next two shots struck the beast under the ear, and he turned his head. The fifth shot hit the bear at the base of the skull, penetrated the brain and killed the animal instantly.

The bear's head (not skull) was 20 inches long and 14 inches wide and the body weight was around 1,400 pounds.

Another brownie was taken with a .220 as a man surprised it at close range. Jim Woodworth, author of *The Kodiak Bear,* and his partner were hunting seals on Afognak Island just north of Kodiak. His buddy had worked his way around some large boulders when a bear stepped from behind one. The hunter poked the rifle toward the bear's head and squeezed the trigger. The bullet, a .220 Wilson Arrow, hit the bear in the mouth, exploded at the bottom of the brain pan and killed the bear instantly, breaking every bone in the skull.

Not all hunters, however, have had the good fortune of these isolated small bore examples. Many are the stories of men who have exhausted several magazines of ammunition only to see bruin continue his death-dealing charge. Gust Jensen shared with me a time when he and his brother were charged by a sow with cubs. "I had a .270. He had a .30-'06, and we were pretty good shots, we don't miss very much. She spotted us; and she started.

"I think I was the first one, I kneeled down good and I started shooting, and I know I was hitting her all the time. When my gun went empty, my brother started shooting and I start loading. And that bear was within five feet of us before she dropped. She had blood pouring out of her face. When we skinned her out, we found we had shot the heart out. I don't know how she ever came that far. We shot her about 15 times — I emptied my gun twice for 10 total shots."

More than one monster bear has been stopped only after two or three men bombarded it with a dozen or more bullets. In one case three men were tracking a wounded bear which attacked them. Paul Polson, Woren Knapp and E.H. Pomeroy were hunting their winter's supply of meat in the fall of 1905. They were around the mouth of the Little Delta River on the Tanana Flats when the bear charged.

They commenced shooting rapidly, knocking him down with every shot, but he would regain his feet and continue the charge. The final shot that dropped him for good at 50 feet was a neck shot. The bear had been hit 14 times, and any one of the shots would have proved fatal within 10 or 15 minutes.

The December 1941 issue of *The ALASKA SPORTSMAN®* carried an account by Robert E. McCully describing a bear's power to absorb lead: "When a bear charges a man, the man must shoot fast and true or he is crushed as one would crush an ant. I have seen a bear that was blasted by nine shots from .375 caliber rifles before he went down to stay. His heart and lungs were blown to bits and his spine smashed before his death-dealing rush was ended. And any guide will say that this is not an isolated case. The vitality of these gigantic brutes, their ability to absorb the most terrific punishment, is astonishing even to guides who have witnessed the deaths of dozens of them."

Hal Waugh used to say that his .300 H and H converted into a .375 Weatherby would stop any bear with one shot, and those who knew Hal could not recall any bear needing more than one salvo from that weapon.

John Graybill of Peters Creek tells of shooting a bear in the head without killing it instantly. His shots "shattered the skull, broke the skull to pieces, from the impact of the bullet; and that bear just raised cain for at least 10 or 12, maybe 15 minutes before it died."

A diehard bruin visited Clark Engle's camp on the Alaska Peninsula. He was guiding some hunters who'd gone to bed for the night when the bear showed up. Clark hollered at it to scare it away . . . "they don't understand regular English; you got to use certain language, and most of it's four letter words." The bear left but returned shortly, Clark recalls. "He's a woofin'. When they start to woof and chomp their teeth, they're upset. That's a very unpredictable animal right at that point — you don't know if they're gonna charge you, run off or just chew up everything that's around.

"I hollered to the hunters, 'He's back! Don't breathe; don't move; don't do nothin'!' About that time there was a roar of a rifle out of the tent. The bear was standing about five or six feet away from their tent; and the hunter stuck the barrel of his .458 out that tent door and shot that bear — that's well over 5,000 foot pounds of energy that hit this bear. He hit him just underneath the eye, tore the zygomatic bone out, kind of a cheekbone of the bear, and down, broke both jaw bones (we found this out later) and landed underneath the hide. That bear absorbed every bit of that muzzle energy, *every bit of it!* The bear went down and was just like a rubber ball, right back up.

"The bear was so confused it had no idea what happened to it. The bear then came straight towards me; and I turned one loose at it, dropped it, and it got right back up. The hunter shot again and hit the bear somewheres in the rib cage, and the bear didn't even go off its feet — it stumbled but didn't go down. It continued and I hit it again and knocked it down. The bear got up and turned sideways, cleared the end of the building and I shot it and tipped it over the bank, down towards the creek."

That bear would not wander into anyone else's camp. Clark's

awe and respect for this magnificent animal was obvious when he said, "He was a little over a nine-foot bear and weighed on to a thousand pounds. It's amazing what these animals can absorb. They're fantastic animals; I just can't say enough about them."   □

THEY'LL ATTACK
WITHOUT WARNING

"Some people claim to believe that if a bear is unmolested, he will go about his business and leave his human neighbors to do the same. Nine times out of ten, or possibly even ninety-nine times out of a hundred, that may be true; however, it's that hundredth time for which the woodsman must ever be on the alert." (Otis H. Speer, "Big Bears are Bold," The ALASKA SPORTSMAN®, December 1943)

Wilderness Nightmare

The following account was adapted from a story given to me by Al Thompson which was written by his wife Joyce and titled "Wilderness Nightmare." Their nightmare was truly an experience that few people could have survived. Few encounter this giant of beasts in hand-to-hand combat and live to tell about it. Joyce's story is a tribute to their preparation, experience, cool-headedness and determination.

"His head was huge and round, and he looked like gray driftwood in the moonlight. He towered above us momentarily as we lay in our Visqueen covered leanto, then he roared down upon us, trying to tear me from my sleeping bag. A scream passed from my lips, which was never heard above the rage of the huge brown bear. I knew it would be a sudden death, with his strong claws ripping through my flesh; or perhaps those powerful jaws would break my neck first. I could see no way of coming out of this alive and was sure I was going to die.

"Dying was the farthest thing from my mind in September 1972, when my husband Al Thompson and I planned our back-packing trip for trophy moose into the Kenai National Moose Range on Alaska's famed Kenai Peninsula, an area mostly closed to aircraft or tracked vehicles. We planned to catch the last 10 days of moose season, which closed the end of September. Al was archery hunting; but if time ran out and he failed to get one, I would shoot one with my rifle. We only wanted to take one moose and had arranged for horses to pack out the meat should we succeed.

"The night before leaving, we gathered our gear together into one spot, double checking and eliminating any items we could get along without. Al was taking his 65-pound bow and glass arrows tipped with razor sharp, black diamond delta heads. He would carry his .44 Magnum revolver, and I would take my .30-'06 rifle. We finished by stuffing our gear into two very full packs.

"The next morning a friend dropped us off at a horse trail where we would start our hike, thus eliminating our leaving our truck along the road for 10 days.

"We adjusted our packs and started down the trail on a typically beautiful Alaskan fall day — the leaves were golden, it was warm and sunny, and the smell of Alaskan autumn filled the air.

"Eight and a half bone-weary hours later we reached the area where we wanted to camp. Every muscle in my body ached and my feet were sore. As it was almost dark, we made a hurried camp, fixed something to eat and turned in for the night.

"The next day we developed our camp into a very comfortable one. We built a leanto out of logs and clear plastic, placing boughs on the ground for a mattress and covering them with a plastic floor. The front of the leanto had a plastic flap to close out the cold night air. Al built a makeshift table from a piece of wood we found. We gathered an abundant supply of firewood and picked up paper and litter left behind by others.

"That day we saw small bulls which Al passed up. We marveled at the ancient ritual of rutting moose during mating season — the bulls come down from above timberline, paw a 20- to 30-inch area and urinate in it to attract feminine company.

"On our third day we started out at daybreak and spotted two bulls with 60-inch-spread antlers calling to challenge each other, but Al was unable to get close enough to either for a shot with his bow. We walked about eight miles. The day had been sunny and warm, but the warmth disappeared with the setting sun. After eating our evening meal and cleaning up camp, we sat enjoying the magical quality of our campfire. The moon rose full and bright and bathed our camp in moonlight. The campfire glowed, and the only sound was the crackling of the fire. I placed more logs on the flames, put on a pair of long underwear and crawled into my sleeping bag.

"Before crawling into his bag, Al located matches, a light, placed his .44 magnum on a piece of yellow paper towel for easier spotting and laid my .30-'06 by his side with the safety off and a shell in the chamber. Unlike me, he left his sleeping bag partially unzipped for quick access to a weapon. The combination of a warm sleeping bag, a tired body, and the crackling of the fire soon had me drifting off to sleep.

"I was awakened about 4:00 A.M. by Al's whispering into my ear. He had sensed something and whispered to me not to move as something might be out there in camp. I listened, straining to hear a sound which might locate an animal. As I kept watching into the moonlight night, I saw the silhouette of a brown bear move alongside of me.

"Al did not see the bear from his position. The animal was only inches from me, with just the plastic between us, and it didn't make a sound. It seemed to be moving away, when all of a sudden the bear was on top of me. He plunged through the top of our leanto with a bellowing roar. This was Al's first sight of the bear.

"Al grabbed the rifle; but with the impact of the bear, the rifle flew from his grip. For a fraction of a second the bear appeared confused as the logs broke and the plastic tore. He stood on his hind legs, towering over us. He was enormous, like a huge, gray driftwood log.

"There was no time for Al to locate the .44 revolver. He knew the only way to save me was to immediately distract the bear from me to him. He also reasoned that if he turned his head in search of the revolver, the bear might instinctively go for his neck, thus killing both of us. As the bear dropped to all fours, Al grabbed its head with his left hand and slugged him with his right. The bear grabbed Al's left forearm in his jaws and by standing up, pulled Al out of his sleeping bag, tossing him through the air.

"He landed at the foot of the leanto. Like a flash the animal was over him. The claws ripped through Al's right side, almost penetrating the lung, and pinned Al to his chest. His teeth raked along Al's skull and managed to grip the scalp. The bear picked Al up with its mouth and one foreleg and ran on three legs.

"With Al dangling by his scalp, the bear stood straight up shaking his head violently as a cat with a mouse. Al's feet never touched the ground. The bear ran a distance of approximately 25 yards, and a large portion of scalp tore loose from Al's head causing the bear to momentarily lose his grip.

"While all this was taking place, I rose, realizing the heavy weight of the animal and the horrible noise was gone. Al's sleeping bag was lying beside mine, empty. I had not seen Al's struggle with the beast because my head was covered, and I was baffled as to where he and the bear had gone.

"I stood up in my sleeping bag, pulled it down and stepped out of it. Searching for a weapon, I saw the .44 revolver lying on the yellow piece of paper towel. The rifle was not in sight. Where was Al? Where was the bear? Even though it was not total darkness, I could not see any movement or forms nor hear any sound. I had a strong feeling of danger and of the bear charging me at any moment.

"My first impulse was to run, to get away from the area. My common sense told me my best chance was to stay in this clearing and in camp as the bear would overtake me, and heading to an area of denser cover would only tend to give him a more secure feeling. My next thought was to stick the revolver in my waistband and try to climb a tree. Unlike black bears, brown bears do not climb trees unless they pull themselves up by using the limbs.

"I was dressed completely in white, including socks, which must have made me very visible as I moved in the moonlight. The trees were large with no limbs low enough for me to reach. Dismissing any chance of escape, I cried 'God, please help us,' and braced myself, holding the revolver in both hands. I may not kill a charging bear before he got me, but I would not give up my life without a fight.

"As Al was being carried by the bear, he thought, 'What a hell of a way to die.' Then he thought of me, faced with the shock of my having a dead husband, miles from anywhere or anyone, and having to hike out of there alone. He became angry, and a strong will to fight for survival overcame him.

"A brown bear is capable of dragging off a full-grown moose. His strong legs and claws can move boulders and huge hunks of earth. A blow from his paws can break the neck of a moose or another bear. No man could come close to matching his strength. Al realized his only chance was to convince the bear he was dead.

"When the scalp tore off and the bear momentarily lost his grip, Al fell onto a hump of moss. He grasped the hump with his right arm, holding his face and stomach down to keep from being ripped open, took a deep breath and held perfectly still. The bear cuffed at him, leaving horrible claw marks all along his side and shoulders. He bit into Al's back twice, while standing over him, looking for a sign of life. There was none. Al's playing dead displayed remarkable self-discipline, as the pain was excruciating.

"Then I heard the bear. He was moving away from me, heading toward cover in the direction of the little lake in the area. As I stood listening, trying to locate him, I heard Al call to me. He was running toward me. Moving closer to him, I could see his knit shirt was torn and he was covered with blood. 'I'm hurt bad, but I'm going to live,' he said. In the next breath he ordered, 'Find the rifle, quick!'

" 'Where do you think it is?' I asked.

" 'Look at the end of the leanto; it may have landed there,' he replied. As he wiped the blood from his eyes, he held the revolver while I searched for the rifle. I had to feel around for it in the darkness. I found it and also a shirt for him to hold on his head, as blood was pouring down over his eyes.

"Our minds were working fast, lining out immediate things to do. A fire! Got to get a big fire going! Thanks to the dry wood, kindling and paper we had collected on our cleanup this was quickly accomplished. In a few seconds the flames were high.

"Al slumped on the sleeping bag. He was cold and started to shake. The temperature was about 25 degrees. He must have lost a great deal of blood and was possibly starting to go into shock. Got to get him warm and look at his wounds. I pulled our sleeping bags close to the fire for him.

"We started to check his wounds. He had been badly mauled. I looked for spurting blood which would indicate bleeding from an artery. His legs were uninjured. He had a large hole in his side under his right arm from the bear's paw. This required a large compress which we had included in our first-aid kit.

"I had sewn large game bags from unbleached muslin for this hunt. The material was new and clean. I tore the bags into long strips to use for bandages.

"Al's head was very bloody — half of the skin on his forehead was missing, from the bottom half of his left eyebrow extending back into his hair. Due to all the blood and poor light, I did not notice part of the scalp was gone. I thought it had been torn back and was still attached.

"I wrapped his head around and around several times with bandages which were quickly soaked with blood. His left arm was badly chewed, and the pain was very severe. He instructed me to take my knife and cut off the shredded piece of flesh that was hanging from the largest wound. There appeared to be a great deal of muscle and nerve damage.

"All I could do was to squeeze a tube of first-aid cream on the wounds as far as it would go and wrap up his arm. I had placed some strong tea in the fire and gave it to him to drink, along with some aspirins. During the process of bandaging, it was necessary to watch and listen for any sign of the bear's return.

"We still had three hours to wait for daylight. The night air was causing the water to freeze in our plastic water jug. Up until now I hadn't noticed the cold even though I had no shoes on. I found my shoes and clothes and quickly pulled them on. This was the longest three hours in my life. I talked loudly, often repeating myself just to be making noise. Al lay resting and drinking strong tea. I circled the fire, listening for any noise in the brush and watched for any moving shadows. It took a large share of the wood we had gathered to keep the fire bright until daylight.

"As daylight approached, I moved more freely around camp but never without my rifle. We discussed our plans for the trip out. It was still too dark to start down the trail. I prepared a pack to carry which contained a space blanket, matches, candy bars, canteen of juice and a sleeping bag which I would pack just prior to leaving. We wanted to get as far away from this camp as Al was able to walk in case the bear returned — if I had to leave him and go ahead for help, he would stay warm in the sleeping bag until I could return with a helicopter.

"I got Al into his socks, shoes and wool trousers and made a sling for his arm. We put a piece of foam rubber against his neck and secured a nylon rope from his sling over his back to his belt to keep the weight of his arm from pulling the sling against his neck.

"I gathered most of our possessions and threw them into the leanto for what protection it would offer, as it was still half intact. We left enough disarray to alert any passing pilot that something was wrong.

"I stuffed the sleeping bag into the pack and helped Al to his feet. The hours of lying and the loss of blood made him dizzy for a moment. The possibility of having to stay alone while I went for help formed in his mind but vanished when his head cleared. He wrote a note on the back of one of our maps indicating the time, date, that we had been attacked by a brown bear, needed a doctor and were trying to walk out.

"At 6:50 A.M. we started down the trail. Al carried his .44

revolver in his right hand, and I followed with the pack and my rifle. The brush was thick in places, and we stayed close together preparing for another bear confrontation. A short way from camp we saw fresh brown bear manure in the trail. Since we had not seen any such sign on our way in or while hunting, we had good reason to believe the brownie that attacked us had passed through here sometime during the early morning.

"Al set a fast pace, and my walk was hurried to keep up with him. After covering a few miles, Al put his revolver into his holster and I put my rifle on my shoulder. He kept up the same pace even up the hills. I was forced to rest a few seconds on the steeper hills.

"It was a beautiful, clear, sunny day; and as the ground thawed, it became slippery. After about 10 miles I found myself getting behind. It was miraculous the way Al was covering ground. He had lost several pints of blood, was in a great deal of pain, his head rested on his shoulder (as a result of being hit on the side of his head); and yet, he was still going strong. We passed up several good clearings where a helicopter could easily land, but he didn't want to stop. With God's help and Al's determination it appeared he was going to walk all the way out.

"As we neared the road I became concerned that I might have to leave Al and hike several miles into Soldotna. Al reached the road ahead of me and was resting when a lady we know drove up and saw Al beside the road. She was on her way to Soldotna, and as I arrived, Al was asking her to notify the troopers to send an ambulance and call the hospital.

"We had hiked out two hours quicker than we had hiked in. Al was totally exhausted and in great pain — face, hands and bandages covered with dried blood. Ten minutes later we heard a siren. In another 10 minutes state troopers and the ambulance arrived. Al explained it had been an unprovoked brown bear attack. They carefully lifted him into the ambulance, and I crawled in back with him. As we hurried over the gravel road, one of the troopers held up Al's wounded arm.

"The Soldotna hospital had been open only for about a year, and we were thankful for it. Since this was Sunday, there was one doctor on call. She had been alerted and was waiting in the emergency room. While undoing the bandages, she noticed the missing piece of scalp. After seeing the extent of wounds and noting the amount of work ahead, she instructed the nurse to try again to locate the surgeon who was fishing. Another doctor arrived and asked if we had any idea where the scalp was. Al told me where it would most likely be in relation to our leanto.

"Al went to surgery while I returned with some troopers to our camp via helicopter. The miles that had taken us hours to cover were behind us in minutes. I stood by the leanto suggesting the most likely place to start looking, and soon one of the troopers spotted a great deal of blood. He followed the blood trail, found the scalp, put it into a clean plastic bag covered with a special solution, and we departed while the remaining troopers stayed to investigate the scene and look for the bear.

"On coming through the emergency door, I noticed a pair of hip boots — they must have found the surgeon. The doctors worked on Al for hours — cleaning, cutting away dead flesh, stitching some of the wounds and leaving others to drain (for later stitching). The piece of scalp was cleaned and stitched in place. It was about 11:00 P.M. before I saw Al in the recovery room. He was in critical condition. He had been given a shot to make him sleep.

"Our friend Mary insisted on staying with me, and I went home about 12:00 A.M.; but I could not sleep. When I closed my eyes, I was haunted by the memory of the bear and the bellowing roar, as I was for many nights to follow.

"I spent the next day with Al whose face and left arm were swollen. He had been given four pints of blood and large doses of drugs to counteract infection so common in animal wounds. He would receive two more pints of blood later. He was so weak it took two nurses and me to help him stand by the bed. He said, 'How'd I ever walk that far when I can't even stand up by myself?'

"I saw no change in Al during the next two days. He looked so pale and swollen. On the drive home that evening tears began to fill my eyes. I felt so helpless.

"The next day I walked into his room and saw a change. Color was showing in his cheeks, and he looked better. He would have a long struggle ahead of him, but he was going to make it.

"During our ordeal many good friends and local people volunteered their services. Some donated blood, and others sat with me. Troopers and wardens became commonplace as they stopped by to check on Al, who is a game warden.

"The media picked up the attack story and distorted the facts. Several days later I heard a report that the guilty black bear had been destroyed. Other false reports indicated we had camped next to a moose kill or Al had wounded a bear with an arrow (a broken arrow in his quiver had dried blood on it from the previous year's moose kill). I was angry with this misinformation and concerned about the possibility of another hunter being mauled by the same bear before moose season ended.

"Another hunter *was* attacked a few weeks later in the same area. He scared the bear away, but it stalked him and charged a second time. The hunter was able to wound the animal, and it left him. He was not seriously injured though his wounds were similar to Al's as only the right canine tooth punctured the flesh. If it was the same bear, it showed no normal fear of human scent.

"Al wanted to destroy the bear and returned to the woods for two days with other officers, but his commissioner heard of it and wisely instructed Al to stay home. Despite intensive searches, the bear was never found. Al feels the bear may have died from its wounds during the winter.

"During the next year, Al underwent two more surgeries for skin grafting on his head and forehead. The scalp never took. Through several months and hours of painful exercising, he has regained most of the use of his left hand and arm and continues with his profession as a warden.

"I keep telling myself the chance of the same thing happening again is too remote to consider; but when I camp out, I find it takes longer to fall asleep, and I find myself listening intently for any unwelcomed sound. I also believe my love for the wilderness, climbing mountains, walking along game trails, looking out over miles of beautiful country will be strong enough to overshadow the nightmare that was for real. And I thank God for giving us a second chance."

I Buried My Ice Ax In Her Skull

Determination and experience played a key part in another most unusual hand-to-hand man-bear encounter experienced by hunting guide Guy George of Valdez. In August 1973 Guy was guiding for another guide, Howard Knutson, and had taken two hunters into the Wrangell Mountains in search of Alaska's famous Dall sheep. Guy spent a few days at the 5,500-foot level with Ed Blecker and Charlie Shockley of Anchorage, and they were returning to camp with their trophy.

"August in the Wrangells can give you chilly nights when your tent will freeze stiff, with the days so warm that even a light jacket is too much. It had been light for hours, but the sun had just come over the mountains and was shining on the 100-pound pack on my back, which contained all the camp gear, plus one sheep and the horns and cape. It was warm under that pack, so I was wearing no jacket — just a T-shirt. As always, I carried my ice ax.

"Charlie and Ed were behind me, still coming down the mountain, by the time I had reached the bank of the Kotsina River. I was making my way through the clumps of berry bushes and small trees that lined the bank and had just come over a small hill when I found myself face-to-face with a grizzly.

"She wasn't more than five steps away from me, and it didn't take her a split second to react. She laid her ears back and came right for me, clicking her teeth. The first thing I saw when she charged was the flash of her claws in the sun. They looked just like knives. I thought, 'Oh, God, I wonder what she's gonna do to me.' Then I was out of time.

"There was no time to shoot. She would have nailed me before I could get a shot off. I reached down with my left hand and pulled my ice ax up into my right hand. She was so close to me I had to swing downward to hit her. The ice ax connected just above her left eye, and I felt the ax go into her skull. By that time she had knocked me off my feet; and as I fell backward, she flipped her head, and the ice ax came out of her skull. I was flat on my back, held down by the 100-pound pack that I couldn't get off; and she went running by me on my right, snorting and clicking her teeth and tearing up the brush and ground.

"She ran off to the right a little way, and that was when I heard a noise to my left. There was a little cub not three feet away from me. Up to that time I hadn't realized she had a cub. Being between that wounded bear and her cub put me in about the world's worst position, and just then the cub started whining.

"That grizzly whirled around and came at me again with her mouth wide open. The froth was foaming out of her mouth, and her eyes were blood red. I thought, 'Oh, God, not again.' Then I realized how angry I was and said, 'I'll kill you, you son of a bitch.'

"I was still on my back, but I swung my ice ax again with my right hand as hard as I could, and drove the spike end of the ax all the way through her throat. It looked as if she had swallowed the ax, because the handle was right in the middle of her mouth. I thought she was gonna bite down on the handle, but she didn't.

"She flipped her head up and to the right, almost jerking me (and my pack) off the ground. That's when I hung on for dear life, thinking she might jerk the ax out of my hand. The spike had gone through her windpipe, and she was making funny gurgling sounds. Then she flipped her head one last time, and the ax came out of her throat.

"Blood was running out of her head, and I thought she was going to try to finish me off; but instead, she lurched over my feet and got between me and her cub. The cub was right next to me, and it followed its wounded mother, which staggered off through the bushes still making those gurgling noises. As I saw the last of her, she was trailing blood, but she had her cub; and I was still alive.

"I think I had some help from Somebody Upstairs. Self-preservation runs very high in all of us, and I doubt that anyone knows what he can do until he is called on to do it. In a situation where your life is at stake you defend yourself with whatever you have at hand. My ice ax saved my life.

"Why I used that ax the way I did was probably instinct, but I have had lots of experience carrying a stick. I was born and raised on a ranch in Montana. We had Angus cattle, and one of my jobs was to retrieve or treat newborn calves in the field. Those Angus cows will charge you when you catch their calves, and I always carried a stick with me. They'd scare you half to death, if you're not used to it, a big cow blowin' and chargin' at you. I'd just slap them on the nose with my stick when they came up to me. I've smashed a lot of old moose skulls while walking along with my ice ax, so this thing with the bear was just a natural reaction. If I hadn't had the experience with the cattle, I might have done something different. It was automatic." □

THEY'RE
UNPREDICTABLE

"Bears had again proved to me that their behavior pattern is strictly an individual matter, dictated by instincts of the moment. There are a few hard and unchangeable facts that a bear hunter learns early in the hunting game, if he is to become a good bear hunter. And one of these is that he will still be learning about bear on his final hunt." (Hal Waugh, Alaskan Master Guide, "More About Bears," ALASKA SPORTSMAN®, March 1964)

"The grizzly is one of the most courageous and intelligent of all beasts, and also entirely unpredictable." (Frank Dufresne, former Director, Alaska Game Commission, "North America's Grouchiest Bear," ALASKA SPORTSMAN®, December 1963)

Where Are My Berries, Papa?

When four-year-old little Ella May Lindberg left her Sitka house alone in July 1921, it was with one thought — blueberry pie. She told her mother if she would bake a pie, Ella would get the berries. Ella wanted a surprise blueberry pie for her papa. She knew about a prize patch of berries where she could fill her pail. Ella had not given any thought to the large bears that roamed the woods near her Baranof Island home. She was really too young to understand anything about bears.

Almost two hours after Ella had left the house, her father Hans, superintendent of the U.S. Horticultural station at Sitka, arrived and queried about "Baby." He was shocked to learn she had last been seen walking with pail in hand toward the woods. He immediately sprang into action, meeting at the blacksmith shop with all available men, distributing his two 12-gauge shotguns and .22 rifle. He carried his .30-40 rifle himself. The men spread out in a half-circle and slowly began combing the woods. They were to fire three shots if anyone found Ella May.

A half-hour later Ella's father heard three shots and rushed toward the sound. One of his companions confessed that they hadn't found Ella, but they'd discovered some large, fresh bear tracks. In a frenzy Ella's father plunged ahead of the others into the dense brush, hoping against the inevitable. He tried to force all negative thoughts from his mind — she could be mangled by a savage bear, she could be partially consumed, she may never be found. He was overcome by a father's grief for his little one.

He called frantically to Ella, reassuring her that he was near, coming to her aid. Shortly he stumbled from the brush tangle almost bypassing the still, small form lying on the ground.

It was Ella May. She lay in a patch of blueberries, chubby little body peacefully sleeping, with her empty berry pail nearby.

He fired three signal shots and turned to his daughter who was awakened by the commotion. Her first words were, "Where are my berries, Papa? I had a whole pail full of blueberries." Completely surrounding the berry patch were large bear tracks evidencing where Ella's berries had gone.

Guides and bear men with years of experience who know bruin best say anyone who thinks he knows what a bear will do knows more than the bear. And Charles Madsen, Alaska's "Dean of Kodiak Guides," said, "Bears are like women; they never do the predictable thing."

Two Mothers Meet

If there is an absolute to be made about bears, it is precisely that — the most predictable thing about a bear is that he is unpredictable. Countless experiences have occurred demonstrating the bear's unpredictable nature.

Half a century ago Dolly Harcourt's mother was walking the beach with her two youngsters on Kodiak Island when she encountered a sow brownie and her twins. The mothers froze and assessed the situation. The lady had never seen a larger bear.

Both mamas directed their offspring toward the shoreline trees.

Mrs. Bruin stood on hind legs examining her human counterpart, and Dolly's mother picked up a chunk of driftwood declaring to Mrs. Bruin, "I'm ready for you." Tense moments passed slowly, and then the bear dropped to all fours. She turned, collected her cubs and departed — much to the relief of Dolly's mother (personal communication from Dolly Harcourt of Ketchikan, Alaska).

He Smelled The Back Of My Neck

Just after World War II Duke Short of Admiralty Island sat upon a stump on the edge of a clearing trying to call a Southeastern blacktail deer in for a shot. His rifle leaned against a stump at arm's length. He wore the same shirt he'd worn the day before while packing out a deer, and it was saturated with dried blood. After a while he became aware of something touching his back. He heard a bear sniffing the dried blood on his shirt and fought a nearly uncontrollable desire to flee.

He sat perfectly still for several moments while the bear sniffed his shirt. Then he felt the moist, warm nose of the bear on the back of his neck. Moments later a deer sounded across the clearing, and the large brownie ambled off through the trees.

Joe Beaty, now of Anchorage, told me about a friend from his Kodiak ranching days who "was sitting up one night in the summer when it was light all night watchin' a cow that a bear had killed. He was sitting up leaning back against a spruce tree, and he went to sleep. The bear came up back of him and snuffed at his neck. I guess Tom carried the branches as he went up the tree."

Alaska's Governor Bowled Over By a Brownie

More than one man has been within arm's length of a powerful brown/grizzly with every reason to expect the worst, only to have the bear turn and leave, master of the situation. Two specific examples come to mind, one involving Alaska's Gov. Jay Hammond and the other a hunter in Southeastern Alaska.

Back in his guiding days Governor Hammond was off Becharof Lake in one of his camps photographing bears along a small stream. He was guiding the owner of Mepp's spinner company, Todd Sheldon, and his son Mike, both fast friends. They'd been filming for some time from the low saddles bordering the stream and decided to move over to the water and follow the streambed upstream.

Normally Hammond would have rejected the idea because of

the high concentration of bears in the area; but the wind blew from the men to the stream, and they'd already spooked one bear from that locale. Governor Hammond said, "We started to thread our way through the brush. I was carrying a sawed-off 12-gauge shotgun which I pack for close quarter work of this type. I had some packets of film and canisters of film in my pack which were rattling and making noises, so I wasn't terribly disturbed about coming on bears and surprising them.

"Todd and Mike were creeping through the alders behind me in very dense cover. We'd been picking our way through these alders for some time when I pulled up an alder with one hand and put my foot down while looking a bit to the right. All of a sudden that foot came up in my face and bowled me over, as the only 20-foot brown bear I've ever seen in my life erupted from that clump.

"I can't say that he actually hit me; I think it was the brush. He didn't hit me with his paw, but whether or not he'd bowled me over with his belly or the brush, I couldn't honestly say since it happened so quickly.

"Regardless, the bear bowled me over, and made one lunge, again standing upright. He made some rude noises deep in his belly and made a lunge then, fortunately, turned and fled at the same time I threw up that shotgun. Fortunately, I did not fire it. The other guys were right behind me and went down like a couple of dominoes.

"It happened so quickly that we hardly had time to become unduly alarmed. In reflection, it was a rather interesting experience and the only time that I've actually been touched by a live brown bear."

A Bear Awakened Him

A hunter in Southeastern Alaska sought a rumored monster bear on Admiralty Island early one morning. That morning the bear did not make his usual appearance at the salmon stream, so the man decided to try for the bear in the evening. During the interim a cozy sand bar beckoned him, and he fell victim to the morning's warmth and dozed on the bar.

Some time later he opened his eyes and discovered a stump-sized, hairy leg next to him. A big, damp nose touched his cheek, accompanied by a salmon-scented breath. The hunter lay breathless, awaiting the powerful blow that could send him to bear hunters' heaven; but it never came. The bear circled him then passively padded across the sand and into the forest.

In many precarious situations where man is completely at the bear's mercy bruin almost seems indifferent. It seems as though some bears recognize man's ignorance and innocence for what they are and hold no grudges. As much as man blunders about in bruin's back yard, the bear takes it in stride.

Mexican Standoff At Arm's Length

Many years ago Andy Simons had guided a young photographer to a stream on the Alaska Peninsula. Typical peninsula weather greeted them, rain poured down upon them throughout the night as they tried to sleep beneath a canvas boat they'd arrived in. Bears were plentiful in the stream below the riverbank, and their splashing and grunting kept the young man on pins and needles.

One old boar sloshed around, roaring his defiance, and Andy hoped the old gent would remain with his relatives. The man eventually slumbered, but the youngster kept his loaded rifle close.

In the wee hours of the morning Andy awakened and gazed toward his partner who had just gasped. Andy surmised the lad was having a nightmare as he sat bolt-upright, ashen faced. The guide followed his partner's gaze to the open side of the boat which they'd disguised with tall rye grass.

A monster bear's head was framed by the grass, rain dripping from its thick fur an arm's length away. The bear was in complete control. The men were robbed of any action, because it would have been futile. Only after staring them each in the eye and inhaling their scent did the bear seem placated. Finally he withdrew his keg-sized head from their scanty shelter and ghosted into the fog-like drizzle.

Frank Dufresne And a Sneaky Bear

In many instances the bear almost seems too kind for man's ignorance. Once Frank Dufresne was filming along a well-used bear trail when bruin walked past his log blind. The bear seemed to stiffen slightly and raise the hairs on the back of his neck as Frank guessed the bear had gotten his scent. The animal continued without so much as a look in Frank's direction and walked up the trail around a bend. A half-hour later Frank rose to go.

As he turned, he found himself face-to-face with the same bear. It had circled and silently eased into the position of the observer. How long he had been there Frank never did find out.

Playmates

Bruin almost shows a human understanding regarding man's innocence. Three-year-old Evelyn Berglund set out to find her mother and father one August morning in 1920. Her brother told her that her parents were at the fish wheel at Nation, Alaska, on the Yukon River. Evelyn wandered along the stream and encountered a sow with three cubs but not her parents. Thinking they were puppies, she tried to catch the cubs. They frolicked with her for some time as the sow watched her and fished nearby. It wasn't long, however, until her father called from the distance and the game ended. The bears sifted into the underbrush. Evelyn's father never saw the bears, but he saw their tracks mixed with hers.

A Lively Pelt

A black bear was discovered at Bell Island by Bob Lane of Ketchikan. Bob was delivering the mail, and when the caretaker did not appear at Bob's usual horn-tooting signal, he decided to go to the caretaker's cabin. On the dock Bob discovered a large black bear. It angered him that some hunter would leave such a trophy, and he drew his knife to skin it. With his knife in one hand and a handful of fur in the other he received the shock of his life — the trophy exploded in his hand, leaving Bob with his knife, a handful of fur and a pretty rattled complexion. The last time he saw the bear, it was scratching and digging for the big timber! (*The ALASKA SPORTSMAN®*, March 1956)

Denning

Although bears follow general patterns of behavior, they are ultimately unpredictable as individuals. Under normal circumstances bears hibernate in the winter. They eat fish. Bears will flee the area if they get man's scent or see him. Sows with cubs will fight to the death to defend their offspring if they cannot retreat with dignity. Invariably, once man has pigeon-holed Mr. Fuzzy Wuzzy, some "weird" bruin comes along and disproves *Homo sapiens'* stereotype.

The life of the North American bears follows a cycle of the seasons. He is born in the spring, is fed and educated by his mother throughout the summer and fall and hibernates in the late fall. (U.S. Public Health Service biologist Raymond Hock of Anchorage differentiated between true hibernation and sleep in the 1950s. He said that bears were easily awakened, had cubs and were warm enough to melt snow, and their temperatures were much higher than true hibernaters like squirrels.) Bruin emerges from his den the following spring.

Dens vary in size and type. A den is usually a cave but could be an indentation in a tree's root system, under the alders or a pile of brush; in some cases the bear digs a hole on the side of a slope and lets the blowing snow blanket him for the winter. The den is slightly larger than the hibernating bear, not too roomy.

An interesting denning study was reported in the April 1977 issue of *ALASKA*® magazine. "Denning activities of grizzly bears were studied in the eastern Brooks Range between April and November in 1972, 1973 and 1974. Active dens were found by tracking bears through snow or by locating bears fitted with radio transmitters. In the fall of 1973, 71% of the newly excavated dens were constructed between October 5-12, although some grizzlies were observed foraging and did not den until after November 7.

"Similarly, of eight dens located, which were used in 1974, six, or 75%, were excavated between October 3-9; one about September 27; and one between October 19 and November 1.

"A total of 52 dens were found; 20 of these were located shortly after they had been prepared for use during the oncoming winter and 32 others were found after they had been used.

"In 39 instances bears dug dens in well-drained areas above the permafrost layer and in 13 cases natural caves were utilized. All dens were located in moderate to steep terrain with the exception of three dens, which were dug into riverbanks on the coastal plain. Mean elevation of den sites was 3,200 feet, and 46, or 88%, were located on southern exposures.

"When caves were utilized, in every case a bed was constructed of moss, woody and/or herbaceous material. Most dug dens collapsed after the bear's departure."

Bears do not always hibernate for the entire winter. Many bears leave their dens periodically during a mild winter when food is accessible. A couple of winters ago there was at least one grizzly prowling around Indian, Alaska (within 25 miles of Anchorage), in January. The grizzly was no doubt calling on the locals for any readily available grub that wasn't nailed down.

Interestingly enough, the pads on a bear's feet "shed" their hard, cracked skin during hibernation. The feet are soft and tender making early travel difficult after first leaving the den. The bear's worn, dull, blunt or broken claws manicure themselves during the sleep process — they are moderately pointed and long as he leaves his den in search of his first spring meal.

They Will Eat Humans

Meals for spring bears normally include plants (wild rhubarb, wild potatoes, skunk cabbage, hellebore shoots), insects, rodents (and small mammals) and occasionally carrion from the previous winter. Later in the summer they eat berries, mammals and salmon (some bears never see a fish; they live high above timberline or in an area that salmon cannot reach).

Bears are often compared with pigs. They are omnivorous, eating about anything they find, and they frequently wallow in bear wallows where available.

For many years man believed that bears did not eat human flesh, but in recent years in Alaska some humans have been eaten by bears. Captain Robert Penman of the Alaska State Troopers told me that most of his experiences with bears involved getting called to either pick up human remains or attempting to find persons who had been mauled, injured, or eaten by bears.

Penman has come to expect to find certain things. "Bears mark their kills. Usually they walk over and around a kill, and if it is a male bear, he marks the area by urinating and leaving his scent. Bears don't usually eat their kill immediately unless they are suffering from extreme hunger. The body of Lee Precup, an Illinois visitor, who in 1976 was killed by a grizzly bear in Glacier National Monument, was mostly consumed over a period of several days.

"The National Park System prohibits the use of firearms in their parks, which I personally feel is a bit ludicrous because dangerous bears constantly confront visitors in these areas in Alaska. Understandably campers are a bit reticent to go into these parks without a firearm.

"Once a bear makes a kill it usually covers it in a pile of vegetation and dirt it scratches up, and then it allows nature to take its course in a sort of tenderization process. Usually a bear will lay up where he can view or be near to his aging kill, and it protects it from intruders. It is under these circumstances that many bear attacks on man occur.

"The bear feeds on what he wants, covers it up, and returns again and again, just like a dog burying a bone.

"One man, whose body was found on Baranof Island in 1964, had been hunting. He had a tin hard hat on, which we found. I also found what was left of his Model 70 Winchester rifle. The bear tried to tear the rifle apart and almost succeeded. He bit completely through the stock and put a dent into the barrel and bent the barrel a half-inch, apparently in a sweep of his jaws. He either had bitten through or clawed through the aluminum hat that the hunter had been wearing; and I'm sure that it was a swipe of the paw that tore the side of his hat right apart.

"All that remained of the body was a portion of the jaw bone, a part of the pelvis, and a small portion of one humerus, just enough to put into a small sack. Everything else was consumed. The surrounding area was completely uprooted, including small trees up to four inches in diameter. Sort of a little clearing was made by the bear, and the body of the victim was covered over in a mound.

"It was very grisly, as all these things are. The bear that eats a human, totally consumes it. They break the large bones for the marrow, and crack the skull open for the brain. Bears don't waste any part of the body."

They'll Eat Each Other, Too

Another trait of the brown/grizzly is his cannibalism. The most common form of eating his own kind is the boar which kills and eats cubs to gain amorous favors from their mother. She will defend her cubs to the death against a boar, but once they are dead, she goes into her reproductive cycle and comes into heat again. Consequently, boars often kill and eat cubs.

In Calvin H. Barkdull's article about the Pybus Bay monster ("The Killers," *The ALASKA SPORTSMAN®*, June 1954) he said, "When I was fairly close, a cub came bawling and crying out onto the open beach, followed closely by the monster of Pybus Bay. He seized the cub in his mouth, jumped on it with his forefeet, tore it to pieces and gulped it down while the mother tore into him from the rear and sides. He showed no interest in fighting the sow.

"It is neither hunger nor laziness, as one might suppose, that makes cannibals out of those old boars. If the sow bear is allowed to nurse her cubs, she will not reproduce again for two years. If the young cubs are killed, she will reproduce the next year. Knowing this, the cannibal boar will follow the sow with a cub and kill the cub if he gets a chance. In a short time the sow comes into heat, to the gratification of the boar."

Bears feed upon other bears that have died or have been killed. This could explain the lack of bear remains in the bush. In the same article Barkdull described the kill site of a bear he had shot. "I landed at the bear carcass. Half of it was gone, and the rest was torn apart and dragged around. I had always heard that bears were cannibals. Here was proof. The great bear had torn open the stomach of the dead bear and revealed its contents — a young fawn and a small brown bear cub, feet, teeth, skull, bones, skin, everything."

Some Run and Hide
Some Are Plain Ornery

A great deal of misinformation has been printed about these big Alaskan bears. Unfortunately bears get blamed for a lot of things just for being themselves. Many people believe that bears attack man on sight. At the other end of the spectrum are those who have no idea that a bear will charge at all.

Under most circumstances a person in bear country will never see a bear if the bear doesn't want to be seen. Joe Beaty, the rancher, has confronted dozens of bears on his ranch and told me, "I believe that they'll get away from you where they can. I've been as close as five to six feet from a Kodiak bear. We've actually run 'em off kills where you'd think they'd fight for it. I've never seen the time when I thought the bear was out to get a man. I know they do, and I respect them."

Bears usually try to avoid man. But some bears react very aggressively toward man's intrusion into their territory. In past years when it was legal to hunt on the same day that the hunter has been airborne, guides flew over bears looking for a respectable trophy. A master guide from Anchorage, Keith Johnson, who has hunted bears for years, commented on the ferocity of big boars and sows.

"If you look at a lot of bears with an airplane like I have, you'll see bears come right off the ground and tear down trees and alders. I saw it this year one time when a bear crouched like a cat, first time I had ever seen that, and lunge and jump. We were looking at the bear a little too close and we got out of there because it was not a good situation.

"We took an 11½-foot bear back in 1966, and he come clear out of the alder patch; and there were big chunks of alders that went end-over-end right up out of the patch. It was really a ferocious attack. He was batting the alders away to get at the airplane.

"I saw an enormous sow this year, probably the biggest sow I ever saw in my life. I think she was eight, eight-and-a-half-foot, just a really big, dark colored sow. You rarely ever see anything like that; sows just don't get that big. She had three little babies, and boy, she was mad. Made one pass to look at her, and she roared right after the airplane, lunging, swinging and fighting, three or four feet off the ground."

Bears usually don't want to be bothered and will leave peacefully; but they reserve the right to scare the living daylights out of you and leave the scene with dignity. Clark Engle told me about a close call he had at McNeil River while backing up Jim Faro, who was darting with tranquilizers and tagging bears for the Alaska Department of Fish & Game. The men were in heavy alders when they encountered the bear known locally as His Majesty; and ". . . he was coming at full charge, I mean *full charge!*

"When a bear charges, they don't normally come straight at you. They come at you dog fashion, a little bit sideways. [Bears normally charge on all fours, much like a big fluffy dog chasing a house cat. They do, however, lunge and bite while standing on their rear legs.] They give you a good shot right at the side of their front shoulder, up alongside of their head, which is a deadly area to knock 'em down.

"This all happened in a split second, so fast that it was kinda fuzzy in my mind. I screamed and cleared my rifle from the alders, threw my safety off. Just before it got to me, it turned, not more than three feet from the end of my barrel.

"Even if I'd shot that bear before it turned, the bear would have gotten me. You're talking about a thousand-pound bear; he'd have rolled over the top of me, and killed me or broken me up.

"All that bear was telling me was, 'Hey, you're in my territory, Mother! Get outa here. I don't want you around.' "

A mother bear is a determined customer, but she will not always attack an intruder. Jim Allen, a former colleague at Dimond High School in Anchorage, told me about the time when he and a fellow worker walked the Tenakee Hot Springs trail one day for a change of pace. They were working for the U.S. Forest Service on Chichagof Island north of Sitka in July 1960. It was a 16-mile hike, and they decided to leave their standard Forest Service .375 Sako rifle behind. "We encountered a sow and a cub going our way on the trail. They were 300 yards ahead of us. She would look back once in a while, completely unconcerned.

"She and the baby were going toward Tenakee, so we decided to see if we could be compatible. She would walk a little ways, and we'd walk a little ways, and she'd look back. None of the hackles up or anything — she was just completely unconcerned about us. She stayed on that trail until she was within about three miles of Tenakee. We bid her a fond adieu; and she went about her business, and we went about ours."

More than one sow has panicked in similar situations and hit for the high country, leaving junior behind. So it can not be stated for a certainty that sows will fight for their young.

Generally speaking, bears spend their winter months in hibernation; they eat what nature provides (which includes hundreds of salmon for the majority of Alaskan bears); the bear will leave an area where man is if he can do so gracefully and if it is not a panhandler (in a park setting); and sows will defend their cubs.

Sometimes, however, they'll turn the tables. They're individuals, and what is true of one is definitely not true of all.

They're an unpredictable and superb wild animal. They're smart, they're fast, and they're deadly. They're a four-pawed keg of gun powder wrapped in a fur coat that can explode at any moment. The man who meets bruin when the fuse is lit should have the firepower to stop him.

When You're 13, Bears Are Even Bigger

The late Bill Freeburn, then 13, son of salmon canner Larry Freeburn, recalls an action loaded week that had him up a tree at least a couple of times on Kodiak Island in the Karluk River country. One bear had a movie camera banged off his nose, but it didn't bother him.

Wrote Bill in "Darn Lucky," *The ALASKA SPORTSMAN®*, October 1952: "We decided to get up early in the morning and go fishing on the Karluk River, only a 40- or 50-minute hike from the head of Larsen Bay. At daylight, which was at 2:00 A.M., five of us started out. There was Milt Guyman, the skipper of the *Sunde*, a cannery tender, Buddy Dana, his engineer, Jack Baker, the Larsen Bay radio operator, Dad and I.

"When we got there we found the fishing was just as good as it had always been, and with Dardevle lures we were snagging king salmon and big steelheads with every cast. We finished fishing about 7:00 A.M., or rather Dad decided it was time to leave if we were going to get to the cannery in time to start work at 8:00 A.M. Everyone wanted to go back except Milt, who wanted to stay and fish for a couple more hours.

"No one had ever heard of a bear's coming near a group of people who were talking and making a lot of noise. Not even Charlie Madsen or Glen Collins, well-known guides. So we decided to leave the gun with Milt and head down to the beach.

"Well, I guess we would probably have been all right except that we took back a couple of king salmon, and we had to carry them down to the beach. On the way we had to cross some open country, and after we had reached the other side we started across a small area of brush and climbed the small hill on the other side of it. As we reached the top we were looking down into the last small meadow we had to cross before going into the final patch of brush to the bay. A boat would be waiting for us, to take us back to the cannery.

"We were just starting down when Dad spotted a bear in the meadow, smelling the tracks we had made on the way up. There is no place to go in this country, and very little time to go there in when you see a bear, so Dad told us to get up a tree. I was in no mood to argue with him, and I don't think Jack and Buddy were either. So we all made tracks for the trees we saw about 30 or 40 feet away.

"Did I say trees? They were little more than bushes, and there were only three of them. My dad, Buddy and I scrambled into them, leaving Jack Baker, the radio operator, who was carrying the fish, to get into the one across the trail a hundred feet away. Thinking quickly, Jack tossed the fish he was carrying into the brush and scrambled up his tree.

"I was still climbing when I realized that the bear was under Dad's tree. He must have come for all he was worth when he smelled those fish. It was lucky for us that he was not a mean or man-hating bear. He was just curious. Dad had Buddy's old-style movie camera, which weighed about four and a half pounds. His bush was so wobbly he couldn't get the camera steady to take a picture, so he hit the bear between the eyes with it. He told us later that the bear was so close to him he thought he was going to rear up. The heavy camera didn't even bother the bear. He didn't hurt it except for chewing the strap off. He didn't seem bothered even when we threw our reels at him, but when he came too close under my tree I tossed my hat at him and he took it and tore it to shreds. I still have the hat at home in Seattle. After that he circled our trees for a short time, then ate the fish, walked off in the brush and disappeared.

"When he disappeared, Dad called to Jack, who was in the tree across the trail. Dad told Jack he wasn't asking him or telling him, or anything else, but since he was the farthest away from the bear and out of sight, did he think he could get out of the tree he was in and get back to the beach and bring the boys back with a gun?

"Jack said he would try. He got down and ran all the way to the beach, only to find that the boat was still on its way up the bay. He says his legs haven't been the same since that trip to the beach and back. When the boat got to him he told the boys, and they started back up the trail with a gun.

"In the meantime the bear had come back near us, and Milt, who had quit fishing, was coming down the trail behind him. He didn't see the bear until we hollered to him, and just as the bear was coming back up the hill he shot. The bear took off, wounded, into the woods.

"That was the longest hour and a half I've ever spent. Afterward Dad asked me if I wasn't glad I did what he said and climbed a tree. I sure was! Being in the woods and doing the right thing is serious business and no picnic."

Then a few days later, Billy and friends had to climb trees again (and the Karluk area trees aren't all that big, either). An airplane pilot in the group, Vince Daly, was one of those climbing trees to get above the bears. He said later he thought of his flying instructor who had preached to him constantly about gaining speed and altitude and he concentrated on just that. In this particular case, with the bear apparently a really peevish one, and the height of protecting trees so marginal, it seemed best (in the 1950s) to kill the offending animal.

Not too long after this, Billy's summer was enlivened by another encounter . . . this one in a brushy creek area. In company with Verne St. Louis, cannery winterman, Billy was hiking back of the Larsen Bay cannery. He says, "We walked up to a small dam behind the cannery and when we started back we decided to come down the creek.

"Down on the creek we saw nothing but bear tracks and trails, and they were not just from a bear passing through. He lived in that country and owned it, and we could tell that right now. We walked through places that looked to us as though it would be the same as walking through a lion's den.

"Soon Verne shouted, 'There he is!'

"I couldn't see him — not that I was anxious to — but I jumped up onto a log, and then I saw him. He was about 40 feet away, standing up and looking at us. When I say he, that does not necessarily mean that it was a male. It might have been the old sow that's lived behind the cannery for years. She may have had new cubs, and we may have got between her and her cubs. At any rate, she charged.

"We didn't know she was charging at first. In fact, when she dropped to the ground we thought she was going to take off. Although the brush was too thick to see which way she was heading, Verne thought she was going and let the hammer down on his gun. It was an 8mm French La Brelux. All of a sudden we heard her breathing a big 'Whoosh, whoosh, whoosh,' and the brush started to crash. Verne shouted for me to get up a tree, but there wasn't time for anything like that. I jumped behind a tree about three feet from me.

"The bear was only about 40 feet away when we first saw him, and now we saw him again, about 20 feet away and coming hard. As soon as Verne had heard him coming he'd tried to pull back the bolt he had dropped on the gun, but it was too tight to be pulled back so easily and he had to pump another shell into the chamber. By that time the bear had run into the tree I was standing behind, knocking me flat on my face.

"It was just about that time Verne shot and hit the bear in the chest. He was only about 10 feet from the bear, the tree and me. Just as he shot he slipped and fell, and when he fell he yelled. With the bear that close it looked as if there wouldn't be much left of Verne. But the yell must have scared the bear. He turned, and when I thought he was working Verne over he was just turning into the brush on one side of him.

"It reminded me of the many times I'd heard how fast bears are. You just wouldn't dream they could go anywhere so fast as they do, and they sure aren't very pretty, coming at you with their mouths open and slobbering all over the place.

"And boy, talk about scared! It's a fact that I could feel my heart beating right up in my throat.

"Bears surely aren't very good things to fool with." □

SOME WILL CHARGE,
SOME WILL BLUFF

"Whatever you do, show your readers how quick and nimble bears are. People just don't realize the speed and agility of bears." (Ralph Ertz, Registered Guide, personal conversation)

"They're deadly, there's no two ways about that. At 25 yards, you'll probably get one shot; if you miss that shot, then you'll be a dead man." (Clark Engle, Master Guide, taped interview)

"Before I realized it, the bear was on me. All I saw was a brown wall of fur." (Creig Sharp, mauling victim, taped interview/story)

Not Just One Bear . . . Five!

In the fall of 1959 Jim Allen, of Anchorage and a former Dimond High School teacher, was hunting in Southeast Alaska with his friend Bob Bryant. They were hunting off a bay in Peril Strait. After looking at 15 bears, they spotted a good one about 500 yards away, so Jim left his partner on the stream bank. Allen carried a peep-sighted .348 lever action rifle as he stalked through the six-foot-high grass.

"When I got to where I could hear the bear fishing in the stream," he later told me, "I stood up from a crouched position to get an idea how far away he was. As I rose to my full height and looked over the grass, five sets of brown bear eyes focused on me.

The nearest bear was 40 feet away (every year they get closer and closer, and I still have nightmares about this).

"They stood there in that classic brown bear stance, on hind legs. Massive shoulders and front legs hung cocked at either side. Pigeon-toed paws held hooked, razor sharp claws. Powerful necks, nearly shoulder width, supported keg-shaped heads. Nickel-sized, pig eyes six inches apart pierced mine. Those rubbery nostrils tested the air.

"I've watched bears run. You couldn't outrun one. I was now in a position where I couldn't have made it to a tree or gotten up into a tree. I don't know whether I could have done anything. I felt so stupid with that little bitty peashooter in my hand. I thought, 'What a useless thing. What am I gonna do?' "

The closest bear was only three bounds and two seconds from Jim. Time stopped.

Brown/grizzlies are well known for their false charges. Many people are unaware of this trait, and even those with considerable experience in the out-of-doors readily agree, however, that it is impossible to determine whether the bear is bluffing.

The bear that is bluffing often roars a challenge of defiance and lunges toward its victim, stopping short — quite often rearing up on its hind legs, looking in the trespasser's direction and testing the wind with its nose skyward and its head moving from side to side. Bears have notoriously poor eyesight, and their "charge" is frequently just an attempt to get close enough to identify its assailant or get his wind. Standing on hind legs gives the bear a better sight picture and is the stance he uses when squaring off against other bears.

Time is interminable at this point. The bear may remain only a few seconds, turn, then leave; or this explosive situation may last several minutes. The bear may repeat this scene many times. It seems as though, given the distance, the time and the chance, the bear will withdraw from the confrontation with its pride intact.

Such was the case with Jim Allen: "At this point all five bears dropped to the ground and lit out of there up the stream. It seemed like I heard them for 10 minutes busting through the brush. When Bob got up to me, he said I was as white as a sheet, and I was just staring. I guess I was in a little shock too, as I started shaking. It is the only time in my life when I was petrified."

When Jim looked over the grass expecting to see one bear, he discovered that not one but five bears had been fully aware of his presence for quite some time. They did not charge; they did not bluff; they just left peacefully.

The Bluffers

Jim Baum, a Federal Aviation Administration worker, was walking with a companion near Cold Bay, on the Alaska Peninsula, when a large brownie surprised him. "My first reaction was strictly on impulse. I started to run just as fast as I could. I ran about 200 feet and looked back.

"The bear was right behind me coming full speed, not 30 feet away. I stopped and started hollering just as loud as I could several times, trying to get the bear stopped. He kept coming about a couple of more jumps. I jumped towards him then, raising my arms and hollering at the same time.

"When I did that, the bear stopped. I really surprised him I guess. He stopped and stood up on his hind feet then pounced down onto his front legs, stamping a few times — a couple of times he just went up about halfway.

"He kept beating the ground with his front feet, legs stiff; and he also growled and barked like a dog, off and on. I kept hollering, and I couldn't get the bear to leave. A 10-knot wind was blowing from my left to my right, and I thought that maybe if the bear got my scent, he would leave. So I started to circle the bear slowly to the left.

"The bear started circling to my right; and we circled in a clockwise direction, evidently he was trying to pick up my scent, he let out a big 'WOOF!' and he turned and jumped about three jumps away from me.

"Then he wheeled around again and beat the ground with his front feet again like he was making one last bluff. I jumped toward him about two steps and hollered. Then the bear turned around and started walking off. He stopped every now and then and turned around and looked at me.

"Looking back, running was the worst thing I could have done. The bear probably mistook me for a caribou, as they are in the area. It would have been better for me to remain calm and to wait to see what developed. I would recommend standing still first, then walking backward slowly."

Some people have been able to avoid injury by standing still or moving slowly away from alerted bears. A Canadian prospector, Fred Lypa of Edmonton, was surprised by a black bear. It made for the man, whose only weapon was an ax. He waved it at the bear and dropped matches into the dry grass as he backed toward his distant tent. Seven hours and several miles later Lypa reached his rifle inside his tent and dispatched the tenacious beast. (*ALASKA SPORTSMAN®*, August 1966)

The Bear Got The Ram

Another persistent bear challenged Warren "Canuck" Killen of Bettles Field, Alaska. The Killens were boating supplies up the John River when Warren spotted a Dall sheep on the mountain and left his wife picking berries while he stalked the animal.

After shooting and cleaning the ram, he tied it to his back. He attempted to unload his .30-'06 which was jammed. Electing to clear the weapon later with proper tools, he began his 10-minute hike to the boat.

A large grizzly interrupted his return by grabbing the ram from behind. Canuck was determined to keep his sheep and smacked the bear with the butt of his rifle. The bear swiped at him, but Canuck avoided it. Bruin lunged for the sheep, and Canuck slid from his strap and backed away. As he looked back, the bear was savoring his prize.

A Bear In Hot Water

Many people have escaped untold harm by being near some means of protection — house, vehicle or weapon. In 1955 three-year-old Christine Young was outside the Half Way Inn on the Alaska Highway playing when a grizzly, which was feeding at a garbage dump nearby, chased her. She beat the bear to her porch and through the door. Her father Stan Young grabbed a kettle of hot water from the stove and doused the bear as it reared up on the screen door. A visitor fetched his .38 pistol from his car, returned, and ended the bear's shenanigans.

Bear Meets Car

More than one person has had a run-in with *Ursus* while inside a vehicle. In September 1948 Pete Svendberg of Stewart, British Columbia, encountered a grizzly along the Salmon River near Hyder. Pete figured the road was wide enough for both of them and started around the bruin. As the car breasted the critter, he swerved and jumped onto the car hood. The bear could not grip the metal and slid off backward, raking gashes in the paint. Pete skedaddled for home.

Bear On The Roof

Mr. and Mrs. Sizelove of Long Beach, California, pulled off the road near Slana Cutoff to spend the night in their mobile home. A growl alerted the couple. Matt looked through the trailer door window and discovered a grizzly staring back. While Matt got his .22, Mrs. Sizelove banged a frying pan on the drainboard. The bear climbed on top of the car and then began ripping on the trailer. A shot in the paw discouraged the bear, and it fled.

This Bear Came For Christmas Dinner

A most unusual bear encounter developed near Homer, Alaska, about 1966. Bill Reynolds was four years old. He and a brother had gone sledding up a hill near their log cabin. It was the day before Christmas, and their mother was preparing Christmas foods while their two older brothers worked on a large igloo behind the cabin.

Bill's brother slid down the hill ahead of him and briefly disappeared from view. A few moments later Bill heard his brother yell something and saw him sledding rapidly down the hill. Bill jumped onto his saucer sled and began his descent. He soon discovered why his brother had disappeared and what he had yelled about.

Bill slid past a shallow hole from which emerged a very angry brownie. The boys barged into the cabin with the bear hot on their heels. Their mother bolted the door, but the bear knocked it from its hinges. They ran out the back door and took refuge in the igloo. Meanwhile the bear polished off the Christmas fixings and fell asleep on the cabin floor.

When Bill's father returned that night, the family decided to spend the night in the igloo. The floor was covered with straw, and it was warm enough for the family. First thing Christmas morning Dad Reynolds stole into the cabin, got a rifle and dispatched the still sleeping bruin.

With One Hand Yet

Another man had the presence of mind to hang onto his weapon after a surprise encounter with a brown. A Tlingit Indian, Jim Kasko, was hunting deer off a bay in Tenakee Inlet when he walked around a bush and met a bear head on. Both reacted on impulse, the bear lunging for Jim and Jim holding out his left arm to stave off the bear's jaws. It chomped down on his arm; Jim shoved the barrel of his .30-'06 against its chest and squeezed the trigger. The shot seemed only to enrage the beast, but Jim was able to chamber another round and break the bear's neck with his final shot. (*The ALASKA SPORSTMAN®*, December 1941)

This Bear Died Hard

Another hunter, Calvin H. Barkdull, got the scare of his life from a big bear that he described. ("The Killers," *The ALASKA SPORTS-MAN®*, June 1954) Barkdull got off a couple of quick shots at a bear "before he reached the creek in the bottom of the ravine. At the creek he jumped into a deep hole and went completely under, but came up blowing pink froth from his mouth and nose. His eyes were green as two big emeralds. He was the most terrifying sight I had ever seen.

"He started to climb out of the water hole on the bank toward me. I could see by the pink froth trailing from his opening and closing mouth and dripping from his big fangs that he was hard hit through the lungs. . . .

"I pressed the trigger. The cloud of black powder smoke cleared away and I saw the froth-flecked body slip back down the bank and roll over and over, the big paws clutching and grabbing at nothing.

"I was sure he was dead, but no such luck. He got up, stood broadside to me, blood streaming from several wounds in his body and from his nose and mouth. His great head was swinging from side to side and he was grunting, 'Uh, uh, uh!' I drew a careful aim for the base of his ear. He went down in a great, sprawling heap at the roar of the rifle, and when I heard that long, guttural death groan, I knew he was dead.

"My two companions had heard the shooting and now came to my assistance. We skinned the top half of the bear, but could not turn him over until we had cut off his fore shoulder and hind legs. Then we turned him over and skinned the back. One man carried the rifles. It was all two of us could do to carry and drag that skin to the boat on the beach."

A Lucky Slip

Although bears are normally very sure-footed, a few people have been fortunate in having a bear slip at an opportune moment. Brian MacLellan of Palmer told me about a close call two cheechakoes had on his childhood homestead in 1958. The MacLellans had just sat down to supper in their trailer-leanto across Knik Arm from Anchorage when they heard excited yelling.

Two men rushed onto their porch and blurted out their story. They had walked around a bend in the road and met about a ton of brown bear face-to-face, a sow and twin cubs. She came for the men. The hunters unlimbered their rifles and thought they were firing, but they merely jacked the loaded shells out onto the muddy roadway.

Just before the bear reached them, she hit a mud puddle, slipped and went down. She skidded along then rolled over. Righting herself, she called to her cubs, ignored the men and carried her bruised pride and behind into the undergrowth.

Downhill They Came Huckety Buck

Another close call involving a bear slipping was told to me by Chuck Wirschem, a fellow teacher at Dimond High School. A student of his and his father had just shot a moose and were packing it out near the Little Nelchina River about 1970. Dad was quite a distance ahead of the lad. The boy reached the bottom of a steep hill and looked back up the muddy trail. Chuck explained, "There, around 30, 40 yards behind him was a grizzly bear just snorting and frothing at the mouth.

"He stood up on his hind legs, hackles were up, jowls peeled back; and, boy, here he comes, huckety buck! The only thing the boy could think of was to get out of his pack as fast as he could. He was standin' there waiting. He didn't know what in the heck to do. Here comes this bear running full bore downhill; and the lad kinda did the old matador trick, and just spun out of the way off to the side.

"The bear put on his screechers to get stopped; and it was muddy enough that he just slipped and rolled over a couple of times, kept on going and the boy never saw him again."

A Wrestling Match

A charging bear shows little consideration. He usually catches man when he's least expecting a warm welcome from *Ursus*. The man is often unarmed and must rely on his quick thinking.

In July 1946 Bud Thayer, a welder in the Northern Commercial Company shop in Fairbanks, was charged by a young brown bear which his hunting party had just wounded. Bud, Lew Hall and Harold Myers spread out to look for the wounded yearling. Bud happened onto the animal which bounded toward him, and he jumped into a stream. The man and bear grappled until Bud was nearly threadbare and the beast had torn one of his boots off. A partner arrived and declared the man the winner with a well placed bullet.

Busted Him On The Nose

A Southeastern Alaska resident, Handlogger Jackson, was counting salmon in September 1956. He walked upstream carrying his walking stick. He hadn't gone far when a black bear exploded from the brush and keyed on Jackson. Handlogger thought maybe the bear was blind and deaf as it failed to heed his warning. He continued waving his stick and yelling to no avail.

When the bear's teeth were only 18 inches from Jackson's legs, he swung the heavy stick down across the bear's nose. The animal shut its eyes, ducked its head, turned and vanished without so much as a whimper.

Any Weapon Will Do

Shouting at a bear sometimes yields positive results as Alaska guide Harry Boyden discovered. He and a friend went looking for a lost horse. They had a packhorse carrying their supplies when they neared Harry's cabin on the Chitina River one evening. Harry hurried ahead to prepare a warm meal.

He was almost to his cabin when he saw a dark object and assumed it was his lost horse; but it was a grizzly. Harry wasn't concerned and began cursing it and waving his ax. The bear made straight for Boyden who figured it would stop.

When the bear was but a few feet away, Harry swung his ax; but the bear swatted it from his hand. Harry quickly doffed his wool cap and hit the bear in the face several times with it.

Bruin stayed on all fours, snapping and growling. Harry started backing up, tripped and fell. He grabbed a three-foot length of cottonwood and began poking the bear with it as he rose and backed toward his cabin where horse bells hung. Harry reached the bells and set up a clatter which caused the bear to back into a clearing in front of the cabin.

Harry's partner arrived with the packhorse, and the men got into the dwelling. Bruin stayed near the cabin all night but didn't bother the horse. At dawn the bear greeted the men as they opened the door. Harry's partner threw several chunks of firewood at the bear before it retreated into the woods.

A Real Ax And Gun Battle

Another ax wielder nearly met his Maker several years ago while trying to recover his rifle from a bear den in the Interior. Athabascan Indian Jimmy Huntington, now of Galena, was a youth of 16 at the time and happened onto a bear den. He decided to kill the occupant. He left his four-dog team and sled in the deep snow and began poking for the den entrance with the rifle stock.

Not being able to find the bear, he poked the rifle into the hole up to his shoulder. The bear growled and snapped the rifle from his hand. Jimmy resolved to get his rifle back by killing the bear in the tradition of his ancestors, with an ax.

He chopped an opening on top of the den and noticed what he guessed was the bear's head. After turning his dogs loose, he returned to the hole and swung down on the bear. He hadn't hit the bear a deadly blow, and the animal boiled out of the hole. One more swing of the ax cut off half its face.

A second bear emerged from the den, red-eyed and wild. Jim's dogs sprang into action, attacking the bruin which responded to the challenge by sending one several feet through the air. Shortly, another bear bounded out into the fracas.

As it came down to all fours beside the den, Huntington dispatched the first bear with a blow to the spine. He disemboweled the next bear with an upward thrust of the ax. The bear swung at him and laid open his arm beneath his heavy parka but was unable to pursue him.

He approached the third bear which swatted his ax from him after he sliced across its nose. He made a dive for his rifle in the den and managed to grasp it, turn and fire at the bear as it filled the entrance. The shot blew the bear's brains out, leaving Huntington wiser and thinner.

Saved By A Thermos Bottle

Several people have avoided serious consequences with bears by striking with whatever was handy. One such encounter involved Jim and Julie Carlson of Valdez. In October 1975 they were walking along the Richardson Highway to their truck in the failing twilight when they surprised a sow with cubs. She charged immediately, knocking Jim to the ground and dragging Julie across the road. Carlson jumped up and accosted the sow with his Thermos bottle. The bear dropped Julie and sauntered off. Mrs. Carlson sustained a broken leg and received 46 stitches to close her wounds.

The Friendly Visitor

One of the most unusual accounts of a man hitting a bear and living to tell about it involved a nearsighted old prospector. In 1927 the Susulatna man was working his claim alone when he picked up a specimen. He held it close to his face and adjusted his spectacles.

He felt a hand on his shoulder. Then another hand was placed on his other shoulder. Delighted that one of his many friends had come to visit him, he turned to greet him.

Staring into his startled, bespectacled eyes was a 400-pound black bear. Paralysis overcame the prospector. The two stared into each other's eyes. The bear was evidently intrigued by the reflection of the sun on the man's glasses and reached out his hooked claws, pulling the spectacles partially from the miner's nose.

At this point the man swung his rock sample with vigor onto the side of the bear's snout. The startled bear dropped to terra firma and left. (*The ALASKA SPORTSMAN®*, January 1939)

Keep Your Legs Inside The Tent
Sometimes a bear will erupt from the brush, grab someone and take off. When the Bering River and Chickaloon coal fields were in full swing, two men slept in a tent along a salmon stream. One man's barefoot leg protruded from beneath the blankets, seemingly an irresistible temptation for a passing bear. The bruin chomped down on the guy's leg and started off through the brush, dragging the helpless, screaming prospector along the ground. His partner came to the rescue and killed the bear and helped his friend, whose foot was badly mangled, back to camp. (*The ALASKA SPORTSMAN®*, June 1954)

Man's Best Friend
Another old-timer, Old Greg (Gregory J. Hildebrand), was walking along the trail to check some moose quarters he'd hung in a tree on the Chena River when he was attacked by a grizzly. Fortunately one of his dogs was with him for as the bear grabbed him, his dog latched onto the bruin. The dog's intervention allowed Greg to kill the bear and get himself back to his cabin for first aid and rest. (*The ALASKA SPORTSMAN®*, August 1949)

True Grit
A man's determination often supersedes that of his four-legged

aggressor. Olaf Heller, a fisherman living at Auke Bay, was hunting deer at Lisianski Strait when a brownie charged him. Heller got off a shot before the brown damaged his rifle. Bruin clamped onto Olaf's leg, and he whacked the bear on the head with the rifle stock.

Heller was surprised to see the bear break off the attack and wander off. The man had a badly mangled leg with a compound fracture. He pushed the bone back into place, bandaged the wound with his shirt and splinted his leg. Then Olaf crawled six miles through brush to the beach where he was rescued and taken by boat to Juneau. His own first aid saved amputation of the leg. (*The ALASKA SPORTSMAN*®, January 1944) The determination he possessed is essential for anyone who hopes to survive a mauling.   □

THEY'LL REALLY
MAUL YOU

"He grabbed my upper left thigh for a moment . . . I rolled into a ball on the ground and he bit the back part of my left thigh twice, picked me up and flipped me over. I covered my face and neck with my arms and had my rifle in my hands. He tried to bite me in the face and I shoved my rifle into his mouth. He bit it and broke the stock. He sheared the sling swivels right off the rifle." (Creig Sharp, mauling victim, personal interview-taped story)

"He reared up, put his front paws on my chest and sank his teeth into the left side of my head. Then he knocked me over and was biting my left side when I got off a second shot. He took my head in his mouth, but let go and ran off." (William M. Faulkner, mauling victim, The ALASKA SPORTSMAN®, December 1958)

She Dragged Me Out Of The Tree

Al Johnson, a state game biologist, was mauled by a grizzly in the fall of 1973. He had been sent to Mt. McKinley National Park to film moose for the Alaska Department of Fish & Game. He was overjoyed to get the assignment which was the first of its kind. While driving through the park with his Great Pyrenees dog, he spotted a sow grizzly with three cubs which he decided would make outstanding subjects. Al was carrying two cameras and three lenses of 1,000, 300 and 105 millimeter focal length, extra clothing, food and a few other items in his pack when he left the car.

Al is a friend and I was shocked to learn that he had been mauled. He shared his story with me later. "I left Tikchik in the car as I thought she might create problems with the bear. I approached the bear from downwind, always kept a healthy spruce nearby and never approached closer than a hundred yards. For about three hours I followed the bear and took a few pictures using the 1,000 mm lens. This lens, the equivalent to a 20-power spotting scope in magnification, is about two and a half feet in length and weighs 12 pounds.

"The clear fall sky along with the fine colors of the berry patch helped produce some good photos. Some 8 to 10 times I saw the sow pounce with her front paws and then slowly pull the heavy tundra back with her claws. I assumed that when a mouse that she had pinned became exposed, she would gobble it down then resume feeding on berries.

"By the end of the three hours the bear had moved about a quarter of a mile and still never knew of my presence. By this time in the afternoon the available light was getting too poor for the proper use of my 1,000 mm lens; and the bears were beginning to move faster, closer to the road, and into an area void of healthy trees. I decided then to try to call the bear to me so I could take pictures with the smaller lenses.

"I chose the healthiest tree in the area and moved to it. By 'healthiest' I mean the one I thought was most bear-proof. I left all gear except two cameras and the 300 and 105 mm lenses at the tree base and climbed up 15 feet.

"During the next few minutes I called — making a noise that resembled the squeal of a rabbit or hare. A friend and I had been successful at calling a number of black bear in to us using the same method. As soon as I called, the cubs became interested — looking, standing on hind legs and moving about the sow. Not until some five minutes later and close to the time I would have given up calling, did the sow show any sign of having heard me. She looked up for a few moments then headed in an arc and at a fast walk towards me.

"I stopped calling and started taking pictures. At about 50 yards distant I yelled at her, hoping to impress upon her that I was *man*. My yelling didn't cause any visible reaction. Some 30 to 40 yards out she looked back to the cubs. If there were any vocal signals, I never heard them; but the cubs then held back and followed the sow in some 30 yards behind her.

"When she was about 20 yards out, she had increased her speed to a slow gallop; and at that point I recorded a blurred image on film. Either because things started happening so fast or because of my state of mind, my images of some events aren't real sharp.

"Because of the lower limbs I could only hear the sow when she arrived at the tree base. She hit my pack and continued beyond the tree another 10 to 15 yards before she stopped and looked back toward the cubs which by this time were stopped a similar distance from the tree but on the opposite side from her and in full view of me.

"When I glanced at the sow, I realized she was confused — wanting to run but not wanting to leave the cubs. Like a young, dedicated, foolish photographer, I was trying to focus on the three standing cubs. I remember thinking, 'What a fantastic photo!' Unfortunately, I never pushed the shutter button for about then a cub let out a bawl which instantly sent the sow for my tree.

"I felt the tree shake violently. When I looked down, I saw her head and shoulders. The next thing I knew, I was being pulled from the tree. Evidently she had enough momentum and claw power to carry her up to my boot, for that is what she got hold of. I got the impression that had I been up the tree another foot or had I held fast to the tree, she would not have gotten me. The tree diameter at the butt was close to eight inches, and I was roughly 15 feet up; but until I return to measure, I'll never know for sure.

"Two things I distinctly remember while being pulled from the tree. I first remember limbs going through my left arm. I had been in a squatting position with my left arm around the tree and focusing with my left hand. With my right hand I was supporting the camera and readying to depress the shutter button. The second thing I remember was that about halfway down the tree I had a tremendous burning feeling come over my whole body — probably from adrenalin resulting from my realization of 'being had.'

"I had held both arms in front of my face for protection. I pushed once with one leg but decided it was fruitless and I'd best not get her mad. She bit each arm three or four times and made a few lacerations in my scalp with her claws. Fortunately she had the safety of the cubs on her mind and wasn't a hundred percent bent on getting me.

"After I pushed with one leg, I had my eyes closed except once when I looked up and saw her standing with mouth agape, arms open with claws exposed — just like a 'live mount' one sees in a museum with the exception that she was looking to one side.

"After she bit into my right elbow a good one, she grabbed my right shoulder and raised me off the ground a couple of feet. When she let go, I turned a little and came down on my stomach (just after I got on my stomach I remember thinking, 'I hope she hurries and gets it over with').

"I then pulled my head in and clasped the back of my neck with my hands to give some protection to my head and neck. Earlier I was reluctant to roll to my stomach since I knew that would expose my head. I knew that bear have a tendency to go for the head.

"Though she worked me over only a short while, it seemed like ages.

"She next bit the small of my back but couldn't get much of a bite because of my heavy clothing and because of the concave surface. She then stepped forward and bit my head.

"I remember hearing what sounded like the crushing of bone and wondered why I did not die or at least pass out. Come to find out she had only removed a strip of scalp, and it was the scraping of her teeth against my skull and not the crushing of bone that I had heard.

"As I said earlier, I don't remember any pain.

"She evidently figured I wouldn't give her any more problem for I heard her leave in the direction I vaguely remember the cubs moving. Right away I got up and headed towards the road which was roughly 300 yards distant. I turned and looked back once, but I couldn't see much.

"My right eye was swollen shut and I could only see out of my left by holding my head higher than normal. I pulled my coat hood over my head and held my right arm tight against my body to reduce bleeding. I lay down twice to rest before I made the road. Fortunately I lay on the road less than a minute before two vehicles came along.

"In the first was Rachael Sperry, a park employee who, fortunately, at one time was a registered nurse. She quickly checked me over, conferred with the two couples in the second vehicle, then headed to inform park headquarters. The young couples on vacation from California were kind enough to get me into a warm reclining position in their van and then transport me to park headquarters.

"By the time we arrived, a paramedic was there, and he bandaged my wounds to stop the bleeding. I was then transported via automobile to Clear then to Fairbanks Memorial Hospital via a small plane. I can't remember much about the trip except the pain in my right arm, being lifted into the small plane, and smiling when I saw the lights overhead as I was being wheeled through the emergency entrance of the hospital.

"The nurses told me that I was a bloody mess and that they spent over three hours in the emergency room cutting my hair and clothes, and cleaning me for surgery.

"Two doctors worked me over, transplanted some skin from my thigh to my head, patched the torn main artery in my right shoulder and sewed shut some cuts on my head. The puncture wounds on my arms were left open to drain and heal.

"One doctor told me that the paramedic from Healy probably saved my life by stopping the flow of blood — they put four pints of blood into me before I went to surgery.

"After two weeks in the hospital and some fine treatment by the nurses, doctors, my girlfriend, who is now my wife, and friends, I recovered almost to prior condition."

The Slingshot Bear

Having a confrontation with a bear never occurred to Al as he began his photo mission, nor did the two young men who went into the mountains south of Hope on Turnagain Arm anticipate bear problems. In August 1967 Mike Moerlein and his buddy Scott MacInnes, both of Anchorage, went into the Resurrection Pass country for several days of scouting in preparation for the upcoming moose season.

Scott's father, Charley, walked in with the young men, ate a bite, had some tea and returned to Anchorage, leaving the boys to themselves. The boys were excited about their adventure, which would be one of their last before starting school and their ninth grade year in late August. I got the story firsthand from Mike a year later when the two came out for the cross-country team which I coached at A.J. Dimond-Mears Junior-Senior High School in Anchorage. I razzed them about joining the team to learn how to outrun grizzlies.

On the fifth, the day after they'd arrived at the MacInnes camp, they ate a hurried breakfast, cleaned up around camp and headed out, carrying their wrist rockets in case they saw some spruce hens they could bag for table fare. Mike recapped his experience, "We made a trip to the East Creek cabin to get matches because we were low. This was my first piece of luck as you will see.

"Scott and I then continued down the trail toward the east and the mouth of Abernathy Creek. We startled several moose but no bulls, so we decided to cut over on the shoulder of the hill which paralleled the trail — it was higher, and we thought we might see more moose. As we crossed over, we saw several more moose but still no bulls. Once on the other side we started angling up to above timber.

"We stopped often to glass the valley and count the moose; we did this until 11:45 A.M. At that time we decided to start back. We angled back down the hill toward American Creek, still paralleling the forestry trail. We came to a very nice moose trail that was going our way and decided to follow it. After walking a short distance, Scott stopped and pointed to the ground.

"There, outlined clearly in the mud, was a bear paw track. It wasn't very big and went in the opposite direction, so we didn't give it much thought, except we began talking about bears as we walked. Suddenly we heard the most awful grunt or growl and a large brown animal came charging out of the brush. 'Moose!' I yelled and ducked behind a dwarf spruce (the only kind of tree growing in that area, reaching a height of around eight feet).

"Scott started running down the trail, but before he got 10 feet, the grizzly bear (not a moose) had traveled three times that distance through thick brush and hurled himself on Scott. I saw him shaking his head like a huge dog, but I didn't know if he was shaking Scott. I was a little surprised to say the least — this kind of thing would never happen to you.

"I feared for Scott's life, so I jumped out, yelled and waved my arms. I shot the bear with my slingshot. The bear charged me. I ran faster than I had ever run, but he caught me before I had gone 10 steps. As he ran over me, he bit me in the left hip and the left side of the head. I saw him turn around and come back at me, so I, in sheer desperation, grabbed Scott's walking stick and brought it down on his head with all my might.

"Then I jumped up and ran to the highest tree I could find (about nine feet high). The bear took off after I hit him and he bit Scott once more. Then he left for good. I called to Scott to climb a tree, but he said he couldn't.

"I jumped to the ground and my legs just collapsed. I soon had all our stuff picked up and went over to examine Scott. His right leg had a few tooth marks. His left leg was real bad, and he said that his arm hurt worse than anything. I didn't see any blood, so I thought he had broken it. I tied a T-shirt around his leg and made a sling for his arm.

"After bandaging Scott the best I could, I started carrying him down the hill. It was a long, slow walk tainted with the fear that the bear might come back; and Scott could not climb a tree, run or hide. Finally after an hour of walking, I had covered a half-mile with Scott. I left him in a small field with a fire and a lot of wood. Scott told me to run down the trail and get the men that were working on the trail [the U.S. Forest Service maintains the much-used Resurrection Creek Trail].

"The trail was completely unfamiliar to me, but I knew that I could not get lost because it was so well marked. The first five miles were the worst. I kept wondering if I was doing the right thing, and I was so worried about Scott. I thought he might suffer from shock or the bear might come back after him. As I ran, little birds would fly inches from my feet, and I was so wound up it scared the daylights out of me. Every time I turned a corner, there would be a marmot sitting in the middle of the trail; I constantly imagined bear!

"The first five miles were also the coldest, so when I came to an A-frame with some old clothes, I gladly took a badly needed wool coat in very good condition. I guessed this was the cabin that the workers were supposed to be staying in, but when I found that they were not there, I almost cried.

"Once again I had to make a very, very difficult decision. Should I go back and give Scott a sleeping bag and food and then walk out, leaving him alone to spend the night; or should I keep running out and risk not being able to make it back with help before dark? I decided to go for help. I ran all the way except where the trail was too rough.

"I finally reached the highway, peeled off my coat and started to wave down a car. The first two cars were going the wrong way, but then one appeared. I stepped into the road and started waving my hands and coat. The car went by me, and my heart sank because I didn't know how often the road was used. As I turned to watch it go down the road, I saw that it had stopped, and I started running toward it. When I got there, I told my story to the driver, his wife and kids. 'Hop in,' he said. The nearest phone was at Cooper Landing, so he gave me a ride there.

"Minutes later we pulled up at Cooper Landing. Walking up the steps, I started feeling very conspicuous. Sweat was still running down my body, mixed with blood and rain water. My hair was messed up because I had left my hat to mark the trail. My shoes were muddy and I had my hunting shorts on.

"When I went in, I asked for advice. I was advised to call the United States Air Force Rescue Coordination Center in Anchorage. The time was 6:30 P.M. I asked for a 'copter to pick me up so I could point out Scott for them. They wanted to know what the weather was like, how high the ceiling was and how fast the wind was blowing. They said they would consider all the facts and then call me back. Meanwhile I called Mom and told her not to worry, and cleaned up a little.

"The people that picked me up took me to their cabin and fed me supper. When we got back to Cooper Landing, the people there had called the Air Rescue back. Air Rescue had a 'copter on the way. At 8:00 P.M. we heard the machine. As it came over the hill, we saw it was a big banana helicopter.

"It landed and one of the crewmen jumped out and motioned me to hop in. When I got in it, they gave me a head phone that lessened the noise. They strapped me in my seat. While flying, I signed some papers for them. We flew over the trail that just hours before I had been running over.

"I settled down to think about Scott. I was really worried because he should have been expecting me at 6:00 P.M., and it was now about 8:30 P.M. I didn't have much time to think though, because the co-pilot asked me up front. I unstrapped myself and walked up front. It took me a minute to locate the place where Scott was, but I pointed where I thought he was. I spotted the flame from his fire and then pointed out a place where I thought they could land. They thought it was a good place and dropped a flare. The 'copter made a very safe landing. I jumped out the already open door.

"I waited outside while the doctor got ready. The doctor, his helper, and one more man from the crew came with me. We walked down the trail to where I had marked it, turned left and walked about two blocks. I stopped on a little rise and called to Scott. I heard him yell, so I lunged down the hill full-speed ahead. When I came to the creek, I just splashed through and ran over to Scott's fire.

"I saw Scott just the way I had left him except that he had a smile on his face a mile big. I was so happy I just stood there.

"Soon the men caught up. We put Scott on the stretcher after a short examination and started the hike out. Going over the rough part took all four of us to carry the stretcher. We finally came out on the trail and made it back to the machine in about 20 minutes. We took off eight minutes later. I sat at Scott's head on the way back, but talk was impossible.

"We landed at Providence Hospital's heliport 20 to 30 minutes later. Scott was rolled into the hospital and doctors started working on him right away. I stayed outside to talk to the Alaska

Fish & Game, the police, a reporter and my mother. It seemed like I had to tell the story to each one too.

"A nurse stuck her head out the door at last and asked if I was bitten at all. I told her I was and that I would be in soon. I went in and they washed my bites, but I had to wait until Scott was all done before I could get sewed up; and that was almost two hours. The doctor found no broken bones. Scott was walking three days after the attack, and I walked out of the hospital that night. All I can say about the whole thing is that we are two of the luckiest people in the world."

He Got More Than Water

Mike and Scott never did find out why they were attacked, and neither did a skipper who told John Graybill of Peters Creek his story several years ago. John told the tale to me second-hand. He and two friends went to Valdez and located a boat captain to take them out to Green Island to hunt deer in the early 1950s. John said, "The captain was a tall, slim fellow; and I noticed his face was pretty badly disfigured, it was a mass of scars and his lower jaw was a little lopsided. He stayed on the boat all the time, mentioning that he was afraid of running into bears although there weren't supposed to be any bears on Green Island. The skipper had had a bad experience a few years previous, and that's how he came by the scars.

"He told us that with this very same boat he was doing some fishing, and they needed fresh water. They pulled in where there was a fresh-water creek. He took the skiff, leaving his two mates or hired hands on the boat to do some work, and went ashore for water.

"The captain walked up the creek, entered the undergrowth and the people on the boat couldn't see him anymore. Somewhere along the creek, he ran into a bear which attacked him.

"It bit him in the side. The skipper said it took his breath away. The bear just acted like it was matter-of-factly going about a job. There was really not much pain connected with it. The bear was chewing on his leg or arm and broke a bone. Angered, the skipper dug his thumbs into the bear's eyes. The bear promptly came alive and shook the daylights out of him.

"That was the only really painful thing about it, that terrible shaking. And he said that's when the bear bit him in the face. He remembered having a hard time breathing while the bear was biting him in the face; and he could hear the bones crunch.

"The captain said that the bear dug a shallow hole, dragged him into it and kicked leaves and dirt and pulled moss over him. He lay there for possibly an hour or two then started back for the boat, dragging himself out of the hole, which was just a shallow depression in the ground — it wasn't a deep hole.

"Where the bear come from he didn't know, but it was on him again in a flash! It shook him up pretty bad again, slapped him around a little; and then it buried him in the same depression again — pulled the dirt, sticks and limbs back over him. That time the skipper stayed put, he learned his lesson the first go around.

"In the morning he could hear his crew walking up through the brush hollering for him. They got ashore somehow although he had the skiff with him. They were hollering for him, and he tried to holler back and let 'em know that there was a bear around. But because of his broken jaw and everything, he couldn't really speak plain; but he made noises.

"When he was lying in that depression in the ground the night before, he knew the bear definitely came back once because he heard it breathing and walking around him. He didn't hear it leave, so he assumed it was still there when these fellows came walking up the creek.

"They came right to him and helped get him back on the boat and to a doctor."

Wabash Bill And The Sow

Another boat captain had a similar experience on a deer hunt. Bill Riodan of Southeast Alaska left his *Wabash* afloat in the bay and had one of his crew row him ashore in his dory so Bill could replenish the meat supply with some fresh venison. He shot a deer, cleaned it, loaded it on his back and started for his ship. He came to a large, downed tree, placed his weapon atop it and began to climb over when a mammoth sow reached from the other side of the tree and raked Bill right down into her bed.

She ripped and tore his arms, neck and back, taking fist-sized mouthfuls. She stopped only when Bill ceased moving. When Bill regained consciousness, the cubs were dragging him about while chewing the deer on his back. Their mother's eyes were glued on their intruder. He moved, and so did she.

Bill tried to shield himself by kicking at her, but she grabbed his thigh, crunched it to splinters and shook him violently. He blacked out again.

When he came to the second time, it was totally dark — unless he was blind. Bill dreaded the thought of moving but forced himself to, discovering the bears were gone. He dragged his mutilated body downhill, and crawled into a muddy hole, a bear wallow. He crawled, drank water and crawled again. He managed to make it to a creek, dragging his mangled leg, and that's where his crew found him two days later.

They took him to the hospital in Juneau where doctors dressed 42 wounds. They felt the mud and vegetation of the bear wallow saved his life, serving as a poultice and a compress to seal his wounds. Large chunks of flesh were missing from Bill's body, but he lived. (*The ALASKA SPORTSMAN®*, June 1954)

Bear In The Alder Patch

Wabash Bill hadn't been looking for a bear when he stumbled onto that sow, but Coast Guardsman Creig Sharp, stationed in Anchorage, was. He found what he was looking for, but the results weren't exactly what he'd expected. Creig had heard many tales about wounded bears and the hazards involved in digging a wounded animal from the brush.

Following a small, wounded black bear is completely unnerving, but when you start along the blood spoor of his big cousin, you face the ultimate heart-stopper, as Creig discovered one spring day in 1977. He and two partners left Anchorage on April 25, 1977, for Kodiak Island. They landed at Karluk Lake equipped with a rubber raft and planned to spend two weeks hunting bears.

The men spent their mornings and evenings looking for animals with their spotting scope and binoculars. They saw bears, but none were close enough to pursue until the evening of the 28th. Kent Whisnant wasn't feeling well that day and stayed behind while Creig and Gary Grinde left the U.S. Fish & Wildlife Service cabin at 4:00 P.M.

Creig told me, "Upon our arrival at the point, we started spotting for bears again. We had only been there for a few minutes and we spotted two. They were about 300 yards from each other and at least 2,000 feet up the side of the mountain across the lake from us. One was a big cinnamon-colored bear and the other was a blonde-shouldered bear of much larger size, which we recognized as the bear we had seen the day before. After we had watched them for about 15 minutes, the blonde started moving up the mountain.

"They were right at the end of the alder line and the start of the snow which went all the way to the top of the 3,600-foot mountain.

We hopped in the raft and crossed the three-quarter-mile stretch of lake to the other side. Taking our hunting equipment, we climbed the mountain through very heavy alders until we broke out into the snow and the grass-covered slopes. We skirted the side of the mountain about a mile and a half and then sat down for a few minutes rest, as our lungs and legs ached from the climb.

"Much to our surprise, the big cinnamon-colored bear that we had spotted walked right up over a slope out of an alder patch in front of us about 80 yards. He hadn't seen us, even though he had looked our way a couple of times. He just continued up the mountain.

"I had a .340 caliber Weatherby Magnum with a 3x9 Redfield widefield scope on 6-power. The rifle was sighted in dead at 200 yards, and I was using 250 grain Nosler factory-loaded ammunition. I had a left front, almost broadside shot, and aimed a little low into the shoulder. When I fired, the bullet hit and knocked the bear up over on his back with all four feet sticking up in the air. As I tried to get another round into him, my rifle jammed! The bolt extractor had slipped over the spent casing, which was still in the chamber. I pushed the ammo down into the magazine and shoved the bolt closed and opened it again.

"The case came part of the way out this time so I grabbed it and threw it to the ground. I chambered another round as the bear sat up. Just as I readied to fire again, he rolled back over on his back; and when he came up, he had done a complete tumble and started to tumble down the mountain. I fired another shot, which was later found to have hit within five inches of the first shot.

"The bear was hit hard twice and fell down over a 200-foot embankment into an alder patch. Gary and I ran for the edge of the cliff to look for him, but couldn't see him anywhere. We skirted down the hill through the snow leaving a wide berth between us and the alders in case the bear decided to come out for us. After circling the alder patch, we crossed a blood trail two and a half to three feet wide.

"Gary and I stopped for a 10-minute rest and figured we would have to track down the bear through the alders. We started after him, following a trail of blood for a distance of about two and a half to three miles. He went up over hills and down through alders that were so thick we had to crawl on our hands and knees to get through them at times. The blood trail was so heavy, it was on the bushes as well as the snow. We found two spots where he had stopped and rooted out the alders, just breaking them off and leaving pools of blood.

"I shot the bear at about 7:15 P.M., and it was now about 9:15 P.M. We had tracked him for two hours. We stopped on a steep descent facing down the mountain. The alder patch was so thick that visibility was about 10 feet in any direction except toward the lake where we could see the water through the branches. Ahead of us was a trail of broken branches and blood leading toward the lake. We knew the bear had gone down that way.

"After discussing what to do next, we decided to get the raft, go back to the cabin and finish tracking the bear the next morning. It was getting dark and a slight drizzle of rain had started.

"I turned to go down the trail and had taken only 8 to 10 steps when I heard a big roar and a rushing sound from behind my left shoulder. As I turned and looked back, I saw the bear charging at me full speed. He was only six or seven yards away. I tried to fire but couldn't turn completely around as my right foot was caught in some alders. I turned back to my right just as the bear hit me.

"He was coming so fast I had the impression that he was going to overshoot me. He started to skid, stiffened up his front legs and just kinda bounced up to me. He grabbed my upper left thigh for a moment as I was turning and then released his grip. I rolled into a ball on the ground and he bit the back part of my left thigh twice, picked me up and flipped me over. I covered my face and neck with my arms and had my rifle in my hands. He tried to bite me in the face and I shoved my rifle into his mouth. He bit it and broke the stock. Then as he was letting go, he tore the sling off. He sheared the sling swivels right off the rifle.

"Gary was about 8 or 10 feet up the trail from me while the bear was on top of me. He stood there and fired three shots into the bear, hitting him in the lung area, shoulder and the neck. One of the bullets passed through my ankle up my leg — the bullet shattered all bones in the ankle and fractured the two large bones in my lower leg. The bullet hole was nine inches deep from the bottom of my foot.

"After the third shot, my partner accidentally hit the floor plate release lever on his rifle, and the other three rounds fell out just as the bear dropped me. Looking up, the bear headed for Gary, changed his mind, turned back down the hill and ran over me as he left. The force tumbled me up to a sitting position facing downhill. I raised my rifle and fired, hitting the bear in the left rump cheek as he retreated. The shot knocked him down in the alders about 100 yards away where we couldn't see him but could hear his bellering.

"Gary came over to survey my injuries. I told him I thought my right leg was broken, and I had been bit a couple of times on the left thigh (at that time we didn't know I'd been shot).

"Worried about the bear returning, we reloaded our guns and started down the trail. Gary tried a fireman's carry to transport me, but he couldn't pick me up because of his smaller size, and the thickness of the alders kept him from standing up completely. I scooted down about 400 yards through the alders on my rear, lifting my legs with my hands up over the branches as we went. It took us 45 minutes to get out of the alders and down to the lake.

"I didn't really feel any pain while the bear was biting me. I didn't realize how badly I was hurt until the bear ran over the top of me on his way down the hill, then I noted that my right leg was broken because my foot was free and just flopped around. It wasn't until we reached the beach that I started to stiffen up and feel the pain.

"It was about 10:30 P.M. and very dark when Gary left me both rifles and covered me with his shirt. He had only a T-shirt, pants and boots on as he started the three-mile run down the beach to the raft. On the way he encountered another bear and had to jump into the lake and swim around him several hundred yards to get past him. He got to the raft, shoved off and got only 50 yards off-shore when he ran into shallow water, hit a rock with the prop and sheared the shear pin.

"After trying to row the boat, he gave up. The wind was blowing, it was raining and foggy. He wasn't making any head-way. It was then he found a nail in his pocket, made a shear pin, and then headed into the wind to pick me up.

"I lay on the shore for about an hour and a half until Gary was able to get back to pick me up. We later learned that the bear was right on the other side of the hill from me — about 150 yards, but I hadn't heard him at all. While I lay on the beach shaking from the cold and pain, a fox ran up to me and tried to bite my foot. It was then I shot him with Gary's rifle.

"When Gary arrived, he helped me get into the raft, and we headed back to the cabin. Kent had gone to bed but had left a Cole-man lantern burning so we had a faint light to steer toward. The blowing wind and four- to six-foot swells on the lake were almost too much for our small raft powered by a three-horsepower motor. The going was slow as we had several inches of water in the raft caused by a hole in the bottom. As I lay in the bottom, I thought the raft would swamp at any time.

"We finally reached the cabin and Gary ran in to get Kent up.

They carried me in, put pressure bandages on my left thigh and then cut off my right boot. There was a large hole in the bottom of my foot, and we assumed it was a bear bite until the next day when the x-rays revealed bullet fragments.

"After Gary and Kent changed all my clothes and put me in two sleeping bags, I drank a lot of hot coffee and soup to keep me from shaking. I still shook for about three hours and the pain intensified to a degree that was almost intolerable. I tried to keep my mind off of it by talking and thinking of a lot of other things. Kent stayed up and talked to me all night.

"Gary left the cabin about 4:30 A.M., took the raft and floated down the Karluk River about eight miles to Portage Campgrounds. Some fishermen there pointed out the eight-mile overland trail he had to take to Larsen Bay. After crossing into the bay, he met a commercial fisherman who took him up the bay in his skiff to the town of Anton Larsen.

"They located a man who had a radio in his house, and called the Coast Guard Air Rescue Service which dispatched a helicopter with two doctors on board to pick me up. They arrived at 12:30 P.M. and flew me to the Air Station dispensary in Kodiak. First aid was administered and x-rays taken. I was then flown via C-130 aircraft to Elmendorf Air Force Base Hospital in Anchorage."

Creig spent several months under doctors' care. They were greatly concerned that they might have to amputate his leg (should it get infected); but he recovered. His bear was located the day after Creig left for Anchorage. It was quite dead less than 200 yards from where he'd awaited rescue. The hide squared 11' 2" and the skull scored $29\frac{5}{16}$".

Two Bears Attacked

Considering the severity of attacks — the bear's ferocity and number of wounds inflicted, it is amazing that many men survive. Ron Cole who, with his wife, Darci, lived in a cabin on Lake Creek in the Susitna valley north of Anchorage, encountered a male and a female brown bear near his cabin, and as a result he will never be the same as he was. It was a spring morning when he surprised the mating pair, and they attacked him on sight. The bears were within 25 feet of him, and he didn't even have time to unholster his .357 Magnum pistol or reach a tree, though there were many in the area.

The sow was first to reach him, and she opened his head with a single swipe of her paw. He blurted out, "God, forgive me and please make it quick." (Ron Cole, "I Was Dying But Not Dead," *ALASKA*® magazine, June 1976) The sow bit into his face and ripped the front of it away. She seemed to be eating his head. He tried punching her with his fists to no avail. He noticed his right hand was useless, and decided to play dead — a decision which took great self-control as she bit him all over.

She then roared away through the brush, but the boar stood with forelegs on Ron's chest, licking at his face and scalp. The sow ran around Ron several times about 50 yards away before returning to him.

She slapped him a couple of times, but he lay motionless. Then the animals broke off the attack and started off through the timber, growling. Ron stayed still for several seconds before rising. He looked in the direction of the bears through his good eye, a costly mistake.

They saw him and renewed their attack. Ron tried to run but ran into a tree. He tried to climb it, but then one bear bit his foot and flung him several feet from the tree. He landed and tried to protect his stomach. Again, he tried to feign death. An eternity later the bears were gone.

Ron managed to get to his Lake Creek cabin and his wife Darci, who tried to give him a drink by pouring water into his face and allowing it to run down his throat. Darci got Ron into their cabin and tried to cover and comfort him before leaving on a three-mile run for help. Ron was rescued and taken to Providence Hospital in Anchorage, where six doctors worked on him for seven hours.

Ron had lost half his blood; much of the flesh had been shaken loose from his bones; most of the bones in his face and foot were broken; he had a broken rib and a broken knuckle in one hand. The doctors used several hundred sutures to repair his wounds and wire him back together. Ron wasn't all too eager to meet that sow again.

Sows Can Be Mean

Sows can be ferocious, especially if they are surprised with their offspring. In the fall of 1952 while hunting moose near his Kenai River cabin, Henry Knackstedt, 39-year-old fisherman-home-steader, met a sow. He was walking along a game trail when he discovered that a sow with cubs had evidently passed just ahead of him. He took a detour and paralleled the trail a couple of hundred yards away. Unknown to him, the bears had left the trail at the same spot, and they lay just ahead of him in his pathway.

He walked along lost in thought until a growl brought him back to the present. He looked up and into the raging eyes of a thoroughly angry mother brown bear not more than 15 feet away. He shouldered his rifle, but noticed that the bolt did not pick up the shell as he slid it forward; and then the bear was on him. He brought the weapon up in front of his face and looked into a mouthful of death. She knocked the rifle from his hands and pulverized him with a paw.

He came to a short time later in a pool of his own blood. The one swipe of her paw had loosened his eyelids, broken his left eye socket and cheekbone (they hung by shreds of skin) and left the left side of head a mass of blood and gore. She had bitten or clawed part of his skull away, exposing his brain tissue to the air. His packboard was missing a few mouth-sized pieces, no doubt saving untold damage to Henry.

He was able to find his rifle and summon help with distress-signal shots. Henry mended in a Seattle hospital.

He Fought Barehanded

Dick Jensen, a bush pilot who lived at Naknek, and his wife also surprised a brown bear and cubs and managed to escape. They were walking into Naknek around 3:00 A.M. July 21, 1973, after having beached their fishing boat the night before in the fog and hiked over 20 miles on their homeward journey. Unbeknownst to them, a bear family pilfered food from a garbage can along the road. In the early morning hour and in their exhausted condition, Dick and Charlotte failed to notice the bears until they were only a few yards from them. Charlotte screamed and ran toward a nearby cabin.

The cubs lit out for the brush. Their mother and Dick reacted on impulse. She exploded, sending gravel flying in her rage to get to Dick. The rage she felt was matched by that of Jensen. Anger filled his being, and he determined to lick this four-pawed hellion with his bare hands.

Dick didn't have long to wait. She swung, and he kicked. Her three-inch shredder-claws missed, but his foot didn't. As he sidestepped and kicked, his foot found her midsection. He kicked and gouged and punched.

She towered over him on hind legs and chomped onto his skull with her teeth. His scalp ripped, but he felt no pain. Next she chomped onto his left shoulder, lifted him free of the ground and shook him viciously. Then she dropped him and moved off in the direction of her cubs. She looked back, saw Jensen rise, returned and mauled him severely around the face and the neck before leaving for good.

Charlotte had made the safety of the cabin's interior and convinced the two strange young boys (whose parents were not home) that she and Dick needed help. She was beside herself with concern when Dick stumbled to the door, voiceless. The older boy (13) found a key to his parents' truck and drove the Jensens for medical help. Dick needed emergency medical treatment, and the closest available center was Anchorage.

Arrangements were made, and he was flown to Anchorage and taken to Providence Hospital where an expert medical team (Doctors Milo Fritz, Jack Smith, Doug Smith, Don Addington and Chei Mei Chao) began work on him at 8:30 A.M. that same day. Dick made an astounding recovery and returned to his Naknek home.

The Mauling of Knut Peterson

Knut Peterson, now living in Tok, was also on his way home when a grizzly altered his plans. In August 1949 he had spent the night visiting his friend Ole Hougland at his cabin on the Slana River about 50 miles from Tok. The next morning Knut started the mile hike to his car from the cabin and had gone a quarter of the way when a grizzly came out of nowhere. He thought he might escape if he could make it to the Slana River, only a few yards away. The 700- to 800-pound grizzly caught him first.

The bear mauled Knut mercilessly, dishing out more than most men can take. Moments after the attack began, it was over and the bear was gone.

The only clothing that remained on Knut was the waist of his pants. All he could see of himself was torn flesh and muscle. He had a broken right arm and wrist; his right thigh looked like so much fresh ground round; the muscle was torn away from his thigh bone; the right side of his face was bitten in two (from below his right eye, cutting off part of his nose and cutting his upper lip in half); his lower jaw was broken (his lower teeth came out with the jawbone pieces); Knut's windpipe was exposed, and a large chunk of his scalp was torn off.

Knut didn't really think there was much hope for him, but he headed for Ole's place anyway. Once Ole got his friend comfortable he went as quickly as possible for help. Knut was taken down the river to the highway and by car to Chistochina and from there by plane to Anchorage. He spent almost a year at Elmendorf

Hospital and it took two and a half years for scar tissue to cover his bare skull. He survived; but Knut hasn't gone out of his way since then to look up any grizzlies.

Attack at the Moose Kill

Even though man has a way of meeting bears, he's not necessarily looking for them. Forest H. Young, Jr., of Haines, Alaska, wasn't looking for grizzlies in September 1955, but he found them anyway. He and his partner had killed their moose on the Chilkat River and packed part of the meat to camp. They'd left some of the meat and the hides cached in a tree a short distance from the kill, planning to go back after them. Forest continued packing meat for the next few days while his partner, Marty Cordes, returned with the canoe full of meat to Haines. Finally all that remained of the cache was Marty's moose hide.

Marty had returned and decided to shoot a few grouse the morning Forest made his last trip for the hide. When he arrived, weaponless, at the kill site, Young found that bears had taken over — they had covered the remaining gut piles with sticks and moss. Forest went to the tree and began to retrieve the hide when he noticed two bears a hundred yards away. He figured they were grizzlies but wasn't concerned, his bear experience convinced him they wouldn't bother him.

Instantly one of the animals charged him. Still unalarmed, he waved his arms and shouted, normal procedures in such a situation. But this bear wasn't going to be bluffed. Forest jumped for a low branch on a tree and had hardly climbed half a dozen feet when the grizzly cleared the brush and clamped down on his right leg, ripping him from the tree.

When he landed the bear held him down with one paw and chomped on his thigh with its teeth, ripping out a mass of flesh. Forest pounded the brute in the face with his fists — tantamount to a mouse chasing a cat. Their faces were only a foot apart as the boar ripped flesh and clothing. Forest broke his hand pounding on the bear's face, and the beast continued to shred his lower limbs.

Young determined to play dead and fell to his side. The bear stopped immediately and might have left, but Forest groaned in spite of himself. The bear bit him in the side exposing his bladder.

The pain was excruciating; but Forest did not move. The bear took a few more bites, ripping three ribs loose from the spine and opening up the chest cavity. Forest remained silent and motionless. The bear left.

Young tried to relax and tell himself the bear was gone, but the boar roared back two or three times to inspect his victim. The ground trembled under him, and he lay there expecting the bear to rip him apart any moment. After a while it became necessary for the man to turn his face to facilitate breathing and to allow fluids to drain.

It was too much to hope for. Here came the bear again! He must have sensed the man's different position because he lit into Forest anew, spanning his buttocks and biting to the bone, picking him up and shaking him. Forest thought his head would pop off, and he feared his spine would snap. The bear then dropped him and left.

It was some time later that Marty called from a distance. He was aghast when he discovered his partner. Marty wanted to carry Forest back to camp, but the pain was unbearable for the injured man. Marty went to camp to retrieve a sleeping bag, air mattress, some food, water, gas lantern, a shotgun and shells. He took them back to Young, made him comfortable and then headed for Haines and help.

During the next 14½ hours Forest hung on to the thin thread of life. The bear returned a few more times and was frightened away by shotgun blasts. Late that night Marty returned with help, but the bruin was reluctant to give up his victim for he followed them all the way back to the cabin, roaring in the distance.

The next morning a helicopter picked Forest up and took him to Juneau where Dr. Cass Carter worked on him. Young had suffered a severe mauling, which included having a rib ripped out. The extent of his injuries was so critical that Dr. Carter gave little hope of survival unless the victim had received medical attention within six hours. But Forest Young, Jr., *did* survive.

She Tried To Get My Head In Her Mouth

Rod Darnell was a veteran woodsman, a man who had experienced a number of brown bear encounters (including one where he was retreating on a trail from an advancing and threatening sow, striking both her and the brush along the trail with a taken down fly rod, when he fell down on his back . . . striking out with both feet as well as the flailing fly rod, he hit the bear "at least several times" when she was strangely frightened away, probably by concern for her trailing cubs . . . at least long enough for Darnell to climb a tree with his friends whose retreat he had been earlier covering).

The bear in the following account wreaked real damage to Darnell in a surprise attack . . . "Four hours on the operating table, weeks of convalescence — and I was scarred for life. How long did it take the bear to do all that? Certainly less than a minute."

"It was the weekend of September 29, 1957, and I had promised Vern Clemons, my dry cleaner at Triangle Cleaners, across from the Baranof Hotel in Juneau, and Francis (Ree) Riendeau, husband of my counter girl, Thelma, a deer hunting trip to my favorite mountain up from Whitestone Harbor on Chichagof Island.

"My pet name for it was Horseshoe Mountain, because from the beach it looked like a giant horseshoe. To reach the mountain, we had to follow a well-used bear trail up a long hogback ridge to the high alpine meadows where the bucks hang out until snow drives them down. From there we could approach the horseshoe, complete the circle if we wanted to, and come down to the lower end of the horseshoe where the beautiful meadows were.

"I got everything ready, including the clean white flour sacks we always used to pack the meat in, gassed my boat, the *Liability*, and we made the four-hour run to Whitestone Harbor. We anchored, put out the pot for Dungeness crabs, fixed our dinner and went to bed.

"The next morning we were up early. As soon as we had breakfast and packed our lunches we went across the bay with the dingy and outboard. It was just getting light enough to see. Once on the island, we took off, single file, through the brush and trees on a faint deer trail. The trail led to a wide muskeg area at the base of the mountain we were to climb.

"We were almost to the opening when I saw her — a brownie with two young ones behind her. I turned to Vern and Ree and told them to start shouting and making noises to scare her away. She heard us and turned to face her yearlings, but she did not want to go back out into that open muskeg. She turned toward us, bristled up like a dog.

" 'I think she's coming for me,' I said. 'Get ready.'

"I was carrying my .30-'06 in a sling on my shoulder, but I got it off and threw a shell into the chamber. By that time she was almost on top of me. I got a shot off and dove into the ground to protect my face and head, and I threw my left arm across the back of my neck.

"I had heard and read when I first came to the country in the spring of 1934 that when all else fails, just dive to the dirt and play dead. That flashed into my mind when I didn't have time to get off another shot although I had managed to throw another shell into the chamber. She hit my left shoulder about the time I was going face down. Things were happening real fast now. I'm sure I did some praying. I thought this was the end. She kept tearing at me and trying to get my head in her mouth. She would try to pick me up, and that drove me further into the ground. Fortunately, my packboard was protecting my back. Somehow, Vern had a chance to get a shot into her and she rolled off me.

"All of a sudden, everything was terribly quiet.

"I found out I wasn't dead and I could hear those yearlings, their teeth chattering. They had climbed a tree right over us. I told Ree to shoot them as they would bring more bears to us with that particular noise. I can still see those cubs tumbling down. I thought they were going to land right on top of me, they were so close. So, there we were: the Big Mama bear still breathing right by my side and the two cubs close by. Vern gave Mama the *coup de grace*.

"Then, either Vern or Ree started to pull my rifle out from under me. The barrel was pointed right at him and I said, 'Don't! I'm sure I threw another shell in and the safety's off.' Strange how clearly a person's mind can work at a time like that.

"I was bleeding badly, especially from the scalp wounds. Vern, who was also president of the Juneau Ski Club, was an expert in first aid. With all our clean flour sacks we had plenty of material to do the job of binding me up — arm, shoulder and head.

"Where the 220-grain bullet from my .30-'06 hit I will never know, but we figured I must have shot her in the face and damaged her lower jaw; otherwise she would have torn off my left shoulder with that first bite. I only had teeth marks on one side, same as my left arm. But when she kept driving me into the ground and trying to get my head in her mouth, she almost scalped me.

"I was not yet concious of any pain. Vern and Ree got me up on my feet and saw that I could stand. Then they got me between them and we slowly worked our way back to the beach where we had left the dingy. All the time I was telling them what to do in case I blacked out on them. I briefed Ree on the operation of the *Liability* — where the safety switches were located and the valves to the gas tanks. He had had lots of boating experience, but every boat has its own peculiarities.

"They picked up our crab pot and away we went. I suggested they cut diagonally across to Funter Bay cannery where they could radio for a plane and medical help, as I did not have a two-way radio aboard. I also told them that if they saw a large boat out in the strait to head for it and ask them to radio for help.

"As soon as we got outside of the bay, where Chatham and Icy straits join, they spotted a boat and headed for it. It turned out to be the mail boat *Forester,* with skipper Don Gallagher. He radioed in and told them to pick me up in Funter Bay only about five miles away. He also gave me some penicillin.

"It was only about a 30-minute run over to the cannery at Funter Bay. Just as we were tying up, we heard the roar of the Alaska Coastal Grumman Goose, with skipper Joe Kendler, Alaska Coastal's office manager, Floyd Guertin, and young Dr. Don Rude.

"I was in a lot of pain by then. My left eye was swollen shut and my chest really hurt. I had been carrying my binoculars inside my shirt to keep them clean and dry, so every time that bear tried to get my head in her mouth, she put her whole weight on me. The binoculars had been pushed against my chest so hard they had torn the cartilage loose from my breastbone.

"They got me aboard the Goose okay, and Dr. Rude insisted that I lie down on the stretcher, which I didn't want to do as the flow of blood on my scalp had almost stopped. But down I went, which did start the blood flowing again. He didn't get it stopped until we reached St. Ann's Hospital. Just before I went under the anesthetic, someone told me that it had only been an hour and forty minutes since Vern's cool shooting had blasted that mad she-brownie off my back. I heard someone else say, 'And it's a lucky thing.'

"It took Dr. Rude and the nurses the rest of the day to clean me up and sew me together. Four hours on the operating table, weeks of convalescence — and I was scarred for life. And how long had it taken the bear to inflict the damage? I wouldn't have believed it except that Vern and Ree agreed — less than a minute. At that rate I couldn't have survived the attack much longer.

"The word had gotten out that I had lost a lot of blood, so there were lots of my friends at the hospital to donate. I remember my first blood was given by Ideal Wildes, a pioneer Alaska friend of Finnish extraction. So I always say I'm part Finn now; the rest of me is still Tennessee Ridge Runner.

"I never wanted to kill a bear and in all my years in Alaska I've never gone bear hunting. That last night before the hunt as we lay in our bunks on the *Liability* — feeling the gentle motion of the boat . . . thinking of those beautiful fat bucks waiting for us up on the mountain . . . listening to the quack of a mallard on the tide flats behind us . . . knowing in the morning that our crab pot would be full of these succulent Dungeness crabs and the deer at the crack of dawn would be out feeding on heart leaves (deer lettuce) putting on that beautiful white fat that when cooked is sweeter than any sugar . . . that's why we went hunting.

"But brown bear will kill. I don't need any more proof now. I have always figured that the bears were entitled to their place; they were here a long time before I was. They are a great asset to Alaska, and the guides and sportsmen are more than welcome to my share. The big brutes have nothing to fear from me and I wish I could let them all know that. Most of us who live in Alaska feel the same way. We like to live and let live, but how can we let the bears know that?"   □

THEY WILL KILL

"From the evidence, the victim evidently ran from the tent before he met his fate. The tent was torn up, all his gear, jacket, and boots were there, but his sleeping bag was not harmed and there was no blood at the campsite." (John Sarvis, refuge biologist. From an official report regarding Jay B.L. Reeves, Cold Bay fatality, August 1974 and later confirmed in personal letter from Sarvis, February 9, 1979)

"The great hunter lay on his back, his stomach and intestines strewn over the ground, his scalp torn off, and his tongue hanging from his mouth." ("The Forty-ninth Bear," by Katherine Bayou, The ALASKA SPORTSMAN®, *September 1945)*

"Most fatal bear attacks occur very suddenly and under the most unfavorable possible conditions." (Keith Young of Anchorage)

Camping Weaponless By a Salmon Stream Was Fatal
Sixty-knot winds blasted the little tent. With each gust the nearby alder clumps whooshed and shuddered, flailing their branches wildly. A steady drizzle fell in the fading twilight. Below the bank, Frosty Creek meandered through the tundra toward distant Izembek Lagoon, near the small community of Cold Bay on the Alaska Peninsula. Dead decaying salmon littered the banks at

water's edge; and bear day beds, circular pockets of bare dirt eight feet in diameter dug into the tundra, cluttered the banks. A damp chill filled the air, but the lone camper who occupied the tent entertained high hopes for the morrow.

Jay B.L. Reeves, 38 years old and single, looked forward to the coming seven days during which time he would attempt to photograph some large brown bears to add to his wildlife photos and footage at home. Jay was more than prepared for this long awaited opportunity. He'd stocked up on food and film and brought his photo gear to this Frosty Creek setting.

Jay prepared a light evening meal and polished it off while pondering the events of the day. He'd spent an hour that morning talking with Robert L. Jones at Izembek National Wildlife Range's office in Cold Bay, seven miles away. Jay queried the Fish & Wildlife Service about the most likely place to find bear subjects, and he'd decided upon the Applegate Cove/Frosty Creek area. It was an area bears frequented along the salmon stream and had sufficient alder cover for the creatures.

Reeves and Jones had also discussed and agreed that a .357 Magnum handgun would not be adequate to stop a bear. Jones advised Reeves that, although he shouldn't consider the pistol as adequate protection from a brown bear, if carrying the pistol gave him peace of mind, he should take it. Jay decided not to pack the pistol.

Reeves had gotten a ride to Frosty Creek and managed to set up his tent in the blowing wind and steady drizzle. His tent was near Frosty Road where he'd been let out earlier in the day, and he felt safe pitching it along the bank of the stream.

Now he doffed his boots and clothes and slid into his sleeping bag whose cold nylon cover temporarily gave him goose bumps. In minutes he was toasty warm. With seven days to film, where should he start tomorrow? Before he knew it, slumber had overtaken him, and he slept in solitude, though the tent occasionally shuddered from a blast of wind.

The drizzle continued as the salmon wove their way upstream, and the bears fed along the creek's banks. One bear, annoyed or drawn by the flapping of the tent fly, approached Jay's refuge, gathered in the man smell and the faint odor of some form of food. The bear was accustomed to scaring off lesser animals with a guttural grunt as it walked the stream bank.

Bears that heard his cough, left his fishing territory to await their turns. He began coughing and chomping his teeth as he neared the tent.

Reeves awakened from his reverie, thankful that he'd escaped from the bear in his dream. *But* the coughing outside the flimsy shelter continued. Was that the wind or a bear that moved his tent?

The grunting noise he heard was definitely a bear, he'd heard it on too many other filming missions to mistake it.

Maybe he should have brought his .357. Perhaps he shouldn't have set up his tent so close to the bears' feeding grounds along the streambank.

Jay slid from the warmth of his sleeping bag. Fear welled up within him. Maybe the bear would leave. Maybe the food would placate him and Jay could make a run for it. The bear probably only wanted his food. If he had to leave the tent, the bear probably wouldn't follow him down the road.

An ear shattering roar interrupted the *flap, flap, flap* of the fly; and the lightweight tent gave way under 600 pounds of brown bear. Somehow Jay managed to slip through the tent's opening. As he cleared the nylon fabric and sprinted barefoot toward the road, a fear of death gripped him. He ran faster than he had ever run; then he looked back.

The bear was chomping and ripping the tent and its contents. Then the animal saw Jay. Escape was too much to hope for. Jay had seen these creatures run, and he knew he couldn't out-distance one; and he knew his chances of surviving a hand-to-hand confrontation were slim.

The bear was five years old and in prime condition. Its paws were eight and a half inches across, it had good teeth and wore an eight-and-a-half-foot pelt. The bear charged Jay, overtaking him in seconds.

A single swat of the brute's paw knocked Jay to the ground, then he had to contend with jaws. A few savage, ripping bites and it was all over for the photographer. He never had a chance.

The bear clamped onto Jay's left leg and dragged him to the nearest alder clump and began feeding. All through the night the bear fed upon his human victim. A couple of times he left the alder thicket and wandered back to Jay's tent, ingesting some of the food, wrappers and all. By morning there wasn't much left intact of Reeves's camp.

Frank Snodgrass of Cold Bay drove by the camp about noon the next day and noticed the collapsed tent. He saw no human activity and reported his discovery to officials at the office of the U.S. Fish & Wildlife Service. They began an immediate investigation.

It was August 3, 1974, and the Fish & Wildlife Service officials at Cold Bay were concerned for Jay B.L. Reeves's safety. John Sarvis and John Stimpson climbed aboard a helicopter chartered by a geophysical firm and searched the length of Frosty Creek and the outlying area. There was no sign of human activity near the photographer's camp. Chewed and flattened cans of food were strewn about, and a trail of paper and other articles led toward an alder thicket.

Sarvis checked out some alders from the ground while Stimpson and the pilot flew to another spot. On the chopper's first pass 25 feet above the ground a bear erupted from the brush. It hid itself quickly in more alders. Sarvis was picked up, and they continued trying to find the bear.

On one pass they discovered some blue clothing and noticed the alders were torn up. The chopper moved to one side, and the men saw the deceased man's skull. They obtained a rifle and flew above the alders again trying to locate the bear. Suddenly it lunged from the alder cover 300 yards away. The chopper zeroed in on the animal which Sarvis dropped with one .30-'06 shot.

It was getting late, but the crew landed to check the dead bear. Sarvis opened it and examined the stomach, which contained some plastic bags, pieces of human bone, skin and hair. The party left as darkness fell.

Several men returned the next day to check the camp, examine the bear and look for Reeves's remains. The scene they found was a grisly one. All that remained of Jay B.L. Reeves were his belt and belt knife in a sheath, T-shirt, shirt, pants, some ribs, part of his pelvis and his head.

The Jay B.L. Reeves incident above is based on official reports I obtained from the United States Fish & Wildlife Service. Most of the information came from a report written by John E. Sarvis, a biologist then working at Izembek. John is now the refuge manager. Since I wanted all the known facts regarding the fatality, I sent my account to John asking him to comment on it. He edited it and wrote me, "Many of the details in the account are fictitious since no one was with Mr. Reeves at the time of the encounter. The known facts (upon which this account is based) are that a bear was found by Mr. Reeves's remains, which were located in alder several hundred yards from his campsite. Mr. Reeves's remains were found inside the bear when it was killed. No one knows what actually happened that night, whether the bear that ate him was the one that killed him, or how Mr. Reeves died. Mr. Reeves made two errors which contributed significantly to the odds of having contact with bears.

He had food in his tent and he camped on a bear trail on the bank of a major salmon stream, rather than camping away from the stream."

This Bear Also Ate A Man

Bears do not make a habit of killing men, let alone eating them. In the annals of recorded history there has never been a killer bear in the same sense as a man-eating tiger. Bears do not kill two or three men for food; some of the big cats are known to have killed hundreds and eaten them. There are few recorded instances of a bear killing and eating a man. However, there are a few.

Alan Lee Precup hiked alone in Glacier Bay National Monument. He wasn't particularly afraid of wild animals, though his experience with Alaska's giant bears was limited. The 25-year-old from Illinois arranged with Glacier Bay Lodge to pick him up on September 13, 1976, then set out on the 10th to enjoy his stay. Precup failed to show up on the 13th, and a search was begun for him the next day.

On the 16th the Jackson party (Charles Jackson, Colin Milmer, Peter Talbot and Leilani Vega) from Seattle hiked into the White Thunder Ridge area in Muir Inlet, the same area Precup had gone into. The group had been told about the lone hiker and were requested to be on the lookout for him. They were aware of search parties in the area. They planned to spend the 16th camping-hiking and to be picked up on the 17th. Another couple hiked into the area with them and set up their tent about a quarter of a mile away before hiking up the ridge about 11:30 A.M., while Jackson's group put up tents and prepared soup and hot chocolate.

A short time later Talbot noticed a six-foot brown bear approaching along the lakeshore. Jackson banged on pans and shouted twice, five minutes apart. The bear paused momentarily each time but continued to advance toward the group. They gathered their food into plastic bags and stuff sacks and retreated in a light-hearted fashion along the lake to some cliffs when the bear was still 150 yards away at 11:45 A.M.

As they reached the relative safety of the cliffs, the three men stashed the food in trees as the bear systematically tore down their tents, chomped on different items and ravaged their camp. Then the animal started in their direction, right in their steps with nose to the ground as if tracking them. It ignored their stash and continued along their trail as they increased their pace.

They circled the lake and arrived back at their camp with the bear pursuing them at 1:15 P.M. Their concern heightened. They decided to seek safety above camp on the hill. As their speed increased, so did the bear's until they were running in an all-out attempt to reach a knoll, peeling off ponchos and jackets and heaving them in their wake.

The bear was 20 feet behind them when they started up the small knoll. They stopped to recoup and rest, and the bear ran up and stopped across a shallow ditch 10 feet away. The animal showed no fear of the group as it paced back and forth on its side of the gully.

The fun had long since ended. It was now a matter of survival. They tried not to panic, and began shouting and bombarding the animal with rocks in an effort to scare it away. Finally the bear went 30 yards away and sat down. It raised its head and watched them whenever they moved.

About 2:45 P.M. the group saw the couple they'd arrived with. A Forest Service plane also flew over them, and their hopes soared. The plane circled five or six times while they discussed moving down the hill to the couple. They decided to join the others, thinking that the circling plane could buzz the bear if it advanced (they found out later that the plane hadn't seen them).

The parties joined at the bottom of the ridge and observed the bear investigating their recently vacated knoll. They started for the Forest Service boat and reached it without further incident at 3:30 P.M. They reported the bear's unusual behavior.

The Park Service dispatched Ranger James Luthy that same afternoon, and he flew over a destroyed camp in a helicopter. He was lowered to the ground. At the same time a two-man ground team was making its way toward the ridge.

Luthy looked through a destroyed camp and discovered it was Alan Lee Precup's. There was no sign of Alan so Luthy left. The ground team arrived at Precup's camp after the chopper had departed, and they were confronted by a bear. They retreated, throwing rocks at it.

The next day a full-scale search was set in motion at 9:00 A.M. Ranger Luthy and two state troopers arrived at Precup's camp at the 1,600-foot level of White Thunder Ridge. They discovered puncture marks (made by the teeth of a large animal) in several items as well as bear feces in the area. Nothing seemed to be untouched. Among the personal effects they found were Precup's camera, credit cards and a journal. The last entry was dated September 11.

While looking further the rescue party discovered Precup's remains. All that was left of the hiker was his skeleton — ribs were scattered about; all the flesh was missing from his skeleton; arms were unattached; the fleshed and featureless skull was detached and lay in the neck's position; boots and socks were still on the feet; his right hand was severed at the wrist and lay under the page of a book near the remains; and his scalp was nearby. His pants, shirt and jacket were next to his skeleton.

Park Service officials believe Precup was killed the 12th, the day before his scheduled pick up. Park spokesperson Judith Ayers believed the Precup bear was "just about certainly" the same animal that stalked the group from Seattle, and that "the bear killed Alan Lee Precup because it was hungry." (*ALASKA*® magazine, December 1976)

The bear that ate Alan Lee Precup did so because of hunger. Officials who investigated the Jay B.L. Reeves fatality stressed that there was an abundance of salmon and berries in the area at the time of that killing. Incidents like these two are extremely rare.

The Stikine Stalking Bear

Almost as rare as the man-eating bear is the killer bear that deliberately stalks his human prey. On occasion a rogue bear stalks man, and nearly always it is due to some pain or conditioned reflex that man has heaped upon old *Ursus*.

Sunday, October 6, 1940, found five men fishing near Paradise Camp, 27 miles up the Stikine River from the mouth, totally unsuspecting that in a very short time one of their number would be frightfully mauled. They had spent the morning fishing and enjoying their wilderness adventure. Grover Foster preceded them to their cabin shortly before the others decided to call a halt to their fishing for the morning. Frank Barnes started out ahead of the other three men toward the cabin by way of a new trail; but he never made it.

Sometime that morning a sow brownie with cubs walked that same trail, and it became Barnes' lot to meet them.

Frank was packing a shotgun. As he ambled along in the quiet morning peacefulness, he was suddenly brought to full awareness by a monster bear springing toward him. He managed to get off one shot before the bear swiped the weapon from his hands and viciously lacerated his face, head, chest and legs — his scalp was nearly ripped off and one side of his face mangled.

His comrades heard the blast and his shout and ran to him. They found Frank wedged so tightly between two willows that they had to cut him free. They transported him to Wrangell, where he was given medical help and sent on to Portland aboard the *Baranof* on Monday. Frank seemed to be improving, but he died in transit.

Frank's friends reconstructed the incident. The killer had to be a she-bear with cubs. The men never determined if his one blast had connected or not, and it wasn't until almost a year later that anyone knew for certainty.

Thirty miles downstream from the site of Frank Barnes' last fishing experience, Arnold Prussi and his father contemplated a two-week moose hunting trip. Arnold had won a new .30-'06, and he was eager to try it out. He would sight it in on the way to the hunting grounds. The day of departure found the Prussis in high expectations, and they enjoyed their journey up the Stikine.

They were a few miles downstream from Paradise Camp when they decided to pull in to shore for lunch and a little trout fishing. Arnold caught several fish and went in search of a branch for a stringer. He passed the boat on the way to the streamside brush and picked up his new rifle, realizing that he had not yet sighted it in.

He filled the magazine with ammunition and practiced snap shooting (pretending to shoot) several times as he neared the brush. Laying the rifle on the ground, he cut a branch. Hardly had he finished when he saw a brown bear step from the protection of the bushes.

Its nose and head moved in concert, testing the wind and calling on its memory bank to sort out past experiences. Within a few strides it became obvious to Arnold that his father was the beast's target.

The bear began a slow, deliberate stalk. Silently, stealthily, she closed the gap . . . 50, 40, 30 yards. She lowered her body until her stomach barely cleared the damp sand of the river bar. She was easily within striking distance. Her muscles bunched in anticipation. She was within 50 feet of the unknowing fisherman when Arnold drew a bead and fired.

A miss!

Arnold ejected the spent cartridge and chambered a live round in an instant. He pulled down on the brute's back. *Ka-whoom!* A hit! But she continued, roaring, pumping her powerful front legs, trying to reach her prey. Arnold's third and final shot found its mark in her neck.

After several moments of trembling knees and counting their

blessings, the Prussis examined the rogue and found a terribly distorted face — her fangs gave her the appearance of a saber-toothed tiger. Her deformed jaw showed every evidence of resulting from a blast from a shotgun, almost unquestionably that of Frank Barnes.

While I was discussing fatal bear encounters with guide John Graybill of Peters Creek, he shed some interesting light on bears and their relative jaw size. He told me, "I lost a good friend who was killed by a bear, and I've known other people who have been mauled by bears; and it pretty much goes the bear's way. There's not much you can do about it.

"Master Guide M.W. 'Slim' Moore (who knows more about game and bears than all the rest of us dudes put together) once told me there seemed to be a formula on who survives a bear mauling.

"He said he noticed that whenever a fatality results, it's almost always a big enough bear that it can get a man's skull in its mouth and crush. Those are almost always fatalities. The smaller bears leave real deep lacerations on the skull, but they don't seem to be able to get the skull in their mouths and crush.

"I really believe he's right."

Old Groaner

Old Groaner was a man killer. He stalked many men, and on several of those occasions he broke off the attack only at the last moment. This rogue bear was monarch of the upper Unuk River country near Ketchikan. His story is probably the all-time classic Alaskan bear tale.

Old Groaner's story started years ago; but the summers of 1923 and 1935, and the lives of Jess Sethington and Bruce Johnstone were turning points in what probably would have been a bear's normal life span.

In 1923 Jess Sethington went up the Unuk River alone on a short trapping trip. He was a Canadian from Stewart, B.C., and he carried a .33 caliber rifle and a .38 caliber pistol for protection and meat getting. When Jess failed to return from the Unuk, four experienced woodsmen tracked his whereabouts by his old camp fires. The searchers lost his trail at Cripple Creek. He was never seen again; a genuine mystery.

Jack and Bruce Johnstone were gold seekers in the summer of 1933, when they took their first trip up the Unuk. They camped overnight at Cripple Creek. During the night they heard unusual moaning sounds and wondered what kind of creature could make such noises. It was a long time before they discovered the sounds came from a very large, unfriendly bear which they dubbed Old Groaner.

The Johnstones made annual trips up the Unuk, camped each time at Cripple Creek, and had several encounters with the bear. He stalked about their camp, getting braver each time. One night their dog, Slasher, chased the bear from the edge of the firelight a number of times, but the bear kept coming back until dawn.

On three occasions the bear lay in ambush for Bruce. Once his dog saved him, and once he bluffed the bear off by firing over its head several times. In November 1935 Old Groaner ambushed Bruce the third time.

Bruce had taken Slasher and had gone to a quartz showing to stake a claim. He leaned his rifle against a tree and knelt on the ground preparing a location notice.

Suddenly Slasher shot by Bruce, startling his master to his feet. Not five yards away Old Groaner lunged toward the man, distorted jaw and abnormally exposed teeth gleaming. Slasher aimed for the bear's throat, but Old Groaner sent him flying into the brush 20 feet away with a single swat of its paw. The dog's actions gave Bruce a chance.

Bruce grabbed his rifle, swung and fired from his hip. The muzzle was just inches from the brute's shoulder when the gun roared. The bear barely missed him as Bruce recoiled backward from the blast. The animal tried to get up, but Bruce put two more bullets into its determined body and brain to end its life.

The next day the Johnstones and a partner returned to examine the dead bear. The bear's paws were 10 inches across. The hairless hide was so tough they had to use an ax to sever the head. The mystery of the moaning marauder slowly unfolded as they studied the skull. Five bullets were embedded in Old Groaner's skull, and they had been there for some time — presumably 12 years.

The right side of the beast's skull had been completely shot away. The zygomatic (cheek) bone was destroyed. A bullet above the right eye had left a hole that was nearly grown over. The contracted muscles had pulled the muzzle aside as it healed, exposing hideous fangs. The bear's teeth were badly decayed and broken.

The animal's right jaw hinge had been shattered. The hinge had never healed internally (though it had outside). There were two lead slugs (jacketed bullets) from a .33 caliber rifle deeply embedded in over-crusted bone in the underside of the right jaw behind the hinge. Three bullets from a .38 caliber revolver were lodged in the gristle under the right jaw.

The mystery of the missing Jess Sethington had also been solved. He had carried both a .33 and a .38 caliber weapon. With five bullets in the lower skull of an 11-foot brown/grizzly, it is not too difficult to imagine the position a man would had to be in to place them there, nor to imagine a doomed trapper beneath the raging jaws and deadly paws of a brown/grizzly.

The Admiralty Killer

Some believe that "once a bear has killed a man, he charges every one he sees thereafter." (Robert McCully, "A Brownie Had Me Up a Tree," *The ALASKA SPORTSMAN®*, December 1941) There is strong evidence to support that theory, though it would be impossible to substantiate. Old Groaner certainly had little fear of man. The Frank Barnes bear stalked Andy Prussi. The Precup bear stalked the Jackson party from Seattle, and the animal that killed Jack Thayer charged another man.

On October 16, 1929, Jack Thayer, prominent member of the Forest Service and a Forest Examiner, was checking timber on Admiralty Island with Fred Herring, an assistant, when they encountered a large brown bear at close range. They were returning to their boat after cruising timber when they noticed an animal in the brush behind them and off to the left of the trail.

The bear stood on hind legs looking over a bush just 20 feet away. Herring shouted a warning, broke and ran past Thayer to a climbable tree 25 yards away. Thayer carried a .30-'06 with steel-jacket government ammunition. He raised the rifle and fired, triggering the bear's charge.

Herring made the safety of a tree and sat helplessly on a limb watching the beast tear at his partner. Thayer received 59 wounds on the front of his body and 42 on the back. His worst wound was on the left side of his head where a huge chunk of flesh was torn loose from the top of his ear down to his shoulder. There was no artery damage.

Herring went two and a half miles for help and returned with Captain Collen, skipper of the boat they were working from. They brought medical supplies, rendered first aid and built a huge fire to warm Jack, but he died around 10 P.M. His broken watch was stopped at 2:05 P.M., the time of the mauling.

A year later Hosea Sarber, an experienced woodsman, returned to the site of Thayer's mauling hoping to find and kill the beast. Determined not to take any chances, he chambered a shell as he moved along the stream bank. The bear had been very near all the time, possibly winding Sarber and waiting in ambush or stalking him.

Sarber believed that the metallic *snick* of his bolt sliding a shell into the chamber, and his man smell at the fishing ground where it had encountered Thayer the previous year, lit the fuse. No one will ever know what triggered the animal, but in that brief instant, the bear exploded and unleashed its towering rage.

Sarber ran up a leaning windfall that he'd purposely picked out to get above the brush and look for the enraged beast. It was just ahead in the brush roaring and tearing at the foliage. It had temporarily lost Sarber's scent and stood on hind legs trying to locate its hated man-enemy. Suddenly its eyes met the hunter's. Sarber took careful aim, and with one calm, well-placed shot, ended the bear's earthly habitation.

The bear had a long scar near the shoulder which may well have been caused by Jack Thayer's bullet. The locale, the scar and the bear's nature lend credence to the likelihood that it was the same animal that killed Jack Thayer.

Death at the Den

At least one bear has killed two men at one time. Lloyd "Penny" Pennington was a guide who flew over a grizzly as it was preparing to den one fall, and he determined to go after it the following spring. He kept his eyes on the den through the winter and observed in the spring that the bear was out and about. Penny and his client, Everett A. Kendall, flew into the area in the spring of 1956. They snowshoed part way to the cave, rested and had a smoke, then left their snowshoes to approach the den.

"They approached the cave on foot, and as they peered into the cave the huge grizzly charged. Investigators were not certain if Kendall had fired a shot, but Pennington's rifle had not been fired. Searchers found the badly mangled bodies of both men. The bear had evidently just come out of hibernation.

"Vengeful hunters found the mauler two days later. Four men, using two airplanes for spotting, located him near the cave where the hunters had been killed. When one of the planes circled low over the bear, he reared up and swatted at the plane with a large paw. When the men landed and cornered him the killer bear roared and started to attack, when they killed him. The bear, eight feet tall, had not been wounded before. The hunters who found and killed the bear were Whitey Faessler, Joe Leland, Stanley Frederickson and Glenn Griffin." (*The ALASKA SPORTSMAN®*, July 1956)

Another Death at a Moose Kill

Nelson Stimaker, a taxidermist from Cheektowaga, New York, went on a hunt with Alaskan guide Ray Caposella of Anchorage in the fall of 1972. Stimaker took the hunt when a friend in New York had to cancel. They hunted sheep, goats and moose. The hunter was successful on goats and moose, and one day they flew over their moose kill-site and noticed a grizzly on the gut pile. The taxidermist wanted that bear. He related his tragic experience to me five years later in a story called "Killer Grizzly."

"We went out to see what we could do to get him. We spent almost the whole day just watching the bear; we knew he was at the kill which was inside a patch of alders. We were on a tundra knoll about 75 yards from the alders. Below us lay more alders, timber and the lake.

"We'd watched the bear six, seven hours, and we had sighted him a couple of times when he would get up from his sleeping and move around and resituate himself. We could see a glimpse of his back and his head real good; but we couldn't see him good enough to get a good shot through his shoulders. I mentioned to Cappy that I could shoot him in the head. He claimed that if it was any trophy size, we couldn't score him for Boone and Crockett if he had a head shot, so we'd wait till he got back on the moose to be sure of a good, easy shot through his shoulders.

"Time went on. We sat and talked, just waitin' to see what happened. The weather was turning sour, it was getting windy, clouds were coming in, ceiling was coming down. Cappy was getting impatient and wanted to get this thing over with and get out of there before we got bad weather; we didn't know if we'd be there for a few days or what. He was going to try to get the bear's attention, causing him to stand up at which time I could shoot.

"He went upwind of the bear, staying quite a ways away, probably between 75 and 100 yards. He started yelling and screaming, making noises like a dog, and all kinds of crazy noises. The bear didn't respond. We didn't see him at all.

"Cappy came back to me and said, 'Either that bear is deaf or it's possible he could have sneaked out.'

"We sat for another 10 minutes and Cappy was getting itchy again. He was going to go upwind and let the wind take his scent to the bear. He was sure this would arouse him, get him to stand up or come out of the alders. He just told me to be careful not to shoot *him*, and I told him not to worry about that.

"I was lying on my stomach. I had my pack on top of a patch of tundra with my rifle on top of the pack; I was looking through my scope where the bear was lying. When he came up and out, I'd be ready and let him have it good. I wasn't watchin' Cappy at all.

"He went and made all his noises and not a thing happened. It was quiet again. I still wasn't watching, and I assume what he did is figure that the bear did move out, and he was gonna go closer to the alders to take a look. That is what he did, he was moving closer. All of a sudden I heard him yelling to me, 'TAKE HIM! TAKE HIM!'

"I was looking through the scope, and I moved the gun around and still didn't see anything. I took my head away from the scope and looked; and I saw Cappy moving backwards quickly and beginning to raise his rifle and looking at me at the same time yelling and screaming to take the bear. I still couldn't sight the bear at all.

"At that time he raised his rifle and shot. As he shot, the bear bolted out of the alders towards him. They were maybe 30 feet apart. I swung my rifle over, took a shot at the bear as he was charging Cappy. As I was bolting another shell in, the bear had caught up to him, took a swipe at him and missed. Cappy dodged and ran the other way. Again he was telling me to take him; and I swung over and shot again.

"Both these times I shot, the bear didn't react like he was hit at all, nor did he react like he was hit from Cappy's shot.

"As the bear came at him again, Cappy took the rifle and turned it around, grabbed it by the barrel and broke it over the bear's head. The bear didn't react at all from that either, didn't even seem to move his head like it bothered him. The stock of the gun shattered in pieces all over the place.

"At that time the bear knocked him down with his paws, hitting him in the chest. Then the bear grabbed the top of Cappy's thigh in his mouth and quickly dragged him into the alders to the moose kill. At that time I ran down to the alders. I stopped right at the edge, suddenly thinking, 'If I get in there, it's so thick, I couldn't see four or five feet away anyways.' There were a lot of leaves on the trees. You couldn't see anything in those close quarters; and if that bear got anywhere near me at all, even if I did get a good shot in, it may not stop him; and I'd be in the same situation and couldn't help either one of us.

"While I was standing there, I could hear all the growling and Cappy screaming. I looked in there, and at one time the bear had Cappy's head in his mouth shakin' him like a dog shakes a woodchuck. I could see both of his legs at the same time and his arms just dangling and waving above the alders just like he was a rag doll. There was a lot of screaming and growling at the same time.

"I ran back to my pack; I was going to get some more shells. I only had three with me at the time, and I'd fired two. When I reached my pack and before I reached down to get any shells, I noticed that the bear had jumped up on top of the moose; and it was in plain view. I immediately aimed carefully and took a good shot for his shoulders. I could tell it hit him solid. It lifted him off the moose and knocked him over. And when he did fall back into the alders, he growled and carried on and made a bunch of ruckus again.

"It seemed to quiet down a little bit, so I got some more shells, loaded the gun and took some more in my pocket and went back to the alders. As I stood there next to the alders, I was pointing my gun towards the bushes with the safety off and ready to go, holding it at my side. I was scared to death. I knew I had to do something, either that bear was going to come out or I had to go in.

"I couldn't hear the bear moving at all or anything. I started yelling for Cappy; I think I yelled three or four times before I could hear him moaning and making a few sighs. So I walked towards the sounds.

"I was pretty scared. I was trembling. It's hard to explain; you're just terrified at the time. As I got into the thick of the alders, I could see like a clearing in the middle. It was an area about 25 feet in diameter that looked like a caterpillar tractor walked through it, cleaning everything out.

"Cappy was lying on the ground rolling around; and I could see the bear about 10 feet away, lying like it was dead. I immediately brought my rifle up and shot him right in the middle of the skull. The bear kinda lifted off the ground a little bit, wiggled, then didn't move at all. I got another shell in and walked up to the bear, poked the barrel in his head a few times, kicked him a few times. He was dead.

"After that Cappy was still rolling around and kept yelling to me to 'Kill the bear! Find the bear!' He didn't want me in there with the bear being alive. I had to calm him down and tell him the bear was dead. And at that time he asked me to pick him up and hold him. I did, and he wanted me to describe to him what damage had happened to him.

"There was blood all over him, but he didn't have any places where the blood was gushing out of him, didn't seem to be bleeding excessively. There was no great amount of blood in the whole area. There was blood on the bear, and I couldn't tell if it was the bear's or Cappy's.

"He had cuts all across his face, and you could see teeth marks in the side of his head near his temple where the bear had Cappy's head in his mouth when he was shaking him. All the other cuts in his face must have been from when the teeth were going across it, ripping muscles and whatnot.

"He couldn't control his jaw to talk. He couldn't open his eyes because the muscles were ripped so bad. His mouth just kind of hung open, and he talked with his tongue.

"Most of his clothes were ripped off. He had numerous claw marks across his chest where the bear had swiped him. They didn't break the skin; you could see blue-purple marks across where the claws went. He had a good bite mark in his leg where the bear had picked him up and carried him into the alders when he first put him down. I could see white marks and a couple of scratches across his arms where he must have been fighting the bear.

"He asked me if I knew how to operate the plane radio, and I told him I thought I did. He gave me some frequencies to check and to make sure it was an emergency frequency where I could get help the fastest; and be sure to set 'em on that and what switches to turn on. He gave me the location to tell these people where we were. He told me south of Tazlina Lake (we were actually a little southeast of it and we were southwest of the glacier area).

"I asked him if there was anything I could do for him or if he wanted me to move him, and he said no, just leave him alone. I took some jackets and stuff I had and put 'em over him to keep him warm. I had maybe three miles to go to the plane. I took my rifle and some more shells, and I ran as fast as I could.

"I don't think I could do it over again. My lungs were heaving. Nothing seemed to matter, only if I could make it or not. I just kept on going, something kept me running. It was mostly uphill over a lot of hummocks and through a couple of bushes.

"The whole time I was jittery as heck, and I was still pretty shook up. I remember running by one small patch of bushes and a flock of ptarmigan flew out and scared the devil out of me. I jumped and threw my rifle up and was ready to shoot again.

"I had no idea how long it took me. I ran all the way, reached the plane, made sure the radio was on the frequency he said, and turned everything on. I spoke into the microphone, calling for help, and didn't hear an answer so I changed channels a couple of times until I heard someone talking. I broke into their conversation, and yelled a 'Mayday' and gave the number of the plane, location and told them we needed a doctor and a helicopter. I told them a guy had been mauled by a bear.

"I was so excited that they couldn't understand a thing I said. I had to repeat myself numerous times. They finally got a location and the number of the plane; and they understood that I needed a doctor and a helicopter.

"I stood by the airplane instead of going back to Cappy; I knew there wasn't much I could do for him anyway. I really didn't think he was going to live, but I kept hoping the whole time. I heard a couple of conversations, probably to the helicopter and the radio dispatch of what to do and where to go; and I just kept watching for a plane and told them to hurry. They said they were doing the best they could.

"When the helicopter came, they had a state trooper in it, a pilot and a doctor. They looked at me kind of funny because they assumed somehow that there was a plane crash. They really didn't know what the trouble was. The trooper ran out first, and asked what the problem was. I explained that Cappy had been mauled by a bear.

"He wanted to run down there, and I said, 'Let's take the helicopter. It's a lot faster, and there's a place we can land there.' I got in the helicopter and we flew to where Cappy was. Before we landed, we hovered over the scene. The trooper said to the doctor that Cappy didn't look alive.

"When we landed, Cappy was already starting to turn bluish, was stiff. The doctor looked him over and pronounced him dead while the trooper had me describe what happened. They took some pictures.

"The trooper had asked me at the time I was describing the incident if I'd shot Cappy, and I told him that I really didn't know if I did nor not. I said I didn't think I did. Cappy was close to the bear when I was shooting, but every time I did squeeze a shot off, I was sure it was on the bear. I said I honestly couldn't tell.

"We loaded Cappy onto the helicopter and went into Glenn-allen. They gave Cappy an autopsy. His skull was fractured, and all of his ribs were busted with pieces through his heart and lungs. It could have been any one of those things that killed him. He was not shot.

"The next day a biologist went in and checked the bear. He said that there was one shot entering his right shoulder, one shot entering his left shoulder and one in the middle of his skull. Out of the four shots I took, I must have hit the bear once before it got hold of Cappy. If I'm correct, I think the shot when he was on top of the moose was a good hit, and I believe it went through his right shoulder. I assume Cappy missed the bear.

"The biologist said the bear was a boar and weighed approximately 750 pounds. I think he said it would have squared pretty close to eight feet.

"At that time I had to give a report to the troopers, and I was pretty shook up. It was a terrifying thing to go through, and I was upset that I'd lost a good friend."

The Bear Came Back

Many man-killing bears were mortally wounded by their victims.

A Russian-Aleut, Pete Kivian, had a good reputation as a competent bear hunter in his section of Kodiak Island. He wounded a big brown bear in the early 1900s then followed it into the alders to finish it. The bear rushed him and mauled him unmercifully then dragged himself off into the brush. Pete regained consciousness, took off his coat and lighted it — possibly to frighten the bear, start a fire or to use the ashes to stop the flow of his blood.

His friends later found his partially burned coat. They discovered his body covered by earth and sticks. The bear had evidently returned, killed Pete, buried his body, then gone away. Pete's friends found the dead bear nearby.

Maybe The Same Bear?

In September 1955, "Willis S. McBride was hunting with Vic Vukovich in rough country about 50 miles north of Eureka on the Big Oshetna River when they became separated. Vukovich was shocked when he later found the badly battered body of his companion. The bear wasn't around, but signs indicated it had been a large grizzly that killed McBride. Territorial police and other offi-

cials from Copper Center flew to the area to recover the body."
(*The ALASKA SPORTSMAN®*, February 1956)

About 50 miles away from the scene of the McBride fatality
another hunter, Herman Oergel, was killed in the fall of 1957.

"A dead hunter and a dead bear were found only 10 feet apart
near the MacLaren River north of Anchorage on September 7. The
hunter, 61-year-old Herman Oergel of Anchorage, died from
wounds inflicted by the bear. The bear, a grizzly that weighed
600-800 pounds, had three slugs in its body from Oergel's .300
Magnum.

"Oergel, a longtime resident of Anchorage and an experienced
hunter, had gone hunting with Bill Prosser and Mr. and Mrs.
Andrew Cooper of Anchorage. They selected a spot eight miles
south of the Denali Highway on the MacLaren River, and set up
camp on September 3. That afternoon the others stayed in camp
while Oergel went out to look the country over for game. When he
failed to return his companions sent word to Anchorage that he
was missing.

"Two private planes and the territorial police began a search.
The dead man's son, Jack, spotted the body from one of the
planes." (*The ALASKA SPORTSMAN®*, December 1957)

Mysteries

Much mystery and supposition surround many mauling victims
who were killed. It is not always known what happened or even if
a bear killed them. Ralph Reischl was a most competent woodsman and top marksman; a well-known Juneau guide. He went into
the woods of Admiralty Island and did not return. Friends
suspected a brown bear ambushed and killed him then dragged
him off into the woods.

Another man may have suffered Reischl's fate. "A United States
deputy marshal left Juneau to investigate reports of a bootleg still
in operation near Mole Harbor on Admiralty Island. He did not
return, and later his body was found literally torn to pieces by a
monster bear. His six-shooter was found with all empty cartridges
in the chambers, and a bloody bear trail led from the scene of the
encounter. The wounded bear was never found." (*The ALASKA
SPORTSMAN®*, "The Killers," by Calvin H. Barkdull, June 1954)

Lawrence Swensen may have suffered a similar fate. "A
skull and a few scattered, bear-chewed bones, identified by bits of
clothing, are the only clue to the fate of Lawrence Swensen, old-
timer of Steel Creek. Swensen was nearly 80 years old, and had

spent more than half his life in the Forty-Mile area south of Fairbanks. The old man had been in Fairbanks only two months before evidence of his tragedy was discovered. Whether he had been attacked and killed by bears, or had collapsed and died, and bears had found and consumed his body, is a question much disputed by Lawrence Swensen's acquaintances." (*The ALASKA SPORTSMAN*®, December 1943)

Even though many men have suffered ferocious attacks, it is uncharacteristic for bears to charge on sight. In given situations they ignite with demonic fury, and God pity the unfortunate victim. But there is *not* a bear behind every bush waiting for a hapless human. Quite the contrary. Bears are content to live their lives and let man live his, unless they feel threatened for some reason.

Use caution in bear country and remember, all North American bears are capable of attacking and killing a human, even the more common black bear.

Most people take black bears lightly. They find it inconceivable that one could harm man. But more than one black bear has killed a human victim. □

WHICH IS
THE TOUGHER?

"A grizz or a brown is a bear, but a black is a dog. They don't even belong in the same category. I don't have much respect for a black bear as a vicious animal. Lot of people are afraid of a black bear. I respect them; I'm not gonna run up and pet them. There's not going to be any black bears chewing on anybody to speak of unless you've got a unique situation — you got one cornered or cubs, then you're going to have to shoot them." (Keith Johnson, Master Guide, personal interview, Anchorage, June 1977)

"A brown bear will come and stand up, then you got a chance. If a brown bear is coming after you, don't run. You got your gun, just kneel down and wait. He'll come so far then he'll stand up and put his arms up. He'll stand up every time and give you a chance. Boy, don't miss. Get him right in the neck and break his neck.

"Black bear are more dangerous. A black bear comes after you, you better make sure you shoot him now because he's going to get you. He's leaping and he'll just tear right into you." (Gust Jensen, Athabascan Indian and commercial fisherman, personal interview, Anchorage, October 1977)

From Canada

A notable black bear tragedy involved three young men and a black bear in Canada on May 13, 1978. The three were fishing along a stream in Algonquin Park in Ontario when confronted by the animal. It killed all three and began feeding on them after dragging them into the seclusion of the nearby brush. The bear was killed and found to be in superb physical condition.

The Slate Creek Kill

July 22, 1976, found seven men involved in geographical survey work. Six were at their Slate Creek, Alaska, camp, and Robert MacGregor was conducting a magnetometer survey a short distance away. Because of the magnetometer and the nature of his work, he was unarmed.

About 3:00 P.M. John Patrick approached Mike Lancaster and told him he thought he'd heard MacGregor yell for help. John went to their camp, picked up a .444 Marlin rifle and went looking for Robert.

While the men worked at their varied jobs, Mike McEwen also thought he heard MacGregor, and he left his work, together with Henry Tonking. They found nothing, returned and told Charles Nak, who related their conversation to Mike Lancaster.

Lancaster then obtained a gun from camp and returned to the core shack to meet Nak and Henry Hickey. The three left camp, met Patrick, Tonking and McEwen and began a search for MacGregor. They split up and started walking west. Tonking and Nak found MacGregor's notebook and hat on a game trail near a bear-clawed tree. Fifty feet down the trail Tonking retrieved Rob's magnetometer.

John Patrick was walking through the brush about 85 yards from Tonking when he heard noises nearby. He assumed it was the other searchers. The noises persisted. John looked toward the sounds and saw a 200-pound black bear stand up and stare at him. The bear dropped to all fours and charged Patrick.

He yelled "Bear!" In an instant the bear cleared the brush within feet of Patrick, who had shouldered the .444. The rifle roared twice in quick succession, and the boar dropped five feet from the weapon's smoking barrel, dead.

The others moved toward the sound and discovered the dead bear. The men then wandered about the area of the magnetometer and Lancaster found the missing man's scalp 15 feet down-trail from the instrument.

Then they began a grid search, everyone walking in a line. As their search continued, Henry Hickey found MacGregor. He was dead.

The men surmised that MacGregor had taken off his instrument and climbed the tree along the game trail, and that the bear had pursued him up the tree, as the claw marks indicated. Evidently the bear had dragged MacGregor 100 feet off the trail, where it either killed him or fed upon him — there were blood soaked bushes and fresh bear dung. From there the animal had dragged the victim another 100 feet. It was apparently feeding on the man when it stood and faced Patrick before its fatal charge (the victim's right bicep and portions of the buttocks were gone).

Black bears are different things to different people. They may be clowns, thieves, panhandlers, killers or various forms of all. Some are brave; some are cowards. There are blacks that are foolish; others are smart. Generally they flee from man's scent; but some are indifferent and almost contemptuous of man's presence. A number of people have compared bears to humans, which may be valid. It is not hard to imagine shy animals as well as extroverts, oafish as well as stealthy, easy going and cantankerous. Surely a bear's environment and his human contact bias much of man's opinion of the animal.

It would be unfair to stereotype black bears in general because they *are* individuals; however, some black behavior is typical of the species.

He Wanted In The Rowboat

The most common view of blackie is that he is a clown. Any number of incidents substantiate this idea. Joe Hong of Ketchikan had a rather unusual experience while working one summer around 1950 for college money. One afternoon during a lull on the trap-tender he and some friends rowed along the beach.

A young black bear saw them and started their way, paddling along. Whether curious or nearsighted, it swam right up to the boat. The occupants thumped him on the head with an oar. A look of surprise crossed his brow and he double-timed it for the beach.

The bear hit the beach, started for the timber, stopped, stood up on his hind legs and put a forepaw to his head. He looked like the proverbial absent-minded professor lost in thought momentarily. Then the bear dropped to all fours and started for the skiff again. He reached the skiff, got a second helping of oar, bee-lined for the shore and the brush.

That young bear was like a little kid who wasn't sure what had happened and went to make sure it was for real. (*The ALASKA SPORTSMAN®*, July 1951)

The Flapjack Bear

An old-time Alaskan, hermit-homesteader .30-40 Joe of Anan Creek, raised a blackie from cubhood. The bear evidently imprinted the man as her mother, and came to like flapjacks better than salmon. She ate pile after pile of flapjacks with syrup until November, when she disappeared.

Early in May .30-40 Joe began frying flapjacks one morning, heard something bumping around beneath the cabin and looked up to discover his "cub" Matilda walking into his cabin. She sat down on her haunches and leaned back with paws waving in the air. His former pet was becoming a nuisance. Matilda continued her sparring matches as she had the year before, but now she carried a wallop.

The bear proved too much for the old-timer, so he coaxed her into his boat with a plateful of flapjacks and transported her a hundred miles down the coast. Every time a black bear neared his cabin, he wondered if his "pet" had returned.

———

Many people say the black is friendly and easy going. It appears that some are. A trapper told about a sow and twin cubs he'd befriended. He was hanging a caribou he had just killed near his camp. He looked up and saw the animals 30 or 40 yards away. The trapper thought she had a friendly and naturally kind disposition.

He took the scraps from his caribou to the bears and dropped them, returned and continued with his work. The man saved his scraps that summer and fed them to the bears who allowed him to get within a few feet of them without so much as a growl. (From *Sourdough Sagas*)

———

Another Garbage Bear

A common view held by those who have lived close to black bears is that they go out of their way to look for trouble. But in defense of the black bear it can also be said that he is motivated by his stomach and his curiosity; and he seems to possess a certain amount of mischievousness. Chuck Wirschem of Anchorage talked with some prospectors who had a run-in with a black in the early

'70s at their Gakona cabin. Their situation was the result of a hungry, curious black bear and their carelessness. Chuck told me, "Apparently these two guys that ran this old cabin, every time they cooked dinner they took their grease from the pan and leftover garbage bits and stuff, and they'd just throw it out the door. They had kind of a little midden pile right outside the door.

"Every morning about four-thirty or five o'clock, while everybody's sound asleep, this black bear came by and kinda scarfed up the goodies there and left. They knew the bear was around; they could see the sign and tracks and stuff; but they never did see the bear. What they didn't know didn't hurt 'em.

"One Saturday night they were in Glennallen, and they got all drunked up and got back about four-thirty, five o'clock early Sunday morning and decided to cook eggs and bacon and stuff in there, and they had the door ajar. This bear was just kinda curious about where all these good smells were comin' from, and he just mosied right into the cabin.

"These guys pushed the panic button, which I guess anybody could do, and I think they threw a couple of things at it. The bear didn't take too kindly to that. One of 'em got a gun and shot the thing.

"So many of these stories that you hear, there's another side to 'em some place."

The black bear tends to be a loner, and rarely do you see them together unless it is at a food source such as a berry patch or a salmon stream. Unless the mother is with cubs or it is during the mating season, the black keeps pretty much to himself.

That the black bear is a coward is a view shared by many. This may be an accurate view; however, part of his "cowardliness" could be because bears will usually clear out at the sight, sound or scent of man.

More aggressive blacks seem to possess a cantankerousness or surliness, a kind of "I don't care" attitude about everything that gets in their way. It almost seems that the aggressive blacks flaunt their surliness as a show of power — don't get in my way, Bub, or you're in trouble. Perhaps this trait can be explained by calling it a grumpy bear.

The Brownie vs. Blackie Fight
Black bears don't reach the size of their grizzly cousins. A 400-

pound black is considered extremely large by Alaskan standards. Rarely is an adult black a match for an adult brown/grizzly. The famed Cordova physician and former mayor, Will H. Chase, recorded a battle between a big brown bear and a black in one section of his book *Alaska's Mammoth Brown Bears.* An intimate friend told Will about the battle witnessed in the spring of 1914 on a tributary to the Copper River.

The two prospectors who saw the battle were short on meat. Their custom was to shoot sheep for camp meat, so they went up the mountain and bagged a Dall. Since it was late and quite a distance from camp, they retired, deciding to bring in the meat the next day.

Early the next morning the men began the difficult hike up the mountain, their goal the opposite side of the peak where the sheep had fallen. Upon reaching the peak and looking down the other side, they were startled to see a black bear feeding on their sheep; and farther down the mountain a large brown bear was coming up the slope in the direction of the feeding black.

The men opted to observe the coming event instead of claiming their hard-earned prize.

It wasn't long until the brownie arrived. The black, growling, never gave an inch but rose on hind legs to face the brown. The brownie growled, more loudly as it circled. Suddenly the brown rose on hind legs and lunged toward the black, ivory teeth bared and razor sharp claws slashing.

They met head-to-head. The black swung a sledge-hammer blow that knocked her foe off his feet, tumbling end-over-end. He was on his feet immediately. His rage boiled, and he pressed the attack with a ferocity that seemed unequaled. She was only half his size, but she responded to the brownie's bulk and power with speed. She held her ground, obviously determined to fight to the death.

The roaring beasts parried and swung, froth flew from their deadly jaws. Blow followed blow. Blood oozed from wounds on each bear's neck, head and shoulders, mixing with the flecking froth. The animals danced, looking for an opening. The brown knocked the black flying, but she jumped right back to the battle. There was no letup, and the fight raged on.

Each time the brown struck the black bear, she was knocked from her feet; but each time she threw herself back into the fray, and gradually the big bear's endurance started to break under the quickness of the black.

Blood now flowed from the gaping wounds on the larger bear,

and as his life's blood waned, so did his strength and efficiency. He slowed in his sparring, and his blows struck empty air. Breathing became more difficult, but he never let up.

Blood spattered the churned up earth in a great circle around the beasts.

The furious swinging slowed and the bears clinched more, falling to the ground, biting and tearing at each other. Their hind legs now came into play, ripping and slashing viciously at each other's belly and rear legs.

Great, gaping holes opened in each animal's midsection, and their intestines oozed out. Their surging, powerful blows had lost their effectiveness. The bears no longer stood on hind legs but tore at each other while rolling about the slope. Sparring had deteriorated into clinging and biting.

By now the brown's eyes were torn from their sockets, leaving him at the mercy of the lesser black. But the blackie was mortally wounded. With her intestines dragging the ground, she gave her dying efforts for a final attack.

She lunged on the brown and both bears went to the ground, rolling and thrashing. The brown ended up on the bottom, unable to regain his feet and too exhausted to raise his paws.

Gradually the big bear relaxed. He made a final effort to raise a forepaw . . . up, ever so slowly, then it fell back limply. His erratic breathing slowed until he lay still.

The black bear rose, walked a few yards and looked back at her trailing intestines. She sat down on her haunches, red tongue lolling out the side of her mouth. Blood flowed from her ragged wounds as she gasped for breath. She sat looking at her fallen foe, emitted a low growl, rose and wobbled down the mountain toward timberline, only hours from death.

The dead brownie lay eyeless, ears shredded, nostrils ripped through, most of his ribs stripped of their flesh, his entrails severed in many places, and his head, neck and shoulders a mass of bloody pulp. The little sow had proved a match for the boar brownie.

Woman Attacked

Contrary to some beliefs, bears do attack women. In 1960 Mrs. Frances Cannon of Fairbanks flew in to a lake north of Minto to go fishing with Albian Johnson and Ralph Fletcher.

Fishing complete, they sat near the plane eating a picnic lunch when a black roared out from the undergrowth and grabbed Frances. Johnson picked up a stick and pummeled the brute, and the bear dropped the woman and charged him. It was waylaid by the lunch, which it began to devour.

In the meantime Fletcher got a .22 pistol from the plane, walked to within a few feet of the animal and killed it. Mrs. Cannon was much more fortunate than most black bear mauling victims.

The Bear Wanted The Sheep

Several years ago two brothers living on the Yukon River each shot a sheep, dressed them and started down the mountain. The going was tough and required attention to the footing. Suddenly the lead brother was struck by a large bear, which may have mistaken him for a sheep. He dropped his burden and leaped back firing his rifle with his right hand, for the other had been rendered useless by the bear's blow.

The bear then lunged at him, and they embraced in a death struggle, the man using his knife and the bear its fangs and claws. They tumbled down the steep slope, dislodging rocks and bouncing over a cliff to its base several feet below.

The second brother rushed down the mountain and followed the telltale blood to the edge of the cliff. He reached the foot of the dropoff and found the two. His brother was atop the bear, clasped in its arms. It appeared that both were dead, they were covered with blood and not moving.

He carried his brother to their cabin and tried to revive him. The bear had bitten and crushed one shoulder, nearly torn off his scalp, and laid bare his chest. Both arms and a leg were broken; he was covered with bruises and lacerations and his face was almost obliterated.

The injured man was put aboard a steamer, taken down the Yukon to St. Michael and then to the States. Somehow he regained his health over a year's recuperation, returned to his cabin and began killing bears to avenge his mauling. (From *Sourdough Sagas*)

This Bear Wasn't Dead

One of the most severe maulings ever to occur took place in 1950 on the Yukon. Alexie Pitka, an Athabascan Indian, was looking for fresh meat. He had seen a medium sized grizzly on several mornings and debated whether or not he should shoot it.

He'd never killed a grizzly; it would provide an abundance of camp meat; and he had a feeling that if he didn't kill it, it might harm him later. So he began to stalk.

He managed to wiggle his way through the alders until he was 200 yards from the animal. As he watched it across the small lake at the edge of a clearing, he was surprised to discover that it was a black bear. He drew a bead and fired, dropping the bear in its tracks. Alexie watched for a minute then fired a second shot over the bear to see if it would react. It didn't move and was apparently dead.

Alexie approached the animal and thoughtlessly leaned his .30-30 Savage against a tree. He walked up to the bear which lay motionless on its side. When he was within 10 feet of the creature, it sprang to its feet and charged. Alexie felt a dull, jarring sensation.

Later on he opened his eyes, but he was in a fog. Things were blurry and unclear. Where was he? What was that above him? It was furry and smelled rotten.

Vaguely, he started putting two and two together. It was a bear, standing astraddle of him. He was lying on his back, the bear's face a foot away from his — though Alexie was faceless. What should he do? He remembered his knife and debated trying to use it. Alexie figured he had nothing to lose and slowly reached for the handle and drew the knife from its sheath on his belt.

Pitka pointed the blade upward and thrust with all his strength. The bear didn't flinch. Alexie alternately blacked out and jabbed the blade into the brute's belly; warm blood flowed over him. Realizing his helplessness, he finally decided to talk to the bear [many natives feel a kinship with animals, especially bears].

He told the bear to go away and he wouldn't hurt it. He blacked out, and when he came to, the bear was gone. Sometime later Alexie heard the black in the distant brush, roaring in its death throes.

Alexie had trouble seeing, but he knew his only hope was to make the 10-mile downriver trip to the camp where he'd left his family. He began crawling the half-mile to his boat, praying as he went. He constantly wiped the blood from his one good eye so that he could see.

Since it never reaches total darkness in June that far north, he didn't know what time it was; but he continued to drag himself through the brush, pushing with his knees and toes and pulling with his elbows. At last, totally exhausted, he reached the bank where he'd left his canoe, but he couldn't make it out.

He dropped into slumber. When he awoke, he looked downstream but saw no boat. Then he looked upstream and saw a blurry object. Pitka couldn't tell if it was his canoe and was too tired to crawl to it anyway.

He thought it was nighttime as it started getting cold for the second time since the attack. He had not eaten or had a drink for 36 hours. Alexie wanted a drink. He wanted to reach his canoe and get his cup.

Gradually he fought his way along the bank toward the blurry object, hoping it was his canoe. After what seemed like ages, he reached the object; it was his craft. Alexie tried to drink water but there was no mouth to put it into. He couldn't get any water to his throat. Beside himself with frustration, he cried out aloud and prayed for help.

Nearly 55 hours had passed since his encounter with the bear when a friend of Pitka's arrived. He paddled up to the hapless man on the bank and was followed by Alexie's wife and daughter in another boat. They managed to get Alexie back to Kaltag and on to Tanacross. Doctors were amazed that he was alive.

His face was pretty much gone. The right side had been bared of flesh — cheekbone torn away, eye ripped out and the nose gone, leaving only cartilage. Part of his left cheek was gone and his mouth was mangled, the facial skin hung below his chin like a ghastly, red beard. Only three teeth remained in his jaw.

Alexie pulled through; and after plastic surgery and months in a hospital in Seattle, he returned to his Kaltag home. He was more fortunate than some.

Two Who Died

Two other men encountered blacks and sacrificed their lives. Ralph H. Gaier, 55-year-old trapper, was found on his blood-saturated bunk in January of 1953 at his wilderness cabin 100 miles northwest of Anchorage. Evidence indicated that a hungry black bear broke into his cabin. Ralph grabbed a rifle and exited through a window then shot the beast several times through the door. He peeked in and was frightfully mauled by the bear which died outside the door. Ralph made it to his bunk where he was found.

J. William Strandberg was killed at the family mine 160 miles west of Fairbanks on August 18, 1963. According to Odin Strandberg, brother of the deceased, "There was a very bad berry crop in 1963 and I heard of many maulings that year. I've warned people about bears for many years because I've had bears stalk me and I know they can really move.

"The Manley Hot Springs camp had been closed down for a while. We'd go in periodically to check camp. Bill had gone in alone. He made the cookshack late and cooked himself a meal. He was a neat person and apparently he stepped out the door to scrape his plate. Evidently a bear had been attracted by the cooking odors and Bill and the bear must have surprised each other.

"Bill probably tried to frighten the bear, and it jumped him. Unable to reach the safety of the cabin, Bill tried to crawl under his pickup. The bear was apparently enraged and killed him.

"Within the next few days people in the area located and killed a good-sized sow blackie which they assumed was the guilty bear."

They Look "Cute"

The predominant attitude toward black bears is that they are lovable and cute. Few people seem to realize the real danger of this black-coated menace. For some it is the indoctrination of television programs which seldom show the explosive nature of these short-tempered, wild creatures.

The next time you hear someone tell how harmless black bears are, ask them if they've ever heard of Robert MacGregor, Alexie Pitka — or Cynthia Dusel-Bacon, whose story follows. □

"COME QUICK! I'M BEING
EATEN BY A BEAR!"

"Bears usually will kill humans only when surprised or super hungry." (Captain Robert Penman, Alaska Department of Public Safety, personal interview, Anchorage, February 1977)

I first heard about Cynthia Dusel-Bacon over a local radio newscast August 13, 1977. She had been frightfully mauled by a bear while working for the United States Geological Survey somewhere up north, around Fairbanks. My interest in her experience led me to write her at the University of Stanford Medical Center.

This courageous lady sent me a tape with her story. She was more than eager to offer her experience in hopes of helping others avoid a similar situation, and she wrote in her letter (typed while holding a stylus between her jaws), "I couldn't be more pleased about your efforts to amass all available information about bear maulings in Alaska. I can't think of a greater contribution one could make to educate people about the potential danger of a bear encounter. I believe very strongly in what you are doing."

A short time later I received her tape and her story.

"The summer of 1977 was my third summer in the Yukon-Tanana Upland of Alaska, doing geologic field mapping for the Alaskan Geology Branch of the U.S. Geological Survey. I began

working for the survey in the summer of 1975, making helicopter-
assisted traverses in the highest terrain of the 6,000-square-mile
Big Delta quadrangle. The second summer, as our budget did not
provide for helicopter expenses, the project chief and I found it
necessary to map the geology by backpacking, usually a week at a
time. Last summer we were again funded for helicopter transport
after an initial month of backpacking. All five geologists in our
group, after being transported by air to the field area, usually
mapped alone. I personally felt quite comfortable.

"Every summer in the upland area we saw bears. The first one I
saw was walking slowly along on the far side of a small mountain
meadow, and I froze. It didn't see me and disappeared into the
forest. Another time I was walking through a spruce forest and
saw a black bear moving through the trees some distance away.
Again I was apparently not noticed. The second summer while I
was backpacking, I encountered a small black bear coming along
the trail toward me. I had been busy looking down at the ground
for chips of rock, when I heard a slight rustling sound. I looked up
to see the bear about 40 feet in front of me. Startled, it turned
around and ran off in the other direction, crashing through the
brush as it left the trail. This particular experience reassured me
that what I had heard about black bears being afraid of people
was, in fact, true.

I See My First Grizzly

"During my third summer, I saw my first grizzly, but only from
the air while traveling in the helicopter. Although other members
of our field party had seen them on the ground, I felt myself
fortunate to have encountered only black bears. Grizzlies were
generally considered to be more unpredictable and dangerous.

"All three summers I had hiked through the bush unarmed, as it
was the belief of our project chief that guns added more danger to
an encounter than they might prevent. A wounded, angry bear
would probably be more dangerous than a frightened one. She
had therefore strongly discouraged us from carrying any kind of
firearm. We all carried walkie-talkie radios so as to keep in constant touch with one another and with our base camp. And we
were warned against surprising bears or getting between a mother
and her cubs. Whenever I was doing field mapping, I always
attempted to make noise as I walked so that I would alert any
bears within hearing and give them time to run away from me. For
two summers this system worked perfectly.

"Last summer we were scheduled to complete the reconnaissance mapping of the Big Delta quadrangle. Since it covers such a vast area, we needed helicopter transportation in order to finish traversing all the ridges by mid-September.

"At about 8:00 A.M. of August 13, 1977, Ed Spencer, our helicopter pilot, dropped me off near the top of a rocky, brush-covered ridge approximately 60 miles southeast of Fairbanks. I was dressed in khaki work pants and a cotton shirt, wore sturdy hiking boots, and carried a rucksack. In the right-hand outside pocket of my pack I carried a light lunch of baked beans, canned fruit, fruit juice, and a few pilot crackers. My walkie-talkie radio was stashed in the left-hand outside pocket, complete with covering flap, strap and buckle. I was to take notes on the geology and collect samples by means of the geologist's hammer I carried on my belt, record my location on the map, and stow the samples in my rucksack.

"Standard safety procedure involved my making radio contact with the other geologists and with our base camp several times during the day, at regular intervals. The radio in camp, about 80 miles south of the mapping area, was being monitored by the wife of the helicopter pilot. Plans called for me to be picked up by helicopter at the base of the eight-mile-long ridge on a designated gravel bar of the river at the end of the day.

A Nice Narrow Trail

"After noticing, with unexpected pleasure, that I was going to be able to use a narrow trail that had been bulldozed along the crest of the ridge, I started off downhill easily, on the trail that passed through tangles of birch brush and over rough, rocky slides. The ridge was in one of the more populated parts of the quadrangle, as there are a few small cabins about 15 or 20 miles downstream along the Salcha River, and a short landing strip for airplanes about 10 miles from the ridge. Fishermen occasionally come this far up the river, too, so the bears in the area have probably seen human beings occasionally. This particular morning I wasn't expecting to see bears at all; the hillside was so rocky, so dry looking and tangled with brush, it just didn't seem like bear country. If I were to see a bear that day, it would more likely be at the end of the day, down along the river bar and adjoining woods.

"I descended the ridge slowly for several hundred yards, moving from one outcrop of rock to another, chipping off samples and stowing them in my pack. I stopped at one large outcrop to break off an interesting piece and examined it intently. A sudden loud crash in the undergrowth below startled me and I looked around just in time to see a black bear rise up out of the brush about 10 feet away. My first thought was 'Oh no! a bear. I'd better do the right thing.' My next thought was one of relief: 'It's only a black bear, and a rather small one at that.' Nevertheless, I decided to get the upper hand immediately and scare it away. I shouted at it, face-to-face, in my most commanding tone of voice: 'Shoo! Get out of here, bear! Go on! Get away!' The bear remained motionless and glared back. I clapped my hands and yelled even louder. Even this had no effect on the bear.

"Instead of turning and running away into the brush, it began slowly walking, climbing toward my level, watching me stealthily. I waved my arms, clapped, yelled even more wildly. I began banging on the outcrop with my hammer, making all the noise I could to intimidate this bear that was just not acting like a black bear is supposed to. I took a step back, managing to elevate myself another foot or so in an attempt to reach a more dominant position. But as I did this, the bear darted suddenly around behind the outcrop, behind me.

"My sensation was that of being struck a staggering blow from behind. I felt myself being thrown forward and landed face down on the ground, with my arms outstretched. I froze, not instinctively but deliberately, remembering that playing dead was supposed to cause an attacking bear to lose interest and go away.

"Instead of hearing the bear crashing off through the brush though, I felt the sudden piercing pain of the bear's teeth biting deep into my right shoulder. I felt myself being shaken with tremendous, irresistible power by my shoulder, by teeth deep in my shoulder. Then it stopped, and seemed to be waiting to see if I were still alive.

I Tried For My Radio

"I tried to lie perfectly still, hoping it was satisfied. 'I've got to get at my radio in the pack, I've got to get a call out,' I thought. My left arm was free so I tried to reach behind myself to the left outside pocket of my rucksack to get at the walkie-talkie. The strap was buckled so tightly I realized I couldn't get the pocket open without taking off my pack. My movement caused the bear to start a new flurry of biting and tearing at the flesh of my upper right arm again. I was completely conscious of feeling my flesh torn, teeth against bone, but the sensation was more of numb horror at what was happening to me than of specific reaction to each bite. I remember thinking, 'Now I'm never going to be able to call for help. I'm dead unless this bear decides to leave me alone.'

"The bear had no intention of leaving me alone. After chewing on my right shoulder, arm, and side repeatedly, the bear began to bite my head and tear at my scalp. As I heard the horrible crunching sound of the bear's teeth biting into my skull, I realized it was all too hopeless. I remember thinking, 'This has got to be the worst way to go.' I knew it would be a slow death because my vital signs were all still strong. My fate was to bleed to death. I thought, 'Maybe I should just shake my head and get the bear to do me in quickly.'

"All of a sudden, the bear clamped its jaws into me and began dragging me by the right arm down the slope through the brush. I was dragged about 20 feet or so before the bear stopped as if to rest, panting in my ear. It began licking at the blood that was by now running out of a large wound under my right arm. Again the bear pulled me along the ground, over rocks and through brush, stopping frequently to rest, and chewing at my arm. Finally it stopped, panting heavily. It had been dragging me and my 20-pound pack — a combined weight of about 150 pounds — for almost a half-hour. Now it walked about four feet away and sat down to rest, still watching me intently.

"Here, I thought, might be a chance to save myself yet — if only I could get at that radio. Slowly I moved my left arm, which was on the side away from the bear, and which was still undamaged, behind me to get at that pack buckle. But this time the pocket, instead of being latched tight, was wide open — the buckle probably tore off from the bear's clawing or the dragging over the rocks. I managed to reach down into the pocket and pull out the radio.

Come Quick! I'm Being Eaten By A Bear

"Since my right arm was now completely numb and useless, I used my left hand to stealthily snap on the radio switch, pull up two of the three segments of the antenna, and push in the button activating the transmitter. Holding the radio close to my mouth, I said as loudly as I dared, 'Ed, this is Cynthia. Come quick, I'm being eaten by a bear.' I said 'eaten' because I was convinced that the bear wasn't just mauling me or playing with me, but was planning to consume me. I was its prey and it had no intention of letting the 'catch' escape.

"I repeated my message and then started to call out some more information, hoping that my first calls had been heard. 'Ed, I'm just down the hill from where you left me off this morning . . .' but I got no further. The bear by this time had risen to its feet; it bounded quickly over to me, and savagely attacked my left arm, knocking the radio out of my hand. I screamed in pain as I felt my good arm now being torn and mangled by claws and teeth.

"It was then I realized I had done all I could do to save my life. I had no way of knowing whether anyone had even heard my calls. I really doubted it, since no static or answering sound from someone trying to call back had come over the receiver. I knew I hadn't taken time to extend the antenna completely. I knew I was down in a ravine, with many ridges between me and the receiving set. I knew there was really no chance for me. I was doomed. So I screamed and yelled as the bear tore at my arm, figuring that it was going to eat me anyway and there was no longer any reason to try to control my natural reactions.

"I remember that the bear then began sniffing around my body, going down to my calves, up my thighs. I thought, 'I wonder if he's going to open up new wounds or continue working on the old ones.' I didn't dare to look around at what was happening — my eyes were fixed upon the dirt and leaves on the ground only inches below my face. Then I felt a tearing at the pack on my back, and heard the bear begin crunching cans in its teeth — cans I had brought for my lunch. This seemed to occupy its attention for a while; at least it let my arms alone and gave me a few moments to focus my mind on my predicament.

" 'Is this how I'm going to go?' I remember marveling at how clear my mind was, how keen my senses were. All I could think of as I lay there on my stomach, with my face down in the dry grass and dirt, and that merciless, blood-thirsty thing holding me down, was how much I wanted to live and how much I wanted to return to Charlie, my husband of five months, and how tragic it would be to end it all three days before I turned 31.

"It was about 10 minutes, I think, before I heard the faint sound of a helicopter in the distance. It came closer and then seemed to circle, as if making a pass, but not directly over me. Then I heard the helicopter going away, leaving me. What had gone wrong? Maybe it was just a routine pass to transfer one of the other geologists to a different ridge, or to go to a gas cache to refuel, and not an answer to my call for help. No one heard my call.

"The bear had not been frightened by the sound of the helicopter, for now having finished with the contents of my pack it began to tear again at the flesh under my right arm. Then I heard the helicopter coming back, circling, getting closer. Being flat on my face, with the remains of the pack still on my back, and both arms now completely without feeling, I kicked my legs to show whoever was up above me that I was still alive. This time, however, I was certain that I was to be rescued because the pilot hovered directly over me.

Silence

"But again I heard the helicopter suddenly start away over the ridge. In a few seconds all was silence, agonizing silence. I couldn't believe it. For some completely senseless, heartless, stupid reason they'd left me for a second time.

"Suddenly I felt, or sensed, that the bear was not beside me. The sound of the chopper had undoubtedly frightened it away. Again I waited in silence for some 10 minutes. Then I heard the helicopter coming over the ridge again, fast and right over me. I kicked my legs again, and heard the helicopter move up toward the crest of the ridge for what I was now sure was a landing. Finally I heard the engine shut down, then voices, and people calling out.

"I yelled back and tried to direct them to where I was lying. But the birch brush was thick, and with my khaki work pants and gray pack I was probably difficult to see lying on the ground among the rocks. Ed was the first to spot me, and he called the two women geologists down the slope to help him. Together they managed to carry me up the hill and lift me up into the back seat of the helicopter.

"I remember the feeling of relief and thankfulness that swept over me when I found myself in that helicopter, going up and away over the mountain. I knew that my mind was clear and my breathing was good and my insides were all intact. All I had to do was keep cool and let the doctors fix me up. Deep down, though, I knew the extent of my injuries and knew that I had been too badly hurt for my body to ever be the same again.

"They flew me to Fort Greely, an army base in Delta Junction, about an hour's trip. There emergency measures were taken to stabilize my condition. I was given blood and probably some morphine to deaden the pain. An hour or so later I was flown to the army hospital in Fairbanks and taken immediately into surgery. For the first time that day I lost consciousness — under the anesthesia. My left arm had to be amputated above the elbow, about halfway between elbow and shoulder, because most of the flesh had been torn from my forearm and elbow. To try to save my right arm, which had not been so badly chewed, the doctors took a vein out of my left thigh and grafted it from underneath my badly damaged right shoulder, through the torn upper arm, and out to my lower arm. This vein became an artery to keep the blood circulating through my forearm and hand. Four surgeons continued working on me for about five hours, late into the evening. They also did some 'debriding' — that is, removing hopelessly damaged tissue and cleaning the lacerated wounds of leaves, sticks and dirt. I stayed at Fairbanks overnight and then at three o'clock Sunday afternoon was flown to San Francisco.

"By this time our branch chief had managed to notify my husband, Charlie (also a geologist for the U.S. Geological Survey), of my accident. They were waiting for me when I arrived at the San Francisco airport at one o'clock Monday morning. I was taken immediately by ambulance to Stanford Hospital and put in the intensive care ward.

Another Amputation

"Then began the vain attempts to save my right arm. For more than a week I held every hope that the vein graft was going to work. But a blood clot developed in the mangled arm and circulation stopped. The pulse that had been felt in the right wrist and the warmth in my fingers disappeared and the whole arm became cold. Although another amputation was clearly going to be necessary, the doctors felt that they should wait until a clearer line of demarcation between good tissue and bad tissue became evident. Then they would amputate up to this point and save the rest.

"But before that line appeared, I began to run a very high temperature. Fearing that the infected and dying arm was now endangering my life, the doctors took me immediately into the operating room, found the tissue in my arm to be dead almost to the top of my shoulder, and removed the entire arm.

"As if this was not trouble enough, my side underneath the right shoulder had been opened up when the bear tore out and ate the lymph glands under my right arm. This area was raw and extremely susceptible to infection. It eventually would have to be covered by skin grafts, skin stripped from my own body. But before the skin graft could be done, new tissue would have to be regenerated in the wound to cover the exposed muscle and bone. I stayed for weeks in the hospital, absorbing nourishing fluids and antibiotics intravenously and eating high-protein meals of solid foods. Slowly, new flesh grew back to fill the hole, and the plastic surgeon was able to graft strips of skin taken from my upper right thigh to cover the raw flesh under my right shoulder. The thigh skin was laid on in strips like rolls of sod, kept clean and open to the air for many days, until it 'took.' Those operations hospitalized me for a total of six weeks.

It Had Been August 13

"During my long days and weeks in bed I had lots of time to review my experience and ponder some of the questions that had puzzled me on that unlucky day of August 13. Why didn't I simply bleed to death after the bear had torn both my arms to shreds and chewed through the main arteries in each? My doctor explained that because I had been in excellent physical condition and my arteries were young and elastic, the blood vessels constricted and cut off the flow of blood very quickly after the flesh was mangled. Even the open ends of the arteries closed themselves off and kept me from losing all my blood, and my life.

"Had my call for help over the walkie-talkie really been picked up? or was the helicopter merely making a routine run over the area when Ed spotted me on the ground? I learned later that my first call for help *had* been heard by the helicopter pilot's wife, Bev Spencer. She understood it clearly, and immediately radioed her husband that I was in trouble. She gave him what little information I had been able to transmit about my location, and he started right toward my ridge. He had also heard my call, but not clearly enough to be sure of the message. But why did he leave my ridge after he flew over me the first time? And where did he go?

"Actually, Ed hadn't been able to spot me from the air the first time, and realizing that he couldn't fly the helicopter and look for me at the same time, he decided to pick up another geologist first.

"The second time over he did spot the bear, and hence, me, from the air, but he also saw that the terrain was too rough for only two to get me up the ridge to a landing spot, so he flew back to pick up a third geologist from another area. Finally, with two assistants, he made his landing and led the successful search and rescue. I only wish I'd known why that helicopter kept leaving me again and again, though. I didn't need that additional mental torture.

Why Was I Attacked?

"But why did the bear attack me in the first place? I see three possible reasons: 1) the bear may have been asleep in the brush and I startled it; 2) the bear may have seen me as a threat, not only to itself but also to any offspring that might have been nearby; or 3) the bear was very hungry. I do not even consider a fourth possibility, one that has often been suggested as a reason for discriminating against women in similar situations — namely, the possibility that wild animals, particularly bears, are often attracted by the scent of menstrual blood of women at times of their periods. For the three summers I worked out in the bush, I was never approached by any wild animals, and my periods came and went regularly. On the day of the attack I was not menstruating.

"Regarding the first possibility, which I believe is the most likely one, the bear may have been asleep in the brush and woke up startled when it heard me chipping on rocks. It should have had plenty of time to collect its wits, however, as it stared at me and circled me before charging. Although the terrain seemed rather unsuited for a comfortable lair — large, rectangular blocks of broken-off rubble covered the ground and were almost covered by birch brush — this hidden spot may have seemed ideal to the bear.

"It is also possible that the bear was instinctively fearful for the safety of a cub in the area. I never saw any other bear that day, but the helicopter pilot, after he left me off at the Fort Greely hospital for emergency treatment, asked Fish & Game officials to find the bear that had attacked me so that it could be checked for rabies. They did, and shot what they believe to be the guilty one — a 175-pound female. They reported the presence of a year-old cub in the area, but left it to take care of itself. If the mother encountered a strange creature in its territory and simultaneously noticed the absence of its cub, it could have reacted violently out of rage or fear for its cub. The fact that I saw no cub, it may have felt, in sudden panic, that I had something to do with its disappearance.

"As to the third possibility, extreme hunger of the bear, the post-mortem analysis of the bear's stomach revealed only a few berries and some 'unidentifiable substance' that may have been parts of me. I hadn't noticed any blueberry patches on the ridge, so the bear could have been tired of hunting for berries and decided to try for larger game, since it came upon me, either unexpectedly or deliberately, at a distance of only 10 feet.

"One fact is certain: that bear wanted me for dinner — my flesh and blood — and once having tasted it, did not intend to let me get away. But I did get away. Furthermore, I'm up and around again. The bites on my head have healed and my hair has grown back to completely cover the scars. My right side is covered with new skin, my left stump is strong and has good range of motion. I'm fitted with artificial arms and am ready to resume my interrupted careers as wife and geologist.

"It will be difficult for me to operate a workable arm on my right side, where I have no stump, and to manage the use of the arm and hook on the other side, where I have no elbow. But with practice I know that I will eventually be able to make my prosthetic devices and my feet and mouth do many of the things my hands did for me before.

"I plan to continue in my job with the U.S. Geological Survey. Both Charlie and I have loved our work there, and our colleagues have been tremendously supportive of me throughout the ordeal. I'd like to stay with the Alaskan Geology Branch, perhaps specializing in petrography — the examination of sections of three-hundredths-of-a-millimeter-thick wafers of rock under the microscope to determine their mineral composition and texture. With only minor adaptations to the microscope, I should be able to do this work as effectively as I was able to do it before my accident.

"I am determined to lead as normal a life as possible. I know that there are certain limitations I can't get around, having to rely on artificial arms. But I'm certainly going to do the best I can with all that I have left. And that's a lot!" □

A BOY IS BLINDED

This is a remarkable account by a young man, Lee Hagmeier, then of Juneau, who survived a terrible bear experience with a degree of successful readjustment that should be nothing less than a beacon for not just others who might have unfortunate afflictions, but most importantly for all of us who perhaps take life a little too much for granted.

A powerful story.

" 'Lee, Brownie!' Doug shouted as the brown/grizzly bear roared down upon me from the tangle of alders and Sitka spruce along the creek bank. Instantly I thought, 'I've gotta get the safety off!' I released the safety and fired from the hip, a desperation shot.

"As the bear rushed up to me, I turned to my left, defensively turning my right side and back to it to absorb the impact of the charge. He grabbed the rifle stock in his teeth and jerked it from my hand, the force turning me to my right and throwing me onto my back. Then the beast began mauling me.

"A bear mauling was the last thing I expected as my friend Doug Dobyns and I left my Auke Bay home near Juneau, Alaska, on a fishing outing that Monday, July 27, 1959. We hitchhiked to the end of the sawmill road where the creek forks — McGinnis Creek goes to the right; Montana Creek branches to the left. We were fishing about a mile up McGinnis Creek.

"Heavy spruce timber, alder brush and devil's club covered the banks, forcing us to wade in the creek. Dog salmon carcasses littered the ground and bear sign was abundant.

"At this point I chose to go into the woods. I left my fishing pole on the bank and entered the undergrowth with the express purpose of killing a bear. We had jumped one earlier, and this was an ideal place to see another.

"Doug followed at a distance. He had no desire to tangle with a bear.

"I was struggling through the brush when Doug spotted a bear behind us off to our right about 20 feet. It was looking over our back trail. Doug yelled, 'Lee, Brownie!' and I whirled around. At this point the bear charged.

"I was slightly off balance and in a poor position to shoot. I carried my Husqvarna .30-'06 in my right hand and was taking a step forward with my right foot. I fired a desperation shot which missed, and the bear knocked me down and began biting me. First he bit me on the left knee and picked me up and shook me. Then he bit me on the leg and picked me up and shook me. He did that three times. Once I bent up at the waist, maybe that's when he bit me in the side under my left arm. I determined to play dead and just lay still.

I Heard A Popping Sound

"There was a momentary period of time where nothing happened. I closed my eyes. At that instant there was a bite across my face. I heard myself groan lightly, *unnnh*. I heard a popping sound (which was probably the skull fracture), but there wasn't any pain associated with it.

"I was filled with terror and horror, and I really don't remember having any thoughts during the mauling.

'After the bear left, I put my hand up to my face. It was really a mess. I felt bone tissue and flesh. My face between the bridge of my nose and the middle of my forehead was gone. My left eye was hanging down on my cheek and my right eye was gone. I thought, 'My God, I've been blinded.'

"Doug didn't know what had happened during the mauling. He couldn't see what was going on. His view was blocked, and he had climbed a tree only to have the bear rush past a few yards away in leaving.

"Doug yelled, 'Lee, are you all right?' I didn't hear him the first time.

"The second time he called I yelled back, 'No, I have been badly mauled. Don't be shocked when you see me.'

"He approached, knelt beside me and said, 'Lee, I hate to say this; I don't think you'll ever see again.'

"I wasn't ready to acknowledge that and passed it off kinda lightly, 'Well, we'll see about that.'

"I didn't have any pain in my face at all. In fact most of that tissue was numb; several of the nerves for the facial muscles and tissue had been severed so there wasn't any feeling in that area. I did have some pain in my knee and quite a bit under my arm.

"Doug and I stumbled 30 to 40 feet through the undergrowth; I was leading. It was obvious we weren't making much headway, so we decided Doug should go for help.

"He left me, blazed a trail to the creek and stuck his knife in a tree. Downstream he located two fishermen, Clark Meriwether and Ralph Shafer. Clark gave Ralph his pistol, a .45 or .44, and Ralph returned with Doug while Meriwether drove for assistance.

"I was drifting in and out of consciousness, my only thought was apprehension that the bear might return (that probably goes back to having read the story of Forest Young, knowing the bear had come back to him seven or eight times and had lain in ambush).

"When I couldn't move initially, I had some anxiety about that.

"I remember turning my head and hearing blood drip into a puddle below me and coughing up quite a bit of blood that had drained down through my nose area and feeling the blood oozing about the rest of my body also, really not being too conscious.

Rescue

"When Doug returned he found the knife in the tree but had a little trouble locating me. He called my name a number of times, and I finally answered. He said, 'Where are you?'

"I replied, 'Over here,' and they came to the sound of my voice.

"Shafer, who had worked for the territorial police and was aghast at my appearance, was struck by my calm attitude and kept saying, 'Bravest thing I ever saw.' He checked me over to see if there were any broken bones. I remember his hand on my leg and one arm.

"Then the two of them half carried, half dragged me out to the dry creek bed, each one grasping one of my arms over his shoulders. I remember feeling pretty woozy, wanting to lie down a couple of times, and they said, 'It's just a little farther.' I reached up once to confirm that it *was* my eye bouncing on my cheek like a ping pong ball. I was aware that my boots had been punctured by the bear because water came into them as we crossed a creek.

"When we got out to the dry gravel bed, Shafer left to show the others where I was.

"Doug sat on the ground, and I sat with my back against his knees. I remember asking him, 'Am I bleeding very bad?'

"He said, 'No, not too bad.' Doug asked me, 'Do you believe in God?'

"I replied, 'At a time like this it's hard not to.'

"And he asked, 'Do you want to pray?'

"I said, 'Noooo, I don't think so right now.'

"The crew arrived from the sawmill with a stretcher. I remember thinking how comfortable it was and hearing the sound of water rushing beneath the stretcher as they carried me out to the waiting ambulance. I don't remember the ambulance nor the shot of Demerol.

"I don't recall much of the following two and a half days. When my parents came to see me at St. Ann's Hospital in Juneau, I was in pretty bad shape. The wound across my face was so deep that it scratched the frontal lobe of the brain. There was a great deal of concern about infection, a perfect circumstance for menningitis to set in. They gave me one chance in 50 of pulling through.

"Dr. Carter set in a lot of antibiotic swabs underneath the flesh and let nature take its course. At one point my fever did go up pretty high, and my body took over. I remember going through some tremendous sweats — you could almost wring out the sheet.

"During all this time the folks were startled that I was so courteous, saying 'please' and 'thank you.' The townspeople wondered, 'How's he taking it?' and were reassured, 'Never a word of complaint.'

Blind

"When I brought up the subject of my sight to Dr. Carter, he said, 'There was quite a bit of damage.'

" 'You mean, I'm not going to see again,' I said.

"He said, 'That's right.'

"I replied, 'I was afraid of that,' and that was sort of that.

"The rest was just sort of getting myself mended. I worked little wooden puzzles that you take apart and put back together. Those were my first successes, as I was able to take one piece out at a time, put it in, then take two out and put them in.

"Though my seven-week stay in the hospital was longer than I needed, it provided an opportunity for visitors to stop by as my country home was somewhat isolated. At one point Governor Egan came up and gave me an Alaskan commemorative coin.

"At first the people at the hospital didn't want me to have a radio because I hadn't been told that I was blinded; there was quite a bit of news about my accident and my condition.

"The townspeople were really great. The town held a successful fund raising radio auction to cover medical and educational expenses. There were cans in business establishments marked 'Hagmeier Fund.' The Territorial Sportsmen put together a trust fund to which donations could be made. The whole community rallied. I can't give enough credit to the entire state of Alaska. People as far away as Florida and Rhode Island sent cards.

"I went directly from the hospital to Perkins School for the Blind in Watertown, Massachusetts. My parents gave me the choice between Berkley School for the Blind or Perkins, which was close to Massachusetts General Hospital where my plastic surgery could be done.

"At Perkins I started Braille immediately, and I found school very, very frustrating. In class I just felt like I was falling behind, that I didn't have any of the Braille in order to know what people were talking about. I was aware that there was an awful lot of independence around me, in terms of people moving freely.

"I had a tutor for a short time. After I graduated in 1960 from Perkins, I returned for an additional year and a half of post-graduate work to polish up on my Braille (the fundamentals of which are not difficult to learn, but developing the sensitivity in your fingertips in order to discriminate the patterns of dots takes a long period of time).

"Then I went to Chico State from 1962-67 majoring in psychology. I graduated at the top of my class, *summa cum laude.* From Chico State I went to the University of Washington and took the two-year masters program in vocational rehabilitation and an additional four years for my doctorate in educational psychology. All together I have 11 years in university study and 24 years of continuous schooling.

"I suppose after the mauling I could have given up. But I chose to make the most of my life in spite of circumstances. At no time following my accident was there any thought that I might not live. That had a lot to do with my pulling through, a strong will to live. And I had a strong will to adjust to my handicap.

"As a youngster I was a very, very physical kind of person. If I had free time, I was out on the beach tidal pooling, hunting in the woods or fishing. I was very much interested in the environment and enjoyed being out in it.

"Although I was an average student prior to being mauled, I was hard working and had a lot of independence and responsibility at home and had worked summers for several years. By the age of 16 I'd hunted alone, shot and hauled out 22 deer.

Adjustment

"When one has been blinded, several changes are immediate, and adjustments are essential. It was imperative for me to recognize two tremendous shocks: 1) the physical trauma from the mauling and 2) the psychological shock. It was critical that I face the reality of my situation.

"A major adjustment for me was to realize that I was making a transition from primarily a physical person to being more of a mental person. This perhaps best explains my success in college. (Being physically somewhat constricted, I was now mentally reliberated, if you will.)

"Another adjustment is that you are redefining your relationship to your environment, both socially and physically, a new identity emerges.

"Part of my adjustment was to make peace with myself (and this emerged many years after the mauling). In essence I had to acknowledge that when I whimsically chose to kill a bear, that is just to commit the act itself, I was doing violence to that which I loved dearly, the out-of-doors. Also only after I had acknowledged that I had chosen to be in those woods and was responsible for placing myself in a dangerous situation, could I fully accept my blindness and be at peace with myself. (Shortly after the mauling my peers wanted to avenge me by killing all bears in the immediate area of the attack, but over the years my attitude has changed 180 degrees. I have no desire for people to go out and kill bears — that bear was just doing his bear thing.)

"When a person is carrying a weapon, he tends to feel more powerful and in control of the situation, thus developing a false sense of security. There's a difference between having a weapon along for protection and using it expertly in a crisis and time limited situation. I learned that when a person's in bear country, decisions have to be based on common sense, rather than on the power one feels because he has a gun.

"Blindness involves a lot more than just not seeing. You develop foot perceptions so that you're more sensitive to texture and what's under your feet. It becomes second nature, you encounter certain things that provide a cue regarding where you are in your environment.

"Also a kinesthetic memory develops where your muscles and joints have a certain orientation to the environment. Once you're familiar with your environment, you walk, and you know when you've arrived — there's no counting steps and no conscious thought about it (when I'm at work, I walk down the hall and reach my hand out and I'm at my door — it's the kinesthetic memory).

You Hear Differently

"You learn to use your hearing differently. You become aware of sound cues you didn't use before. I was only in the hospital three weeks when I noticed something on my left while walking down the hall. At the time I didn't know what it was all about but now I realize it was actually hearing the absence of space, like walking down the right side of a street that is open to the left, and then encountering a parked car. Suddenly, you pass a parked car, and the sound comes back to you quickly because there's an absence of space. It's like a subliminal echo that comes back; you can hear telephone poles, curbs, open doorways, etc.

"In addition to my sight, I lost my sense of smell. Generally blinded people use their sense of smell a lot. It helps a great deal in mobility.

"As these senses and awarenesses are refined through experience, your world expands and takes form. It has new meaning kinesthetically, auditorially and tactually.

"Another confrontation that handicapped people encounter is the attitude of other people toward them. The blind are subject to certain kinds of attitudes that they have to fight against. There's a tendency to see a blind person as helpless and childlike and dependent when in actuality the only difference is that they can't see.

"In terms of notetaking and organization it is very important for a blind person to acquire methods of communicating with himself. My study techniques developed while I was in the university setting and I became more efficient. I preferred to work with taped recordings rather than individual readers; I seemed to work more readily with the tapes and get the job done faster.

"I arranged for textbooks to be recorded on tape, listened to the information and took Braille notes. The notes were reviewed two or three times before an exam.

"I use Braille more now and the tape recorder less. While in college I recorded lectures by summarizing them quietly into a recorder as the professor spoke.

"I received a lot of support from my parents who learned Braille and corresponded with me. My mother is a homemaker. My father was an accountant with the Alaska Steamship Company when I was blinded. Later he worked for the Department of Education. Dad and I continued to do our fishing on weekends for salmon and halibut. Dad teased me suggesting that if I had not been blinded I may have become an 'outdoor bum.'

"Initially I had developed an interest in working for the Department of Fish & Game. However, I became interested in sociology and psychology and gradually I went on to pursue counseling and therapy. As a blinded person I became increasingly aware of the needs of handicapped people and sensitive to how often our rights are abridged and opportunities denied, because of misconceptions and stereotypic attitudes. This influenced my decision to pursue a career that involved working with disabled people and related issues.

"At this time I'm employed as a vocational rehabilitation counselor for the Division of Vocational Rehabilitation, Department of Education. I'm responsible for working with disabled people, outlining programs and services that will enable them to move into the competitive labor force in an occupation that is compatible with their disability.

"I started out with the Division of Public Welfare, but I felt I was only helping people to survive rather than to grow. What I like about rehabilitation is that it's really assisting people to grow, to maximize the opportunity for themselves, to get to the point where they are carrying their own rehabilitation forward, where they have taken control of their lives and are really independent of support systems. I feel good about that.

"I worked in Seattle from 1974 to 1979 as a pre-vocational program specialist for the Northwest Regional Center for Deaf-Blind Children (serving Alaska, Washington, Oregon, Montana and Idaho). In 1976 I conducted a national workshop in Denver and met a young lady who worked with deaf-blind adults. Although we had never met, we learned that we had attended the same master's degree program at the University of Washington.

Christy and I

"In 1977 Christy and I met again at a workshop in Seattle. We later went to a coffee hour and we talked for three hours with never a lack of words.

"The next day, I wanted to get in touch with her. However, I didn't know how to go about it because I didn't know where she was staying, and Christy is deaf. She called me about that time and invited me to go beachcombing. I responded affirmatively.

"I began sending her typed letters and she sent me recorded tapes. We carried on a courtship between Denver and Seattle.

"Since the time of my accident my desire to return to Alaska to live permanently became ever stronger. Christy was also interested in moving to Alaska. In 1978 the opportunity occurred. Christy was hired for a new program in Anchorage and I accepted a position with the Division of Vocational Rehabilitation. We knew that moving to Alaska together could be a risky business because we really didn't know each other very well. We were married in April of 1980.

"We're an unusual couple because of the fact that I'm blind and Christy's deaf. However, we accommodate each other. I make phone calls for her (she reads lips and has clear speech), and she reads print materials for me. I make sure I'm facing her when I talk to her. If she's in some other part of the house and she asks me a question, I'll stomp on the floor twice for *yes* and once for *no*, and she interprets the vibrations. If she wants to watch television and I don't or if I want to sleep, I turn the sound off. If I want to read recorded books or magazines, the sound doesn't disturb her and she can sleep or go about her business.

"We spend a lot of our time fishing and are rapidly becoming familiar with different areas in Alaska. We aren't familiar enough with the area yet. We also have a cabin near Hope, and frequently spend weekends there. People often forget that along with blindness there is also respectability and a lot of enjoyment.

"Over the years I have learned that my adjustment to blindness is an ongoing process. It involves penetrating those self-limiting beliefs and misconceptions about blindness which I acquired while growing up. When I am clear of these attitudes, I recognize that by doing things a little differently, the limitations associated with blindness are minimal. My attitudinal growth as a blind person has been immeasurably assisted by my association with the National Federation of the Blind and its Alaska affiliate. It is an organization of blind people speaking for themselves."   □

NANOOK —
THE ICE BEAR

"I turned around, and there stood the bear not 15 feet away . . . He just walked right up on us. He didn't know what to do; he was just as startled as we were." (John Graybill, personal interview, Peters Creek, Alaska, January 1978)

*"One bear, riding an ice pan along the shore of the Arctic Ocean, drifted into the harbor of a supply camp . . . while a landing craft was unloading . . . the bear came aboard . . . A blast from a fire hose finally sent the bear back to his ice pan." (*The ALASKA SPORTSMAN®, *July 1954)*

Nanook (the Eskimo word for polar bear) lives in a land of perpetual ice and snow. His creamy, white coat gives him a natural camouflage in his white surroundings. His shuffling, mile-eating gait carries him across ice pans and around massive piles of crushed, pressure ridge ice. Long hair envelops his entire body except for the pads on the bottom of his feet, which seem to grow out of the hair. This hair provides maximum protection to the animal in his frigid wonderland.

Polar bears inhabit the white North, but they are not restricted to the ice; and in areas along the coast Nanook inhabits the land. It is quite common for him to eat berries, lichen, grass, sedges and moss. This creature frequents man's habitations along the coast and has walked *Homo sapiens'* streets, fed at man's garbage pits and inspected his buildings. This is not to imply that you will run into the bear in the northern hamlets regularly, but these animals are seen frequently in some villages — and in North Slope oil camps.

The bear of the North is a loner who spends most of his time roaming the ice in search of nourishment. Bears *do* congregate at food sources, and it is not uncommon to see several of the great white beasts at walrus or whale carcasses. In the late summer of 1914 Arctic trader Jim Allen (not the same Jim Allen mentioned in Chapter 4) witnessed over a hundred white bears at a whale carcass between Point Barrow and Beechey Point. They were in various positions — several lay on the ice sleeping, others were walking on the whale's back and yet others disappeared inside the dead animal's mouth and reappeared out gaping holes in its side.

The bear relies on his nose to guide him to many feasts. Some people contend that he can smell food 12 miles distant. He may not depend heavily on his auditory sense because of the noise created by the churning and grating of the sea ice around him. His eyes have a protective covering that shields them from the sun's harsh glare and guards against snowblindness.

The tiny cubs, seven to eight inches long and weighing one to two pounds, are hairless and pinkish in color at birth. They cling to their mother's hair and suckle there in the protection of her warm fur. Her milk is of the consistency of cow's cream, smells like seal oil and tastes much like fish — similar to cod liver oil. As the cubs increase in size, they become more active and open their eyes about the sixth week. At the end of three months they are introduced to the outside world for the first time.

Their mother teaches them how to locate bird eggs and seaweed as well as how to catch lemmings, fish, ducks and seals (many bears' stomachs contain mostly seal oil when they are gutted; it is said by some that they eat only the seal's blubber and not the meat). These bears eat carrion, and during their lifetime they will travel farther for food than any other bear.

Polar bears often catch seals by standing over their blow holes awaiting a head to pop up through the ice for air. Nanook's neck, shoulders and forelegs are extremely powerful (some people claim their studies of skinned polar bears indicate the animal's left front leg is bigger than its right leg; and tradition has it that polar bears are "left handed"). Sometimes the bears stalk the seals by diving below them, swimming to their blow holes and waiting for the seal to slide into the water from a spot near their blow hole.

Polar bears are no match for walruses in the water. There is evidence that Nanook is afraid of bull walruses and usually attacks females or calves, if any. Jim Allen, the trader, once encountered a battle scene. The surrounding area was red and blood saturated. A polar bear lay oozing blood from a number of wounds where a walrus had run its tusks into the bear. The two-ton walrus was gone, but the bear was dead.

The richness of the polar bears' food creates such a high concentration of Vitamin A in his liver that it is very harmful and usually fatal if eaten by man. Eskimos do not eat the bears' liver. An interesting scientific achievement was recorded in the August 1949 *The ALASKA SPORTSMAN*®: "The liver of the polar bear, long believed to be poisonous because of the religious taboo attached to it by the Eskimos, may play an important role in medical progress. When a polar bear died in a Chicago zoo two years ago, bits of its liver were fed to other animals suffering from various ailments. One of the sufferers, a dog, responded in an amazing manner. Its blood pressure, which had been very high, dropped to almost normal within a few hours. Research workers at the University of Chicago Medical school made efforts to obtain more livers for research purposes. Leon S. Vincent, then principal of the Alaska Native Service school at Point Barrow, agreed to act as agent and offered the Eskimos top meat prices for polar bear livers. The Eskimo hunters promised to bring in the livers but never actually did, probably because of the strength of their ancient superstitions. Finally, through the efforts of Commander Roberts and Lieutenant Krickenberger of the Navy's oil project at Point Barrow, three livers were secured last April, delivered by Wien Airways to Vincent in Fairbanks, and forwarded by him to Chicago. Recent word to Vincent from the recipients hints of the possible development of an antitoxin for tuberculosis from their research. This, believes Vincent, would be the greatest single blessing that could come to the Eskimo people."

Unfortunately many myths or half truths robe the ice bear in mystery. One of the major controversies involving this animal is his aggressive behavior. Old-time whalers, explorers, sailors and traders insist the animal is aggressive and charges man on sight, recognizing him as food; but others claim he is merely curious.

They're Big

The son of famed Arctic trader Charles Brower once killed three ice bears, each of which was nearly 12 feet in length before skinning. And Bud Helmericks, author, hunter, guide and pilot, once reported a bear with a skinned neck circumference of 42 inches.

Eskimos have told of bears that were so large the men could sit cross-legged in the animal's tracks. Several years ago a polar bear was killed and left overnight on the ice. When the hunters returned the next day, they found the beast had been covered with a mound of snow and ice by another bear whose hind tracks measured 17x10¾ inches. The mound-building bear was seen later, and it was estimated to be 14 feet long.

The average size of males is seven to nine feet long and 800 to 1,000 pounds. Females, which are smaller, average six to seven feet and around 700 pounds.

Some say the brown/grizzly is the largest carnivore on earth today, while others champion the polar's size as being greater than the brown/grizzly. Lee Miller of the Alaska Department of Fish & Game told me, "I have examined thousands of these bears and am not sure which is larger. It's pretty well established that the brown has the larger skull, but of those I have measured, the polar has the larger hide. I would like to see any evidence to show one is larger than the other."

Polar bears are perhaps the most powerful four-footed swimmer in the world. They have been seen more than 200 miles from any visible shore ice, paddling about in the ocean. At least two different sightings have been reported of polar bears on Kodiak Island, over a thousand miles from their polar home. One such report appeared in the December 1943 issue of *The ALASKA SPORTSMAN*®: "For the first time on record a polar bear was reported killed on Kodiak Island recently. The bear, described as absolutely white in color, with a yellowish cast in the fur on the back, was identified as unmistakably a polar bear by everyone who saw it, including a teacher at Larsen's Bay who had been in the Arctic, which is its natural habitat. How it got as far south as Kodiak Island, a thousand miles from its home shore, is a mystery, although it is possible for him to have drifted on an ice floe to the southern shores of the Bering Sea and crossed the Alaska Peninsula."

Weismuller Couldn't Catch One

The swimming speed of these animals is amazing, as they are able to catch diving ducks in the water.

Evidently mother bears tow their cubs through the water. In at least one instance a sow was seen paddling along with two cubs trailing in her wake; one had clasped her tail in its mouth while its sibling did likewise to him — the three resembled a tug pulling barges.

Nanook possesses a volatile temper when angered. Several years ago F. Illingworth observed a bear stalking a seal as it lay on the ice next to its blow hole in Ice Fjord, Canada. The bear proceeded until he was nearly within striking distance; then he launched his attack. The seal managed to escape through the hole to safety. The bear was so angry that he pummeled a rock outcropping with his front paws. Illingworth killed it and examined its paws. It had severely injured its left paw, and every bone in its right paw was broken.

Pregnant sows are usually the only ones to hibernate, that being for the sole purpose of bearing offspring. She rarely has as many as three cubs. Sows locate a den in tumbled ice along pressure ridges, snowdrifts or along the coastline where they can find or dig an appropriate earthen shelter or utilize a rock outcropping.

The den is often a two-chambered affair — one a birth and sleeping room and the other a play room for the cubs. The den is oval shaped and has a length of six to eight feet and a height and width of five feet. Naturally some dens are much larger. It is common for dens to have a 10- to 20-foot tunnel leading to the den proper which branches off at a 90 degree angle from the tunnel and has a "room" at each end of the branch (like the letter *T*, the vertical leg forming the tunnel). Most dens have an air hole in the roof.

Nanook has been subjected to a great deal of scientific research the past several years, and den studies have been undertaken by Arctic nations. Jack Lentfer, formerly of the United States Fish & Wildlife Service, was working with Chuck Evans of the University of Alaska in the spring of 1973, looking for vacant dens from the air. They spotted one, landed and began inspecting it.

Jack dug a hole about midway along the 25-foot tunnel (to offer better light) before entering the tunnel. As he slid into the tunnel head first, a blast of warm air and strong bear odor met him; and an angry bear growled somewhere very close below. Jack exited!

Jack experienced another close call while darting bears with tranquilizers with Lee Miller of the Alaska Department of Fish & Game in March 1970. They were in a helicopter from which they shot a sow twice. They waited several minutes until the bear and her cub sat down. It appeared she was going out, so Jack approached her from 50 yards while Lee carried a rifle for backup.

About that time the sow charged. Jack yelled, but she kept coming.

Miller fired a warning shot in front of her when she was within 25 feet of Lentfer, but she pressed her attack. Lee reloaded and fired, killing the bear which was only two yards from Lentfer. They discovered that the darts had frozen, rendering the drug useless.

An Elusive Bow and Arrow Bear

Chuck Wirschem of Anchorage told me about some bears he had chased around the ice in 1971 while he was trying to shoot one with his bow and arrow. "I always had heard that the polar bear was the one that was the most vicious guy, and if he saw you, he'd get after you.

"I stalked four different bears and got within 30 yards or less of each one of them and missed every one of them. I was after this one bear, not a big boar, about seven and a half, eight feet. A big, old cantankerous boar polar bear is gonna give you a lot more problem than a younger bear. I'd shoot an arrow at him and miss, and the bear would take off running (I richocheted one off the top of his back). I was able to cut him off because it was good hard pack, and the running conditions were good. The bear wouldn't run so fast that I couldn't catch up with him.

"I'd cut him off and restalk him. I'd get up 25 or 30 yards from it, and I'd draw and let fly and miss again. A couple of times he stood up on his hind legs and looked down at me and snorted steam. Then he took off on a dead run again. I'd go after him again and hop across the ice floes.

"That game of cat and mouse went on for a full two hours before finally I ran out of gas and was gettin' an awful long way from where the plane was parked. That was my last stalk on that particular hunt, but I remember that one very, very clearly.

"I'd always heard that polar bear were so vicious. I'm sure they are in a given situation; but it's just like anything else with bear, you never say that anything's going to be true all the time because they're so darn unpredictable."

This Bear Walked Right In

Similarly, guide John Graybill shared an experience he had with a polar bear. He and a client had flown away from a wounded bear, pretending to leave and hoping it would leave the water where it had taken refuge and return to the pack ice. After they were airborne, the bear came out of the water, and John landed again. They stalked the animal but couldn't find it.

"I turned around, and there stood the bear not 15 feet away; and he was a big 10' 6" boar, wounded. He had no inclination at all to charge, nor did he seem to associate us with the hurt or the danger.

"I said, 'Oh, my God, there he is, Lee. He's right alongside you.' Lee turned and shot him in the head, and he just fell over. He just walked up on us. He didn't know what to do; he was just as startled as we were."

A man who has stumbled onto a polar bear would be wise not to panic and run as any quick movement could trigger a rush — not necessarily a charge. Many bears have run up to men and examined them without harming them, almost as though satisfying their curiosity.

A Lantern Was His Weapon
In the late 1950s an old Swede, employed to patrol the Miocene Ditch near Nome, walked into a sow with two cubs, face-to-face. He had a lantern and began waving it in a wide arc as she swung her head from side to side, scrutinizing him methodically. He hurled the kerosene lantern at her, wheeled about and dug for camp. That was the last he saw of the beast. She made no attempt to follow him.

The ice bear is comparable to his southern cousins in his unpredictability. Three boars could all respond in the same way or differently — one might attack a camp and sled dogs, the second could run from a bunch of puppies, and the last might take a nap within earshot of man's camp.

The Seal Hunters
A native of Upernivik, Greenland, using nets to catch seals, bent over a seal entangled in his net. He felt a tap on his shoulder. He assumed that it was his partner and continued with his work. Then another, sharper thump caused him to look around. His eyes bulged as the black, shiny eyes of a creamy, old bear focused on

him. Without so much as a "pardon me," the bear stepped past the surprised man, ripped the seal from the net and started eating it.

On another occasion an Eskimo hunched over a seal hole in the ice, harpoon poised. He stood patiently waiting for a seal when he felt a jab in his back. He turned, saw a bear, screamed and fled. The bear ran just as fast, in the opposite direction!

In a most unusual bear encounter two men went out to check their seal nets. They were working some distance apart, and one of them heard a bear coming his way in the crunchy snow. He had only a knife and saw no means of escape. In desperation he flung himself down on the snow and awaited his fate. He lay completely motionless, and in a few moments the bear approached him. Nanook sniffed him from head to foot.

The bear thrust his face against the Eskimo's, black nose rubbering over the man's nose and lips. The seal hunter held his breath with the greatest of self-control, fearing his lungs would burst and hoping the bear would leave. Presently the bear heard the man's partner and galloped off in his direction. The first man fled in desperation and returned with help. They arrived at his partner's net and found the bear, eating the second Eskimo.

You can never tell about polar bears. Several people insist that this bear is timid and will normally flee, even when wounded. In December 1964 a Wainwright Eskimo fired on three bears at a great distance, hitting one. It charged him, and he escaped to the village nearby. Another man was charged by a wounded bear. He ran toward it, and it retreated.

Bears are individuals. Perhaps a young or timid bear will flee, but an old boar, accustomed to having everything on land flee his presence, might walk right up to man. It appears that the controversy of aggressive versus curious bears will persist until enough scientific data are obtained to distinguish between the two.

Many Eskimo legends center around Nanook. In the past they would not shoot a bear that had just left the water. They believed that bullets would not penetrate his thick fur or that the water froze on its hide. They waited until he had rolled in the snow before shooting.

On one occasion some natives said they had shot a wet bear at least 15 times before killing it. They said they found that their bullets had penetrated only one-half inch into his hide. Another wet bear was killed by a shot in the ear, and it was declared that other bullets lay on the ground around the fallen animal.

Eskimos are ingenious and opportunistic. Many tales have been told about Eskimos waiting on the pack ice and patiently watching bears who in turn wait for seals. Many Eskimos have refrained from killing the bear until it killed a seal; then they dispatched the bear and got a seal free.

International treaties restricting take, prohibiting killing in international waters, and prohibiting use of aircraft in hunting, among polar bear harboring nations ensure perpetuation of the ice bear. □

SOME ARE
PLAIN NUISANCES

"Grizzlies do far more damage to hunting camps, and people's homes normally than do brown bears from some odd reason. Biologically they're the same bear, maybe it's because the brown bear is better fed along the fish streams; a grizzly bear's flat got to work for food. Black bear probably are the worst ones on damaging camps. I've had them in my trapping cabin, and they just tore the devil out of it." (Clark Engle, Master Guide, personal interview, Anchorage, November 1977)

"A yearling black bear cub was shot by an irate gardener in Juneau recently. The animal had peeked into windows, rummaged through garbage cans, and foraged through Victory gardens despite the repeated efforts of the police to scare it back into the woods without killing it." (The ALASKA SPORTSMAN®, October 1943)

"Bears are present but not on the menu at Stuckagain Heights, a dining lodge high in the Chugach foothills overlooking Anchorage. To protect its customers, the restaurant ran this ad in the Anchorage newspapers in August: 'Please remain in your car until in the parking lot. Black bears are cute, but they could cancel your dinner reservation.' "(ALASKA® magazine, November 1975)

Bears vs. Beef on Kodiak

Man's confrontation with bruin in Alaska includes, but is not limited to, trappers, prospectors, farmers, loggers, construction people, outdoor enthusiasts and ranchers. In many situations the bear's plight has been in question. One of the most crucial developments for bear versus man was the bear-cattle problem on Kodiak Island that came to a head in the late 1950s and early 1960s.

In 1953 an enthusiastic cattle rancher moved to Narrow Cape, 50 miles southwest of Kodiak, to raise beef on 23,000 acres of land leased from the United States government. His plan was to raise 600 head of Hereford cattle through the summer, butcher in the fall cutting the herd to 450, calve and build the herd back up to 600 where he would level off. There was only one hitch in his plan — bears, of the famed Kodiak variety.

Joe Beaty raised cattle, bruin got wind of the venture; and the feud was on. Beaty didn't want bears annihilating his herd; the Alaska Department of Fish & Game was opposed to the extermination of a magnificent wilderness creature; and the guides wanted some of these animals for clients.

Even though the cattlemen utilized a very small portion of the island for grazing, the controversy raged. I talked with Joe who related his feelings to me in what he called his "bear beef." "Basically the Fish & Game was trying to save their bears, and we were trying to save our cattle. There's nobody more of a conservationist than a farmer or a rancher because their livelihood depends on it. As far as I'm concerned, when I was there raising cattle or if I was still back there raising cattle, I would not want to see the bear killed off on the refuge. They're a great animal.

"But when it comes down to a matter of them or a matter of survival, you've got to do something about it.

"The argument given to us by the Fish & Game was that the only way you could justifiably kill a bear was if you actually saw him kill a cow. They said if you just see him eating a dead carcass, maybe he's not the outlaw; maybe some other bear killed it.

"Joe Zentner, a neighbor, said, 'Well, I saw one chasing Beaty's steers across the road right in front of me. Was I legal to shoot him?' And the Fish & Game said, 'No, he might have just been going to play with 'em.' That's how narrow-minded they were.

"Their attitude made us almost be outlaws to try to hide what we was doing (killing bears that killed cattle).

"Whenever we killed a bear, we were supposed to report it to the Fish & Game, which we did. If you killed a bear in season and had a license, it was legal; but if you killed one out of season and you took one hair of it, then you were trophy hunting and they would nail you to a cross. We couldn't take a toe or anything. Same way with hides. They was bitter because we wouldn't skin out the bears and take them the hides. Once we got into an awful problem.

"We started after a bear at Middle Bay and went up over a hill. We started at 3:30 A.M. and fought our way almost straight up through the snow. The only way to get down the other side was to slide down. We killed the bear several miles away about 6:00 P.M. and didn't get back to our starting point until 1:00 P.M. the next day, with no food in between.

"The bear had a beautiful hide; it was a shame to leave it, but you skin out a bear that size and the hide'll weigh at least 100 pounds, maybe 150 or 200. Fish & Game wanted us to bring in the hide, but you just couldn't on deals like that."

Bears From A Plane

"The shooting of bears on Kodiak was sanctioned by the Fish & Game. We requested it and were a long time getting their permission. They hired a P-51 World War II fighter pilot, mounted an M-1 Garand, eight-shot rifle on a Cub airplane, and shot bears with it on the leased grazing areas.

"The guides got to hollering that the pilot was crossing the boundary and shooting bears on the Kodiak National Wildlife Refuge. I know it wasn't true because I was in the area every time he took off, and he never crossed that boundary line, never shot a bear on the side of the boundary separating the refuge from the grazing land.

"The state grounded him.

"The only time I used traps was when we found a beef kill. One year, I'm sure it was just one bear killed 23 head of two- and three-year-old steers in less than a week's time. It would have been impossible to sit on 'em. My two sons, a fellow I had working for me, and I would usually get to the kills about 9:00 P.M. and sit there til 6:00 A.M. We spent 31 nights sitting at different kills, and from the one where I was sitting, I could see five kills. The bear, I'm sure, was eating others in the brush that we didn't know about because we found the skeletons later.

"The large bear traps then cost about $87.50 and the smaller ones around $50, very expensive. I bought several. Often the bear's foot was so big he'd hit the pan and the jaws at the same time, and we wouldn't get him.

"We set the traps around kills, where he'd killed a critter. I was just talking to a guy the other day that used to work for Fish & Game. He sold 'em a bill of goods that he could trap the Kodiak bear on the ranches. They hired him for two seasons. He was a big laugh to us who knew something about it because he set traps all over that country, and the chance of a bear ever getting in them was remote because maybe there'd only be one or two bear on 20,000 acres in a year.

"I've known of times when the guys would sit on a bear-killed cow maybe for six nights and then didn't go back and the bear would come back that night and eat it. I don't know whether they watched us, but I had a feeling that they did.

"The bear that killed the 23 beef in one week never touched most of them other than to kill them. Not all bears will kill. I've seen evidence several times, particularly when there's snow on the ground when you know there's no question about it, of bear walking right through where cattle have bedded down. If they weren't spooked by the bear, he wouldn't make a pass at them. Other times he'd go in and chase them and kill a bunch. Why they do it, I don't think anybody knows.

"No one bear does the same thing twice, and no two bear do the same thing as the other one. When you say you know something about them, you don't. They don't have habits. As far as I could tell they have no home. They just bed down wherever they happen to be.

"I was there for 15 years and sold out for health reasons more than anything in 1967. I was allowed one bear a year, and I never even got my quota; and I can honestly say that. Not that I didn't want to or didn't try hard enough.

"I lost 46 head in 10 years. It wasn't only the loss of animals, but also the time lost every summer trying to protect the cattle. There's two years I did nothing but work for bear because my complete income was wiped out by them.

"I lost $20,000 in beef to bears, and that's a conservative estimate."

Trailer Courts and Bears

Much of man's involvement with bears stems around the dollar. In Valdez a trailer court was developed along the Robe River. The land was cleared and pads prepared for lot spaces, trailers were brought in, and people began living there. One minor problem plagued the residents of the trailer court — bears. The court was set up right next to a salmon spawning stream which bears frequented in season. School-age children customarily walked along the trailer court road to and from their school bus — they walked on one side of the road and the bears walked on the other side.

This is a classic case where man infringed on the rights and privacy of bears, to the bears' detriment, and to the chagrin of some of the human types. One woman was mauled one night when she returned to her mobile home and surprised a mother and cub rummaging through her garbage can. Who is to blame, man or bear?

Bears often become a nuisance and must be removed or killed. In more than one case, however, man has camped the night on a bear trail, causing the bear to look the villain. Olga Hughes of Anchorage wrote a letter to the editor of *ALASKA*® magazine which was printed in April 1974.

"For 40 years my trail and my friends' trails have crossed those of bears. Most of the time the bears were not nearly as aggressive as the people. A small unpredictable percentage of bears, however, keeps us on our toes.

"Bears come around almost any place in Alaska where there is garbage. A dishwasher at a mess hall in Yakutat went out to dump the garbage after a meal. His small dog followed him. A sow and two large cubs were at the garbage pit and would probably have caused no problem, but the dog decided to attack a cub. The cub promptly slapped him halfway across the street. The dog scrambled to his feet yipping and ran to his master.

"Things then happened so fast that the man had no time to avoid the sow that had come to the cubs' defense. The sow was intent on getting the dog. When the dog ran to the man, she grabbed the man with her powerful front legs, shook him hard and threw him out of her way. She continued after the dog that had scrambled back under the low heavy porch.

"While the sow was busy trying to get to the dog, the man gained his feet and made it inside the nearest door where his calls for help finally attracted someone's attention.

Here, again, is a classic example where the bear was blamed for being a bear. The animal was helping herself in a situation that man had created.

Handout Bears Are Dangerous
Man conditions bears through his association with them.

"Tame" bears can be found throughout Alaska, bears that have been coddled and fed by well-meaning people; unfortunately not everyone who ventures into the bush knows the bears have been fed, let alone which ones are "tame." Peter Gatz, deputy collector of internal revenue at Fairbanks, was fishing on Long Creek near that Interior city about midnight June 13, 1948, when a bear approached him from across the stream. Gatz fled, and the bear followed. Other fishermen stood speechless along the stream; ultimately the animal broke off the chase after 75 yards. Later in town, Gatz learned that the bear subsisted on handouts from a local mining camp where it playfully chased miners around until they produced some victuals for it.

Another situation involving bears in proximity with man and man's disregard for the creature's future and their own well-being is the Alaska oil pipeline that was recently completed from Prudhoe Bay to Valdez. The general contractor for the line would have the general public believe that there were minimal man-bear encounters and certainly no instance where bears drew blood during the construction of the line. Evidence indicates the contrary.

Scores of pictures illustrate the foolishness of men who fed bears from their machines. Pictures abound showing men feeding steaks to bears as well as men holding the little plastic honey-bear bottles and squeezing their contents into the mouths of bears below. Many bears had to be relocated in an effort to reduce man-bear problems. And this callous regard to the bear's welfare contributed to a law making it illegal to feed and/or bait animals, which poses a hardship for archers who would like to hunt bears from the safety of a stand.

Naturally, not all man-bear confrontations are caused by man; and there are hundreds of examples to illustrate how a nosy or surly animal disrupted man's normal way of life and caused him problems.

Nuisance bear situations occur when bears become overly aggressive. Most incidents involving nuisance bears center around an animal that has worn out his welcome around a camp, park, cannery, individual's dwelling or other human habitation. The bear becomes too familiar and his aggression endangers human residents, their livestock or property. Certainly the incidents related to me by Irving Palmer, Jr. of Anchorage would fall into this category.

Irv was working for the U.S. Geological Survey as a supervisory geologist when he had bear problems. In 1967 he was in the

Katalla area of the Gulf of Alaska staying in a geological tent camp. "Brown bears visited our camp in the middle of the night and rolled our meat chest away, making considerable noise banging into things. Our tents were pitched near a small stream west of Palm Point. We recovered the chest the next morning sprung open but unharmed."

Near Cape Suckling two years later . . . "A small building, used to house radio transmitter equipment for offshore seismic surveying navigation, was completely demolished. Size of claw mark scratches indicated a probable brown bear. All material inside was knocked over and bitten. Even battery cells were bitten."

Irv fished in Alexander Creek across Cook Inlet from Anchorage in 1968 with friends. "Three of us flew in and were dropped off. There were already six of seven people there. The plane was to return the next day before noon. We each caught two salmon, then decided to build a fire and barbecue a couple for dinner and to wait until next day to catch our third fish prior to leaving.

"We were. on a point bar with a small 10- to 12-foot-wide slough separating us from the brush-covered edge of the stream. Several people had salmon on stringers in the water. Several brown bears patrolled the edge of the stream all night, watching us and fishing themselves upstream. We kept the fire going all night and they did not come across the small slough. The bears did not seem to mind the people activity, and we made no attempt to scare them away.

"While there, we saw a cow moose jump from one bank of the stream into the stream and run to the other side, followed immediately by a moose calf which in turn was being chased by a large brown bear. After seeing that, we all talked a little louder and put some more wood on the fire."

Bears Are Cabin Wreckers

One other aspect that Palmer touched on was the damage done to cabins by bears. He had flown into Hewlitt Lake near Skwentna in the winter of 1975 to go ice fishing and said, "I stayed in a friend's cabin. The cabin had been scratched by large claws, probably of brown bear, at all window openings. The windows had protective veneer coverings with many protruding nails to discourage entry. A large 2x4 bolt system had been torn off the front door and the door smashed open. Inside, flour was everywhere and large bear tracks were all over the floor and on a couch. We asked the owner about the incident and he told us that nearly all cabins had been so entered on the lake. Sometimes the bears would even rip off siding to gain entry if they were unsuccessful in gaining entry through doors or windows."

Breaking and entering is not uncommon for the four-legged thief. I discussed this formidable creature with Sergeant Bob Brown at the Department of Public Safety, and he showed me some slides of bear damage at Shell Lake. A sow and cubs badly damaged some cabins there. Bear tracks in the snow showed where they had walked up the nail-perforated steps and ripped into the cabins. Several 20-penny nails protruded two to three inches up through the steps and were outlined by large bear tracks — the bear walked right over the nails as though they weren't even there. Bob told me that man's deterrents of this nature usually do not work. There was a five-foot hole in the roof of an A-frame cabin where the bears had exited. Boards and insulation were ripped off the walls from the outside, and the cabins were a mess.

Bears Like Cities, Too

A couple of years ago I heard about the rampaging black bears of Valdez. Seems as though one summer several of the beasts maintained a nightly "beat." They wandered at random up and down the streets and alleys rummaging through garbage cans for food. Bears also have a reputation for visiting the city of Ketchikan, as they do many towns.

One night in September 1960 two Ketchikan officers shot a 300-pound black bear. They had been on the lookout for the bear for several nights before they caught up with it along Ketchikan's main drag. They shot the bear eight times with pistols; but while examining it, they discovered nine bullet holes, one several days old. If ever there was an animal that could have been a danger to a community, it was that bear.

Bears frequently invade cities. *ALASKA®* magazine carried information about the nuisance bears in the November 1972 issue. "Hunger and over-crowding appeared to be major causes of the bears' war on humans. Juneau authorities received 50 bear complaints in a two-week period last summer. Garbage cans and open dumps were prime targets for the invaders. A black bear was shot in Ketchikan after it had killed a pig on the outskirts of the city, and a reindeer herder near Buckland shot a grizzly that was after his herd.

" 'There seem to be more black bears in the area this season than in any recent year,' said Don Strode of Juneau, Southeastern

Alaska supervisor for the Department of Fish & Game. In urging residents to keep garbage out of the bears' reach, Strode also warned against intentional feeding of the animals.

"Black bears are so numerous in Southeastern Alaska, according to Strode, that they have filled the available habitat. This means that there is no space available for additional bears, but more are being born every year. These bears without established territories are now moving into populated areas and are becoming a nuisance."

Polar bears brought their own brand of danger to Barrow in mid-January 1946. They were brought close inshore by the Arctic ice pack and began prowling the village. One bear was shot and tracks indicated a number of others were roaming about. The village hunters who had been unsuccessful on the ice began hunting in town while the non-hunters armed themselves with whistles to call for help should they run into a bear. Bears seem to like man's dwellings.

It Isn't Always A Neighbor Knocking

Dozens of people have been aroused from a sound sleep in the wee hours of the morning by some bear outside wanting in. Eighty-five-year-old Frank Pratt of Jack Wade, 200 miles east of Fairbanks, was awakened September 3, 1949, by his dog's excited barking outside. He grabbed his rifle, went outside and promptly bumped into a large, hairy, smelly object. He turned so suddenly that he lost his balance and fell over the wood pile. Looking up, he distinguished the outline of a bear about to jump on him. His dog Sugar leaped to the rescue, grabbing a mouthful of bear, and Frank retrieved his gun and fired into the black night. Dog and master made it back inside the cabin only to be roused moments later by the bear nosing around in the storeroom. Frank went back outside, threw a box into the storeroom and dropped the bear as it appeared. Not all people escape so lightly.

One proud cabin owner from Fairbanks gloated over his recently completed cabin that was outfitted with finery to the tune of $2,000. A pilot flew over the dwelling and reported that something looked amiss. Upon investigation it was discovered that the stove was overturned, the bed torn up, cans of food chewed, squeezed and emptied, and bear claw grooves tattooed the walls.

With practice, bears become expert at breaking and entering. The U.S. Forest Service vouches for the expertise of these cabin clobbering clowns. Forester Floyd L. Rentfro of Sitka wrote

ALASKA® magazine, in September 1974: "I inspected the Baranof Lake cabin last spring and found it to be suffering from acute brown bear overuse. Apparently our brown friend made his visit early in the spring when the ice was still on the lake. He sledge-hammered the door open, and once inside literally destroyed everything but the built-in bunks.

"All four windows had been knocked out from the inside with sufficient force to ruin the window frames as well as to break the glass. The storage cabinets had been torn from the wall and reduced to kindling, and the edge of the table looked like fancy lace where dainty bear-sized bites had been taken from around the edge.

"The stovepipe was chewed up and wadded into metal gobs and although stove parts lay scattered in and around the cabin, the stove was gone. It was later found in about six feet of water at the edge of the lake, which leads me to believe that the bear packed the stove out onto the lake ice where it sank when the ice melted.

"Within two days our maintenance crew had the cabin back in good condition and ready for the next visitor. Fortunately, most of our cabin visitors are not as hard on the facilities as was this one.

"This incident is not rare or even extreme. It would be rare if none of the Forest Service recreation cabins were torn up by bears in the spring. Our Rezanof Lake, Plotnikof Lake, Gar Lake, Davidof Lake and Kook Lake cabins have all taken their turn at providing spring amusement for bears.

"It is possible that some of these cabins were inadvertently located on a season migration route and have become a part of a certain bear's life as he makes his annual trek from alpine den to ocean beach in early spring.

"The nature of the damage at some of these cabins indicates that the same bear may be making an annual visit. The Davidof bear is an aluminum chewer and plays havoc with the roofing and the skiff. The Plotnikof bear is a styrofoam eater and chews the styrofoam foundation blocks out from under the cabin. The Rezanof bear broke out the same window two years in a row to gain entry to the cabin. Shutters were installed and on the third year the bear planted a big foot in the middle of the shutter on *his* window with enough force to remove shutter, window and frame right out of the wall."

Cabins aren't the only area of bear interest. They seem to be irresistibly drawn to airstrips. A student pilot narrowly missed a bear on Merrill Field in Anchorage in 1940. Tales abound about close calls pilots have had with bears on strips, however, the bears of Yakataga were a step ahead of most bears in 1950. Every time a flight was due to arrive, the ground crew had to check to make sure the bears hadn't been up to their old tricks.

One of their tricks was to kick over the runway border lights. They liked to tear down cables and crawl under planes then stand up. Chewing through two-inch rubber hoses that were used for filling oil drums delighted the bears. The critters became so commonplace a telephone alarm was developed. When the alarm sounded, the men grabbed their weapons and the women and kids took cover. One woman chased a bear from her kitchen with a fly swatter.

A Bear In Camp

Bears also enjoy visiting campsites. One of my students, Lori Meade, had an unforgettable experience with her family in the spring of 1977. She shared it with me: "My parents, sister and I were going to Byers Lake Campgrounds, Mile 147 on the Parks Highway. We were to stay at Byers Lake for two days with my grandparents who live in Talkeetna.

"On our first night out the park ranger came by to sell us a Parks and Recreation state park sticker. We were a little worried at the possibility of bears coming in and raiding our camp, so we asked the ranger if he had heard of any bears in that area. He said, 'No,' and reminded us that no shooting was allowed in state park areas. We settled in for the night with my grandparents in the camp next to us.

"The next morning my dad woke up about 5:30 when he heard the trash cans being knocked over. Then he woke up my mother. He looked out the window of the camper and there he was — a six-foot male grizzly (some way to wake up, with a grizzly looking into your camper).

"My sister Lyn and I were sleeping in the tent, 20 feet from the camper, my parents and our dog Tiki, who had awakened by this time. I imagine she smelled the horrid smell of the bear's breath, as the windows were open. Being the fierce dog that she is, Tiki hid under the covers.

"The bear, not being content with the trash cans, wandered into camp. This bear evidently knew what he was doing. He went straight to our airtight cooler. This cooler was filled with meat and eggs and weighed a good 80 pounds. I know this because I am very healthy, and I couldn't lift it. My father even struggled to lift that cooler.

"No sweat for this bear. He took one paw and swiped it halfway across the camp. Then he waddled over to it and lifted the lid and dug in.

"Up until now Dad couldn't do anything because he couldn't get his gun. The night before, Grandfather, a firm believer in not having or needing firearms while camping, led my father to put his .357 pistol in the cab of the pickup (need I say that my grandfather has changed his mind since?).

Well, the bear just happened to have knocked the cooler about five feet from the door of our tent. By this time Dad was very shaky because he didn't know how much food we had in the tent. So Dad got out of the camper and tried making a lot of noise by pounding a big spoon on the side of the camper. The bear just looked at him and went back to devouring our breakfast of two dozen eggs.

"Dad then got his .357 out and shot three rounds into the air. The bear dropped the package of sausage and looked at Dad. He shot another round, and the bear reared.

"Dad then started shouting, 'Don't say anything! Go out the *back* of the tent, fast! We have a bear!'

"Being awakened at 5:30 A.M. *anytime* is a shock, but with gunfire and a bear in camp!

"Well, Lyn couldn't get out of her sleeping bag, so she took it with her — hippety-hop, hippety-hop. Instead of going out the back of the tent, which Lyn had to crawl under, I went out the front. Off to my right about three feet was the bear. Boy, did I ever boogie to the pickup!

"The bear stood there looking Dad straight in the eyes, not moving. So Dad had one heck of a decision — he knew he only had one round left. He was close enough to kill the bear if he got the bear either between the eyes or in the throat. He wasn't that sure of himself, so he started walking towards the bear and shot his last shot into the air. Finally the bear lumbered towards the trees. He picked up a steak on his way out!"

Talk about a volatile situation. The bear was just looking for a free handout, but it was pretty obvious that sooner or later someone was going to give it a handout or a hand.

More Hungry Bears

Bears never seem to be able to sate their hunger. Some years back Lynn Castle was guiding some Japanese hunters in the Alaska Range. As their pack train arrived in camp, it was evident that bears had frequented the tents and garbage pit. Lynn was awakened late one night by a frightened Japanese who told him of a big bear in camp. It appeared the brute had left, so Lynn turned in again, only to be awakened by his Japanese client, shaking his bed.

But the bruin whose black paw was groping around under Lynn's bunk had no Oriental blood in its veins. Lynn pointed his flashlight at the hairy paw that withdrew, clutching a side of bacon that it bore off into the night.

Unfortunately in situations of this nature man conditions bruin all too often. I helped guide four Wyoming hunters and an Alaskan into the Wrangell Mountains in the fall of 1973. We had a successful hunt with each of the five hunters taking a sheep. We had a 12-hour hike down the glacier to the pick-up location of the airstrip, so Lester Smothers, my brother-in-law, started out with the Carrells from Wyoming. Tony James and I stayed behind to clean up camp and burn any litter.

In the midst of our activity we noticed a mamma black bear and two cubs approaching our camp area. We had gobs of grub left over, and rather than pack it out or destroy it (our packs were full), we opened all our remaining food and fed the bears.

We spread several loaves of bread on boulders around the area, put chocolate Hershey bars on the bread and poured honey all over the bread and candy. We didn't stick around to view the results, but since then I have realized the folly and danger of our actions.

"Tame" Bears

Man conditions bears whether he feeds them or shoots at them. When a bear is accustomed to handouts and easy pickings around a camp, he gets more bold and expects the same treatment from others. By the same token, if a bear is shot at or abused by man, he develops a dislike for man in general. A person's chances for bear related problems are greatly intensified under these conditions.

A former guide in the Gunsight Mountain area told me about different bears around his lodge. He had a young "pet" grizzly that hung around looking for handouts and helping himself to the garbage can goodies. It was not unusual to find the bear in the back yard. The guide's children occasionally met the bear face-to-face while going out the back door. The bear seemed to enjoy human activity and often sat like a big house dog, lazily watching someone wash a car at the lodge.

You can well imagine a person's concern at meeting such a bear face-to-face and not knowing it was a "tame" bear.

Randy Terry and Tom Bentley, two former student-wrestlers I coached, and I were hunting in the area in 1971, and in my ignorance we hung a sheep in a deserted, windowless cabin to cool — about three miles from the same lodge. We were sleeping in that cabin one night when we had a caller in the form of Mr. Bruin. The bear didn't know it, but I had since taken the sheep down to a meat cache. However, the odor from the drippings drew the bear to the dwelling.

We heard the bear padding around behind the cabin and shined a flashlight back there where I was going to get some wood for a fire in hopes of scaring him away. We were a little shocked to see a set of green eyes staring back at us from the wood pile. We shot into the ground in front of the bear and didn't see him again until the next morning. It was a three-year-old grizzly.

We found later that it was the "tame" lodge bear and that it succumbed to a hunter's bullet opening day of bear season while looking for a handout at some cabins in the vicinity.

Other campers had a rather unusual experience in 1967. Some of the boy scouts at Camp Gorsuch north of Anchorage tied up a chum in his sleeping bag, not knowing that a black bear and her cubs were due in camp any minute. The guys were teasing the victim in his mummy bag when the bear family strode into camp and began examining the foodstuffs. She polished off one dish after another and took her morning exercise in between courses — she walked over to the sleeping-bagged boy and strode up and down the length of his bag, then back. Finally enough people arrived, and she bid them adieu.

One nosy camp bear overstayed his welcome in the Wrangell Mountains in 1972 or '73. Two fellow Dimond High teachers from Anchorage were on a sheep hunt. Charley Vandergaw and Chuck Wirschem had a great hunt, and later Wirschem told me, "Our pilot Howard Knutson flew me in on one day, and the next day he flew Charley in. Charley was going to cache our goods at the bottom of the glacier where we were going to get picked up. We went in up at the top of the glacier, and we were going to walk one way down to the bottom and get picked up.

"Charley was in a big hurry at the time, so he grabbed a tree and tied things up, and didn't really tie things up all that high, which was a learning experience.

"We landed up on the top and walked out. I think we spent 16 days on the trip and took a couple of pretty fine rams, found a big set of horns and shot a lot of good film footage. We got down to the strip at the bottom of the glacier, greatly anticipating our cold beer and can of mixed salted nuts. These goodies kept us going that last day with that 120-pound pack when we were about to die. We were very much looking forward to our beer and nuts.

"We came to where the cache was, and a grizzly bear had gotten into it, destroying everything. You have to get caches up 12 or 15 feet in a tree to be safe, and this one was maybe eight feet up. He tore up all the nylon bags, and punctured every single can, including my chili which I was looking forward to.

"He ran away with about a hundred dollars' worth of 16mm movie film, got our brandy and all our chips and peanut butter and jam. It was a pretty expensive bust. We had one piece of satisfaction. When he punched that *Off* insect repellent can, we know that he got a mouthful.

"We resigned ourselves to the fact that we had to go back to eating sheep meat and what was left of our freeze-dried food. We put up the tent and made camp. We were gathering firewood when all of a sudden about 10 yards away here was this bear standing looking at me. It was getting on towards dark, and this was in August and it must have been 9:30 P.M. or 10:00 P.M. or so; and it was getting pretty dark. It just scared the heck out of me. I dropped my wood and ran off to the camp, grabbed my rifle and poked a couple of shots up in the air toward it; and it snorted and ran off into the trees.

"Next morning about four o'clock or so I heard this *hoe, hoe, hoe, hoe, hoe,* a nasal sound like a hog at a hog trough. The bear was snorting and rubbing around outside the tent. I pushed the gun barrel out the tent and cranked off a couple, *karoom, kaboom!* and I heard him snorting, *aarrrr*; and off he ran, into the trees.

"Later on that day Howard came in to pick us up.

"About a week later that bear was still scrounging for goodies when a man and son, and another hunter were there. They came in late in the day, and were going to go after a ram next day. They were in their tent that night, and early in the morning all of a sudden the bear grabbed the tent and started running down the strip with these three inside. One of them finally got a gun pointed up to the top and poked a hole in the tent, and the bear dropped it. They scrambled out of the tent and shot a couple more shots toward the bear.

"A week later Jim Harrower was in there, and he parked the airplane and went on up the glacier after a ram. While he was gone, the bear tore a lot of rubber from his $500-plus airplane tires. He was able to take off and fly back into Chitina by himself and get another set of tires and come back and get the rest of his load and his passenger.

"No one shot the bear that year. No one wanted to shoot it.

"Next year, the same place, Tony Oney and his family arrived for about a month, scouting for sheep and on a family camping trip. They were parked at the same place, and after their second or third day this bear had come by a couple of times and they shot and scared it away. It finally got to the point where Rita and her daughter Mary Lou felt that it wasn't safe.

"The bear came back and Rita finally said 'Enough's enough,' and she shot it. We felt that we had started the whole thing."

In such a situation it is hard to blame the bear. He was much like a pet dog, moseying around looking for something to eat.

Sometimes it is possible to relocate an animal without doing him any physical harm, though the efforts are often futile. In June, 1951, Mike Fuller, an employee of the Alaska Road Commission, captured a young grizzly that had been a nuisance around camp. He decided to take it to Mount McKinley Park, 40 miles away, where it would be protected against firearms. He loaded it into a trailer and transported it to the park, however, when he tried to release the animal, it turned on him and mauled him. Mike recovered but hasn't offered any bears a ride since.

He Liked His Home

Another ungrateful, or lonely, bear showed up October 15, 1976, in Ted Butler's back yard in Cordova, and he shot the big brownie. The bear had been live-trapped in his yard in September, drugged and loaded aboard the state M/V *Montague* and taken toward Montague Island. Fish & Game biologists recorded scientific data on the way to the island, giving it ear tags and a neck collar. As the boat came within 50 yards of the island, the bear was released.

Evidently the animal was still woozy from the drug and swam about in confusion. He finally made for shore and the boat departed. Just 28 days later the animal appeared in Butler's yard — 47 miles from his drop-off point.

Alaska's Gov. Jay Hammond shared some bear-moving experiences with me and made some general comments on the subject. "There were some bears in the Katmai area which were doing violence to camps. Fish & Wildlife wanted them removed to other locations. They'd asked a couple of the airlines, who had a big amphibian, to move them, but they couldn't get anybody that was interested.

"I told them that I would do it if they would accompany the bear with a guy who had another syringe of tranquilizer in case the bear started to become active. Though it was not legal to carry a firearm in the park, I have to admit I kept my .44 magnum.

"There were no problems except we had to fly much longer than anticipated to move the bear to a new location. It was starting to roll around and come out from the tranquilizer a bit.

"It's quite a chore to remove a bear from an airplane. In fact, it took four of us to load him. While in the plane, I put him under a tarp which I strapped down. You have to be very careful because tranquilized bears need to be cooled off quickly or they'll develop respiratory problems. Upon landing, we put this bear in the lake and then held him upright. I have numbers of pictures of holding the bear while he's sitting in the water cooling off with his feet dangling from a float. Rather ludicrous.

"They did fine. We had no problem. We moved one, I believe about 50 miles one time was all; and he showed back at his original location. The ones we moved distances from 100 to 200 miles did not."

When animals become too much of a nuisance, other alternatives are sought. In 1949 brown bears in the Kodiak Island-Alaska Peninsula areas were reported to be depleting the salmon stocks so badly that the canneries recommended a bounty. During the same time the Alaska Native Brotherhood passed a resolution in Klawock asking for a $6 bounty on black bears.

Nuisance Bears

Nuisance bears in proximity of man have been kept in check at different times by allowing hunting seasons on the animals. A prime example is the Cold Bay area on the Alaska Peninsula. When there was a season on the bears, the local residents had little trouble with them; but when the Board of Game rescinded the hunting and protected the bears, the animals became more brazen and aggressive. Around 1974 the bears in the Cold Bay area were protected. Consequently they became more aggressive and wandered into town. A dog was attacked and killed by a bear. Later a man was killed. Then the authorities opened season on bears. It was time to move the bears out of town.

The Alaska Department of Fish & Game allows for the extermination of nuisance bears in extreme cases. They group nonsport kills under the title "In Defense of Life or Property" which covers any emergency bear killing. Lee Miller of the department is one of the most noted and qualified men working with the study of bears in Alaska. He spoke with me regarding "In Defense of Life or Property" and said, "In Alaska persons are permitted to kill bears in defense of life or property only after reasonable effort has been made to protect life and property by means other than killing the animal. In the case of brown/grizzly, black or polar bear, the hide and skull must be salvaged and surrendered to the state.

"In the past 17 years Alaska has averaged a kill of 28 brown/ grizzly bear per year taken in defense of life or property, and slightly fewer black bear. These kills cover a wide spectrum of incidents, some of which could have been avoided while others were unavoidable.

"As the country develops, more pressure is put on our bears, especially our brown/grizzly bears. Their cohabitation with humans often leads to the demise of the bear or occasionally the human. In the 1960s nonsport brown/grizzly kill averaged 16 per year. So far in the 1970s the kill has averaged 41 per year (as of January 18, 1978).

"This is a very real problem that will probably get worse as more people come into the state and more land is put in protected status where in some cases even the carrying of firearms for self protection may be prohibited. To complicate matters more we have TV shows like Walt Disney and Grizzly Adams that lead the misinformed to believe you can walk right up to and talk to the bears. Perhaps what is needed is more basic, straight-forward education on the facts of bear life."

As Lee has stated, not all bears that have been killed in defense of life or property are "legitimate." Some grizzlies were killed by someone who "thought" it was a black bear and so on.

John "Jake" McLay of Lower Ugashik Lake had a legitimate claim in September of 1970. A big brown bear had been nosing around his camp for several nights, pushing and rubbing against the cabins. One night it pressed its nose against the window pane of the McLays' bedroom and awakened Mrs. McLay who looked out the window and into the face of the bruin five feet off the ground. A few nights later the bear pulled a moose hind quarter from a cache 12 feet above the ground. The next day Jake tracked it down and put an end to his cache-robbing days when the bear charged him from the brush.

Just a few months earlier Ernest Mack of Cold Bay killed a brown bear June 27th as it charged his three-year-old daughter who was playing outside her house. The child escaped the bear, and Mack shot it with a 12-gauge shotgun with .00 buckshot.

Another Cold Bay resident gave me permission to include his letter to the Department of Fish & Game after he had been forced to kill a bear in his mess hall. This incident followed Mack's by a week. Also included is a letter from Harold Doland of Juneau.

To Alaska Department of Fish & Game
Cold Bay, Alaska

This is to report the circumstances of a nuisance bear kill at Cold Bay on July 6, 1970.

About 1:55 A.M. July 6 the cook at the Reeve Aleutian Airways messhall phoned me that a bear had broken into the messhall pantry. I went immediately to the messhall and found the bear inside the pantry and shot it three times with a 16 gauge shotgun. The bear died immediately.

Further examination revealed the bear had torn siding off the outside wall to gain entry creating a hole roughly two feet square. Inside the bear had consumed or destroyed one case of bread, one crate of cabbage, one sack of onions, and ⅓ crate of peaches.

This messhall had previously been vandalized by a brown bear on June 25 and again on June 26. On those occasions two windows were broken, an outside door was broken down, and the bear ate or destroyed 25 dozen eggs, five quarts of milk, and ½ case each of apples, cantalopes and oranges.

Calvin Reeve
Station Manager
Reeve Aleutian Airways
Cold Bay, Alaska

Juneau, Alaska
October 6, 1976

Alaska Department of Fish & Game
Subport Building
Juneau, Alaska 99801

Gentlemen:

On October 4th I shot a black bear on our property at Mile 4¼ Mendenhall Loop Road and surrendered it to your department. I shot the bear because it had been destroying our property and disturbing our animals every night for about a month. We feared for the safety of our own children and the other children of the neighborhood as well as the safety of our goats, rabbits and pigs.

These are a few of the things for which the bear was responsible. She:

Caused the mother rabbits to kill their litters.

"Spooked" our dairy goats so that they fell off drastically on milk production.

Tore the box off our fish smoker and crushed in the sides of the smoker. (It hadn't been used for several weeks.)

Destroyed 20 dozen eggs that we had placed in the shop to keep cool, and completely messed up the shop.

Tore off the shop door latch — a one-inch board I had nailed on — in order to get in and further destroy things.

Ate the animals' grain.

Ripped the wires loose on our 26-foot food freezer in the shop, trying to get through a small hole behind the freezer.

Broke out two windows getting into the shop. Later ripped off the plywood I nailed over the broken windows.

Climbed and snooped around our oil tank near the kitchen window, apparently attracted by the odor of food. (We feared she might break this window out, too.)

Climbed around our cars — where we had placed our pigs' food to keep it from her — and apparently damaged some windshield wipers.

This bear was very brazen. We have been on this place eleven years and have had farm animals most of that time. Even with the animal feed to attract them, bears have never been a problem before. Up to now, the barking of our big husky dog has caused all of them to completely bypass our place. This bear was different; she ate up the dog's meat while he stood right there barking at her. Likewise, she just stared at us when we went out and didn't run even when we shouted at her.

I shot the bear only after careful consideration, for our policy has always been one of live and let live. We lived on Kuiu Island for three years (1962-65) amid lots of black bears and persuaded several fishermen not to shoot them. We shot only one bear during that time and that was for meat. But there was a distinct difference between those bears and this one: they ran when they saw us or heard us or if the dog barked. We were convinced this one couldn't be trusted.

We had asked Fish & Game officials to move the bear about two weeks ago, but they were reluctant to do so. I asked my wife, "How are they going to feel if one of our kids gets mauled by this brazen bear?" She then asked me, "How are you going to feel if *you* don't do something?"

Our neighbors have expressed their gratitude for my having destroyed the bear. They were also having problems and a similar response from her and were concerned about their children's safety. (One mother drove her children to and from the school bus because she was afraid to have them walk.) I have also learned that two other neighbors had their guns loaded and were going to shoot the bear the first chance they got. Thus, her days were apparently numbered.

Sincerely yours,
Harold D. Doland

Probably the most-read-about killing of a nuisance bear occurred in Anchorage in June of 1978. My brother-in-law told me that there had been a brown bear near their house on Upper Huffman Road in the Chugach Mountains, and then I began hearing reports about it on the local media. The bear was harrassing residents of Rabbit Creek, Huffman and O'Malley roads — raiding chicken coops and the like. One night the brown bear called when he should have folded.

He wandered onto the Myers' place, ate a duck, chewed on a pig and was eyeballing the family cow when Don Myers sent the intruder to bear heaven.

The Fish & Game Department examined the three-year-old bear which weighed around 300 pounds. This bear would probably be alive and well today in the mountains behind Anchorage had he not wandered into man's back yard. Fortunately not all bears are dangerous; and not all bears in proximity with man need be shot. □

THEY CAN BE FUNNY

"Strangest outcome of a bear attack was experienced by Scott Kronburg of Fairbanks. Rushed near Castner Glacier by a female grizzly and two cubs, Kronburg jumped in a hole and used his pack for protection. The bear smashed at the pack, then left. The uninjured hiker heard a hissing sound and realized the bear had ignited a supply of matches in the pack. The fire destroyed a jacket." (ALASKA® magazine, December 1972)

Bear-man encounters range from the serious to the humorous, and somewhere in between are some interesting and unusual happenings. The majority of the incidents listed in this chapter were taken verbatim from *The ALASKA SPORTSMAN®*, which underwent a name change to *ALASKA®* magazine.

Some interesting developments have transpired with bear genetics. "A male polar bear, a female Alaska brown bear and their impossible progeny in the Washington, D.C., zoo have upset accepted theories about what can be and what can't. Fifteen years or more ago the polar bear and the brownie mated and produced four cubs. These cubs were hybrids, and extremely improbable if not impossible. Of course hybrids cannot produce offspring. So when a male and a female of the polar-brown hybrids produced a cub a couple of years ago, the little double hybrid was entirely impossible. Last New Year's Eve the hybrid pair produced triplet double hybrids. It is quite impossible for them to be, but Dr. William M. Mann, director of the Washington zoo, announced that they had been and are being. Of course double hybrids can't possibly have offspring, so the impossible story has to end with them. Or does it?" (*The ALASKA SPORTSMAN®*, June 1952)

One bear had the good manners to use the phone to make a call at the Ballistic Missile Early Warning System at Clear, but once the party answered, the animal apparently forgot what it wanted to say. "In the middle of the night, a flashing light told police at the officers' listening post that the commander's phone was off the hook. Listening in, they heard heavy breathing noises that sounded as though a struggle was taking place. Police rushing in to investigate were met by a four-foot bear rushing out. They found that the bear had been on top of the commander's desk, messed things up considerably, and knocked both telephones off their hooks." (*ALASKA SPORTSMAN®*, October 1963)

One trademark of bears is their nature toward thievery. "Joe Wood, a homesteader near Sand Lake in the Anchorage district, brought a thoroughbred pig home from a neighbor's, put it in a pen, and was standing at his car nearby, talking to Chet Lloyd, another homesteader. Suddenly they heard a violent commotion from the pig pen. A bear, undaunted by the protests of a sow and a cow, was climbing over the fence with the expensive pig in its mouth. The two men seized clubs and chased the bear, overtook him at the edge of a swamp, and beat him vigorously. But the bear refused to drop the choice porker. Wood ran for his gun, while Lloyd continued to beat the bear. A bullet finished the bear who only then released the pig, somewhat the worse for the experience. The discriminating bear had passed up the ordinary pigs in the same pen in favor of the thoroughbred." (*The ALASKA SPORTSMAN®*, October 1944)

Chocolate Cake Finished Him

"Mr. and Mrs. Frank Miller, owners of Miller House near Fairbanks, were awakened one night by a noise downstairs. Mr. Miller went down to see what was the matter. A huge grizzly bear had forced his way through the screen door and was helping himself to some blueberries and a chocolate cake. The bear made a quick exit through the kitchen window, taking glass, frame, and potted plants with him. Later he visited the storehouse of a closed mine and several neighborhood houses. At last, unable to resist Mrs. Miller's chocolate cake, he returned to Miller House. Mr. Miller was ready for him that time, and he now has a grizzly's pelt to make up for the lost cake." (*The ALASKA SPORTSMAN®*, November 1944)

"Two years ago a grizzly bear raided Miller House, near Fairbanks, and got away with Mrs. Frank Miller's fresh blueberry shortcake, plate and all. Mrs. Miller regretted less the loss of her cake than the loss of the plate, which was one of her most prized possessions. She was pleasantly surprised recently when Mamie Tamura, a Japanese neighbor woman, brought her the plate, which she had found in a clump of bushes while picking blueberries. On the bottom of the plate are the marks of the thieving grizzly's teeth." (*The ALASKA SPORTSMAN®*, December 1947)

Bears get pretty cagey with age. A prospector near Kantishna left his camp for a couple of weeks. He had had trouble with bears taking supplies from his cache, so he decided on a means of deceiving them and assuring himself ample groceries on his return. He wrapped his grub in a heavy canvas, tied a waterproof sheet around it, shinnied up a tree until his weight bowed the tree earthward then tied the booty to the tree and let it spring up. The food hung from the limb of the tree 15 feet from the ground and five feet from the trunk of the tree. The prospector parted with a smile on his lips.

In due time he returned to find the tree, the rope and the canvas — the tree was no longer bent over, the rope still hung from the limb; but the canvas was empty, its contents obviously departing in a safer container than they'd previously occupied.

The Oil Drum Bear

Charlie Evans, one of the five surviving mushers who raced to Nome with diphtheria serum in 1923, told me that when one of his boys went bear hunting, he and a fellow youngster had to resort to their ingenuity to get a bear home. The lads were about seven years old and decided to use some old packing crates for a shooting fortress. They made peep-holes from which to shoot; they then spent the night in a packing crate and shot a bear the next morning.

Since they had no way to skin the animal and were too small to pack the bear, they searched the nearby countryside for a solution. They settled on an empty 55-gallon drum and shoved the bear into it. They rolled the drum about three-quarters of a mile to their boat, loaded the full barrel into their boat and took off across the river to a fish camp where they received help from adults to skin the bear.

Another boatman wasn't as fortunate. An Indian trapper was paddling his canoe one spring while trapping beaver. He had a carcass of one in the canoe and paddled silently along when a bear sprang from the bank nearby and leaped into his tiny craft. The canoe sank instantly as the trapper floundered ashore. In the meantime the bear had clamped onto the beaver and departed.

"Just up the Richardson Highway from the Konrads, Mr. and Mrs. Tom Baumgartner had an uninvited visitor. They returned to their trailer home to find that a bear had broken through the window, eaten part of a plastic salad bowl with some salad in it, stomped with his muddy feet on three of the beds, and departed. They didn't find Goldilocks." (*ALASKA SPORTSMAN®*, October 1963)

The bear's giant appetite is his chief motivator — sometimes his friend, often his betrayer. "Lawrence Carson, wolf trapper for the Forest Service, made camp at Traitors Cove, along Behm Canal north of Ketchikan, one night recently. His tent pitched, he squatted beside his fire and fried a fish caught that day, ate, and rolled into his blankets, slept. In the gray dawn he awoke to find a huge bear in the tent greedily feasting on the leftovers of the fish. Carson whooped, the bear grunted and in the ensuing melee the wolf trapper was subjected to the rare experience of being trampled by a thoroughly frightened bear. Carson showed up in town later, none the worse for the experience, to report that neither he nor the bear had suffered any harm as a result of the encounter." (*The ALASKA SPORTSMAN®*, November 1940)

Nothing But The Best

Some bears are class eaters and prefer nothing but the finest of cuisine. Charlie Evans of Galena told the story about a bear with unusual culinary tastes. His two sons were hunting from their gas boat and left the boat on the river to go into the brush. When they returned, they found a black bear searching a pack on the bottom of their boat. The animal systematically threw the groceries aside and kept digging. It tossed coffee, tea, sugar and finally reached what it was after — two packs of cigarettes. Mission accomplished, the bruin sauntered off into the brush chewing on the cancer sticks.

Many a hunter has returned to a big game kill to discover that a bear has taken the meat elsewhere. Clark Engle, Master Guide from Anchorage, laughed about an experience one of his packers had: "We had a funny situation at our Moose Lake camp. The airstrip was on the top of a knoll which was about a mile from camp. We had a couple of moose down, so I flew in a packer to help pack out meat to the airstrip. I took him in one afternoon and said I'd be back the next afternoon. I was unable to get back the next day because of weather, but I did get back in the next day. There was no meat on top where I'd landed, and I wondered what that packer had been doing.

"Just about that time I looked down the trail, and here he came with a full pack of moose. I waited until he got up there and I said, 'Jim, what have you been doing? Where's the meat?'

"And he said, 'I've been packin' meat for two days now.'

"And I said, 'Where is it?'

"He said, 'A grizzly bear's been taking it. I been packing that meat up here and that bear's been eating it as fast as I can pack it up here.'

"We could see signs of where the bear had dragged it off and buried it about 300 yards away. Jim said, 'I don't know why that blankety-blank bear doesn't go down there and eat the meat instead of letting me pack it up here and eat it.' "

Frank Dufresne told about a cabin-raiding bear that broke into a moonshiners still shack during prohibition. The bear had eaten a barrel of fermented mash then destroyed the interior of the building, slopping molasses all over himself, opening a down sleeping bag and rolling in it, consuming untold quantities of booze and ripping down the moonshiners stovepipe. After jumping on the hot stove, the bruin exited the premises with gusto — through a window, wearing the frame and all around his neck.

More than one old-timer was forced to pull his teeth with pliers and improvise with whatever he could use for teeth until he had a chance to go to a genuine dentist. One old-timer made a set of teeth from gold nuggets and fastened them to plates of soft tin; but the gold wore out so soon it wasn't practical to make another set.

"A set of false teeth made by the late Edwin A. Robertson of Eagle, are on exhibition in the office of a dentist in Seattle. Robertson made the denture by setting mountain sheep, caribou and bear teeth in a plate produced by vulcanizing rubber from an old boot." (*The ALASKA SPORTSMAN®*, March 1941)

Another sourdough fashioned a set of false teeth from sheep and bear's teeth taken from skulls around the cabin, then he ate a bear with its own teeth.

Some bears have as much trouble eating as some of the old-timers. Hal Waugh once witnessed a sow swat her two-year-old cub 20 feet down the hillside. Apparently the young bear bit her while trying to nurse, and she didn't take too kindly to it. As a matter of fact that poor cub followed its mother all day and was last seen some 100 yards in her wake, looking like some forlorn five-year-old kid who had informed his parents that he was running away and had made it to the first corner on the block.

Some bears were a little more aggressive than junior. A sourdough shot a sheep and hung it high in a tree to keep a bear from getting it; but he forgot to tell the bear. The next day part of the sheep was gone. That night the man determined to protect his sheep, so he took it into his tent with him. The man woke up in the middle of the night which was as black as coal. A steady downpour fell on his tent, and he heard the bear outside. The man figured if he was silent the bear wouldn't find the sheep; but he underestimated the bear which promptly came under one side of the tent.

The sourdough promptly went out the other side and wasted no time in getting up a tree. The tent collapsed on the hapless bruin, and the bear proceeded to make a few more openings than the tent's design originally called for. The bear shredded the canvas and demolished the camp for two hours while the old man sat up in his tree contemplating the folly of protecting his meat in a tent.

Bears are fond of fish. Master Guide Keith Johnson of Anchorage told me about a bear that savored a fish dinner one day when he was interrupted. "We hunt some bears on fish streams. One time this guy stalked a bear that was in the stream fishing. He sneaked around the alders and drew a good bead on the animal and shot him. The bear was kind of half in and half out of the water. His head kept bobbing and jumping, so they shot him again. The head kept moving, and he shot the bear again. This continued, and the guide told the hunter not to shoot again until they checked it out.

"They got over there to him, and he had a fish in his mouth that was flopping and jerking the bear's head up and down. He was a dead bear, but the fish didn't know it."

One bear decided his human-fisherman counterpart might have had some luck and decided to take a look on board. Commercial fisherman Gust Jensen told me about his friend: "One morning Billy Nakeekoroff was tied to the dock, and he heard something out there. He thought someone had come into the boat. There was a little window on the door through which he saw a big brown bear looking around for fish on his boat.

"The bear went up to the pilot house and took the steering wheel in his front paws. He was hanging onto the steering wheel and looking around for fish. Billy must have had fish up on top of the cabin in the box, and he smelled that.

"It was a great big bear and had brought a lot of mud into the boat, because the tide was out. Billy stayed where he was down inside the cabin and kept quiet. He didn't open the door or anything. The bear looked around then just walked out of the boat and walked away."

Living Dangerously

Some bears live dangerously. "Dale Clark of Revilla Air Service saw a black bear swimming in Klawock Lake and landed for a closer look. The bear bit the float and punctured it, but Clark made it back to Ketchikan for a patch job." (*ALASKA®* magazine, December 1975)

One man told about a brown bear on Admiralty Island years ago that was ambling down the beach one morning when he came to a boat. An outboard motor hung from the stern of the craft, and the bear moseyed over to it. The bear seemed a little puzzled by the whole affair and gingerly reached out to take a nip of the propeller. The blade made a metallic sound and slipped from the bear's mouth. Satisfied, or befuddled, the critter turned to tend his business on down the beach.

"An Alaskan brown bear unwittingly flirted with death sometime recently when it chewed on a Japanese fire bomb, and never even learned it was in danger. Homesteader Allen Hasselborg of Mole Harbor on Admiralty Island found the remains of the bomb near his home and sent them to the Territorial Museum. A Japanese balloon fire bomb, it was composed of a flashlight bulb, electrical wire, brightly colored paper, a two-foot rattan hoop and synthetic rubber, all bearing marks of a brown bear's teeth. There was no evidence of bomb destruction in the area. Apparently the bomb had drifted across the North Pacific on air currents during the war." (*The ALASKA SPORTSMAN®*, July 1953)

If it's not one mechanical device that gets bruin into trouble, it's another. "Alaska's truck drivers almost unanimously agree that the worst things about the roads are bears and ground squirrels. Although large-scale surfacing projects are under way, most of the territory's roads are gravel. Ground squirrels find them highly suitable places to burrow into and make their dens. Bears, prowling for food, energetically dig out the squirrels, any bear being perfectly willing to dig a hole big as an oil tank to get a squirrel big enough for one gulp. What that does to truck driver's language, especially at night, just isn't fit to print." (*The ALASKA SPORTS-MAN®*, July 1949)

Some bears die of fright when faced with the mechanical world. John Hillborn described such an incident in the December 1937 issue of *The ALASKA SPORTSMAN®*: "Every winter there are bears around my trapping quarters — big brownies who steal my dried fish and break the roof of my provisions shed. I've never had a bear actually attack me. I have had them run at me to scare me away from the fish I was cleaning, though.

"Usually, when I see a bear coming, I shout, wave my arms, and sometimes run at him. He'll usually scamper off in a big hurry. There was one ole brownie who wouldn't be scared, though. She was the one I saw commit suicide.

"I was cleaning fish on the bank of the creek at the time, about a hundred yards from my cabin. I didn't notice Old Bruin until she was nearly on top of me. Then I shouted, but it was no use. She kept coming, and snorted as she came. I could see that she was hungry, and that she didn't intend to be cheated out of her meal. I knew she'd resent my company, so I didn't wait for an invitation to get out.

"I was more angry than frightened, but made good time to my cabin, just the same. My rifle, a .30-'06 Government, was beside the door and there was one shell on the window sill. I threw it in the gun and stepped to the door.

"The bear was turned toward me, and just finishing the last of my fish. I yelled. She raised her head just in time for my slug to catch her in the breast. Then she turned tail and went down the bank to the creek. I wondered 'how in blazes' she'd climb the steep shale wall on the other side, so I ran for the creek, completely forgetting that there were no more shells in my gun.

"Bruin had waded the creek, and there she was, pawing at the loose shale on the other side, unable to climb the bank. She slipped back, and turned her attention to me.

"I remembered that there were no more shells in the gun, but I waved it at her, anyway. I could see that she was far from dead, and had a hunch that I'd better start for my cabin while I had a head start, but somehow, I couldn't seem to take my eyes off her. For a bear, she was acting mighty strangely. She waded nervously up and down the creek for a short distance, but eyed me constantly, and when I'd raise my gun she'd whine.

"Just to see what she'd do, when I was sure she was watching me I took a good bead on her head. To my amazement, she plunged her head beneath the water and left it there.

"I could hardly believe my eyes. Then I thought of the bullet I'd planted in her chest. It had probably done its work, after all. However, when I'd pulled her from the creek with block and tackle, and opened her up, I found that the bullet had struck a glancing blow, and had caused little more than a flesh wound. It was then that the significance of her act struck me. The old brownie, fearing death from my gun more than she did from the waters of the stream, had committed suicide. . . .

"This episode with the bear is absolutely true. Still, it may seem hard to believe, but I can explain her action in no other way than simple suicide."

This Bear Came To Church

Some bears, fearing their encounters with man and not wanting to live dangerously, have taken spiritual steps to enhance their living. "The snow hills and valleys of Alaska have witnessed many strange, weird sights, but few to compare with that which took place at one of the Army posts some time ago. As Chaplain Paul Hicklin conducted open-air services for a group of parka-clad soldiers one bright Sunday morning, a black bear, fresh from his winter's hibernation, wandered solemnly into the group, stretched out in the sun and listened and watched as Chaplain Hicklin prayed and preached. When the services were concluded, the bear got to his feet, stretched, yawned, and lumbered away into the wilderness." (*The ALASKA SPORTSMAN®*, June 1942)

It is often difficult to see the bear's side of an issue, but Kodiak cattle rancher Joe Beaty read between the lines when one of his workers was "attacked" by a bear. "The bear ran right over him," Beaty said. "It came out of the brush and he shot it under the chin as he went over him. The bear wasn't after him. He and the fellow who was hunting with him walked around a spruce thicket, and the bear was in there. The bear must have gotten wind of them, because when he came out, he ran right over that guy."

"I asked, 'Well, Walt, weren't you scared?' He said, 'No, but that bear sure was, I could tell by the look in his eyes.' "

Other men have narrowly escaped bear charges or apparent charges. Two men were hunting one spring when they stopped for lunch. They built a small fire next to a stump. One man prepared their lunch while the other gathered firewood for the already blazing fire 20 feet away. All of a sudden a bear roared and burst from its den beside the stump. Both men scrambled for a tree, snowshoes flying. The bear jumped over one, who had fallen in the snow, and continued on its way. The other man was six feet up a tree and climbing fast with snowshoes.

"He wasn't bear hunting at three o'clock one dark, cold morning last October, but Hans Weidman, who lives just outside Fort Saint John, B.C., shot a bear bare. Wakened by the barking of his two dogs and assorted sounds of commotion, Weidman leaped from his warm bed and got to the back door just in time to see a bear take a swipe at one of his dogs. His rifle and ammunition were in his truck out in the yard, so he made a dash for the truck. The bear made a dash for him but missed, and was just entering the kitchen through the door Weidman had left open when he brought the animal down with a bullet. The bear weighed approximately 800 pounds. Weidman decided he'd better bring his gun inside at night, or else give up sleeping nude." (*The ALASKA SPORTSMAN®*, February 1953)

More than one person has had a close call with bears and used some questionable practices on old bruin. "So intent on saving a herd of domestic goats which were being raided by a grizzly bear that she did not think of the danger to herself, 13-year-old Betty Bishop ran out in front of the bear and started shooing it off her parents' Unuk River ranch by waving her apron, recently. The bear stopped and snarled, but made no effort to approach. George Lemmon, a miner, happened along and saw the episode. He killed the grizzly with four shots from his rifle." (*The ALASKA SPORTS-MAN®*, July 1936)

"Joe Hollinger and Art High, CAA employees of Mile 13, Cordova, had a hair-raising experience with a big brown bear last April. Hollinger was exploring a few miles from the CAA station when he saw a portion of a brownie protruding from a snowbank. Wondering whether the bear was having a nap or still hibernating, Hollinger crept close with his spine atingle and his larynx misbehaving. He got fairly close, saw the long-haired patch of bear move and concluded he'd better let sleeping bears lie for the moment. Next day he and High, armed with .30-'06s, advanced toward the spot. The bristly fur was still there. Silently, cautiously they sneaked up on the bear, whose long hair was astir with the breeze. Rifles ready and nerves tense, they stamped on the ground, shouted and waited. Nothing happened. They shouted and stamped some more. Still nothing happened. They grew impatient.

Finally one of them covered the bear with his gun while the other crept up, not so cautiously, and gave him a swift kick. And still nothing happened. The bear had been dead probably a couple of months." (*The ALASKA SPORTSMAN®*, July 1949)

Bear riding is not recommended, but it happens. "Two high school boys visiting the dredge in the Cache Creek mining district shot a brown bear with a .22 high-power rifle. No one but youngsters would have had the foolhardiness to tackle a brownie with a rifle of such small caliber.

"But it stunned the brute and they thought they had him. Laying the rifle down against a bush, they were admiring the carcass. One boy was astride the bear, the other pulling at handfuls of fur to see how silky it was. The bear came to life, upsetting the kid sitting on top of him, and tore off down the hill.

"The kids were so excited they forgot where they had put their rifle, and by the time they found it he was too far away for them.

"That grew to be a legend too, and the boys were glad when it was time for them to go home. Wherever they went, some miner was sure to call out, 'Hey, Bud! If you're gonna ride any bears today, let me know. We'd like to see that rodeo!' " (*The ALASKA SPORTSMAN®*, July 1952)

Cat and Mouse Bear Game

One "motorist" had an unusual experience with a brown bear while working on the highway near Skilak Lake on the Kenai Peninsula several years ago. The story is told about a catskinner who was attacked by a brown bear. The man managed to keep the blade of the cat between himself and the bear for more than an hour. The machine was nearly destroyed before the brute, weary from the struggle, slipped and the man ran the cat's cleats over the top of the bear. Old-timers call the section Brown Bear Flats.

One man was unable to stay out of bruin's reach. "It was lunch time at Colorado Station one day last July, but instead of a meal road-worker L.P. Rorrison got first-aid treatment. Rorrison stopped work, unpacked his lunch, then walked down to a nearby stream for water, leaving his gun beside the food. When he turned back he saw a mother and her twin cubs sampling his sandwiches. Quite willing to concede, Rorrison started to retire rapidly across the creek, but the mother bear apparently didn't like his attitude. She followed him and slapped him across the rear, then returned to his lunch and with one swat sent what was left of it across the creek after him. Ed Ueeck, a fellow worker, applied first-aid to portions Rorrison was unable to reach." (*The ALASKA SPORTS-MAN®*, October 1950)

Moose and bears have never been on speaking terms. Several years ago a man encountered a cow moose with a calf which a large black bear was trying to get. It was on the White River near the Yukon, and the only escape route was blocked by the bear which kept moving from side to side to stop the cow's efforts. The incident had obviously been going on for some time as the cow could hardly stand on her feet. The man shot the bear and proceeded to skin it out. The cow collapsed on the ground. Every once in a while the man would pat the moose on the head and continue skinning the bear. Finally the man left carrying the bear hide, leaving the moose to rest.

Another moose-bear encounter involved a brown bear . . . "state biologists . . . recently reported a moose-chases-bear incident observed in June 1970 on the Alaska Peninsula. Circling a three-year-old brown bear sow in a helicopter preparatory to immobilizing and tagging, the biologists saw the bear run within 50 feet of a cow moose and her calf. The moose and calf gave chase and pursued the bear for 13 minutes. 'At times the calf was leading the chase,' said the biologists' report. Once the bear was immobilized for tagging, the helicopter had to be called in to drive the moose away from the drug-groggy bear." (*ALASKA®* magazine, September 1971)

Sleeping Bears

"When L.K. Williams discovered a sleeping bear in the hills near Anchorage last fall, he decided to collect a fine rug when the bear's hide reached prime. He visited the sleeping bear at 10-day intervals all winter, turning it over carefully so that the hide would prime evenly. Finally, he took his gun and went out to get his rug, only to discover that the bear had awakened and left." (*The ALASKA SPORTSMAN®*, August 1941)

Sleeping bears are hospitable. "Eleven-year-old Fred Lewis and his younger brother, Harold, got lost last summer on a fishing trip and spent a night as guests in a black bear den. The boys had gone with their father, George Lewis, up Klawock Creek. When he missed them he supposed they had tired of fishing and gone home, but when he returned home they had not yet arrived. A searching party set out immediately with Brownie, the boys' dog, who led them at 5 A.M. to a cave beside the creek. There they found the boys asleep with the bears. Except for a few scratches and tooth marks where a cub had nipped Freddie, they were none the worse for the experience." (*The ALASKA SPORTSMAN®*, December 1947)

There seems to be a general category for school bears. For some it involves tardiness and others arithmetic. " 'Delayed by a bear' was the excuse given by three children when they missed classes at the Ninilchik school one day last September, and the excuse was accepted by Superintendent Donald V. Lawvers with only a few questions about details. The three, Duane and Ray Newton in grade five and their sister, Ia Donna, in grade two, were three miles from home, walking toward the road to catch the school bus, when a big brown bear came down the path toward them at a gallop. The children ran off the path into the brush. The bear continued on its way, but by the time they had collected themselves and reached the road, they had missed the bus. The three are the children of Mr. and Mrs. Frank Newton." (*ALASKA SPORTSMAN®*, December 1961)

"Sometimes a hunter believes he has missed and they all turn out to be hits. It could be embarrassing, if he had gone over the limit allowed by law. But in the years before there was a limit on brown bears, a sourdough from Seward was at Upper Russian River fishing, and jumped a brownie in the brush. It was such close range that he shot at once, before the bear could charge him.

"It flopped down in the high grass where he couldn't see it. In a few seconds it raised up on its hind legs again. He shot it again and knocked it down. It rose up the third time. This time he got desperate because he didn't see how he could be missing it at such close range. This time he shot so fast he emptied his magazine.

"Well, the bear didn't rise up again, and when he got up enough courage to go into the high grass to look for the carcass, he found he had shot three bears instead of one! All his misses were hits. It was an old she-bear with two yearling cubs that had grown almost as tall as she.

"Afterward, back in town, his friends complained teasingly, 'You might have saved a few bears for us, Charlie!'

" 'You didn't come soon enough,' he retorted. 'I couldn't wait till you got there.' " (*The ALASKA SPORTSMAN®*, July 1952)

"An 'educated' bear not only shredded supposedly bear-proof

doors and wrecked several cabins but also burned down a warehouse at Camp Denali, according to evidence on the scene. Miss Celia Hunter, one of the operators of the wilderness camp near McKinley National Park, and Alison Smith flew to the camp early in May and discovered the damage. Miss Hunter, who surmised that the depredation took place last fall, said there was no evidence of human vandalism. She believes the bear ignited some matches while tearing up the contents of the warehouse." (*ALASKA SPORTSMAN®*, July 1961)

Double Double Bears Are Trouble
On some occasions it appears that man sees double. "Charles Martin Cloud of Badger Road, near Fairbanks, Alaska, had quite an adventure recently. He was walking down the trail somewhere along the Chena when he suddenly came upon a black bear. The two eyed each other for a short time, then Cloud ran for his truck to get his rifle. He pulled open the cab door and reached for his gun. Then he looked up. There was a second bear behind the wheel of his truck. Cloud jumped back, looked around to see if the first bear was around. He wasn't, so he shot the second bear. As he was trying to drag the body of the dead bear from the truck, he heard a rustle behind him. There stood his first bear. Cloud had no alternative when the bear started toward him but to shoot the animal." (*The ALASKA SPORTSMAN®*, March 1957)

Sometimes man lends a hand to old bruin. "John Wall, Ketchikan old-timer who has spent many seasons as a stream watchman, practices a good-neighbor policy though his summer neighbors are mostly bears and deer. On two occasions last summer, Wall's helping hand probably saved a life.

"Once when he was crossing George Inlet, near Leask Cove, in his power dory, Wall overtook a black bear trying to swim across and making heavy weather of it. He maneuvered alongside, grabbed a handful of hair on the bear's neck, and steered toward shore. The bear looked up with doubtful eyes and in a feeble show of defiance bared its teeth. They were badly worn and some were missing, indicating old age as the animal's lack of stamina. Reaching shallow water, Wall let go of the bear and sped off. The old fellow dragged himself onto the beach and lay down to rest." (*ALASKA SPORTSMAN®*, January 1962)

It seems like some bears should be in the construction business.

"At least one brown bear in the vicinity of Homer, on Kenai Peninsula, knows about window glass. When Nils Svedlund went out once to his hunting cabin six miles from his Homer home, he found unmistakable evidence that a glass-wise bear had visited the place in his absence. Unable to open the door, the bear had taken out the window, glass and all, carried it 25 feet away and put it down without breaking it. Then he had tried to enter through the window opening, but found it too small. In frustration and rage the bear had then taken a vicious swipe at the tar-paper roof of the little cabin, raking an eight-foot gash with his powerful claws." (*The ALASKA SPORTSMAN®*, August 1951)

Whenever man has a close call with a bear, the bear is usually labeled the villain; but Klondiker Frank Kelley was mighty thankful to the bear he tangled with. He was on his way down the dock, a little tipsy from the hooch he'd taken to give him enough courage for the boat journey to Seattle from the Klondike on the Yukon River. He encountered a chained black bear. The bear was a little touchy from the ill treatment it had received of late from its soldier captors; and it popped up on its hind legs in the classic bear fighting stance. This proved too much for the Old World sourdough who "put up his dukes" and started swinging. The next thing he remembered, his neck was paining him tremendously and he had a good-sized knot on his head.

A passing soldier had picked him up from the ground 30 feet from the bear and taken him to safety. Kelley walked to a window and noticed that his Seattle-bound ship was gone; and thankful he was to see that he'd missed it as it was later announced that the ship had gone down in a storm, with all hands lost.　　　□

SOME TALES ARE ODD,
SOME ARE JUST TALL

" 'And there I was,' Casey said, 'backed up against a cliff with a broken leg, unable to move, and my gun out of reach. This big brownie that I'd wounded charged right up to where I was lying, then reared up on his hind feet and made ready to take a swipe at me.'

" 'Gawsh!' we gasped, all tense from excitement and suspense, 'what did you do then?'

" 'Nothing! The bear killed me.' " (J. Preston Levis as told to Stan Lilian, "We Saw Seventy-two Bears," The ALASKA SPORTSMAN®, February 1941)

"When a bear enters a cabin, he usually helps himself to any food he finds, demolishes everything, and lets it go at that. But the bear which entered Alec Hagland's cabin on Good Hope Creek near Livengood last fall had a more sinister purpose. He broke in, stole some supplies, and also took Hagland's social security card. The Social Security Administration at Juneau has been notified of the theft, and has agreed to see that the bear is not paid any benefits due Hagland." (The ALASKA SPORTSMAN®, February 1946)

In general the bear is an intelligent, courageous, tenacious and curious animal. He doesn't want to give man a hard time, but his nature often drives him to impulsive action which becomes his undoing. The bear becomes the villain when in actuality he would just as soon be left alone. The vast majority of man's dealings with bear, however, are of a passive, harmless and often humorous nature.

The Guvnor's Bear

Governor of Alaska Jay Hammond is a former guide with considerable experiences with bears. One time I heard him tell about the brown bear that touched him which prompted me to ask him for any other bear experiences he'd had. He sent me the following humorously told story which he permitted me to title "The Bear and the Rock."

"Of the times that I've had problems with bear usually it was due to peculiar circumstances, and the bear had a 'mad' on for some reason or other which was most understandable upon final examination.

"When I first came to Alaska, I, like many, felt that most brown bear charged upon virtually no provocation whatsoever. We held rifles at high port expecting a haired-out H bomb to erupt from the brush every time we turned the corner. I spent seven years virtually rubbing shoulders with 'em on the Alaska Peninsula with the Fish & Wildlife Service. I've been privileged to have observed more bears than most over the 30 years I've spent out in the country. I have a great affection, but also a high respect, for the brown bear. I came to see that the typical brown bear charge was a hundred and eighty degrees in the opposite direction. Sometimes you got perhaps a little careless or contemptuous, sometimes you got scared and got a shot off at an appropriate awareness level, finally most kept as your hole card at least a rifle of sufficient caliber in heavy brown bear country.

"I can't say that I've had to actually defend my person from rampaging brown bear except on a couple of occasions. The first time it ever happened I was tending traps over in the Thykakela or 'Big River' area. I was on a narrow creek bed that necked down and was covered with brush on both sides. I had a number of traps on both sides of it.

"All of a sudden out of the brush there came a cow moose with a brown bear chasing her. He couldn't catch her when she took off down this dry river bed. He stopped and started moseying around lookin' for ground squirrels and so forth, tearin' up the ground on the other side of this river bed . . . which wasn't very wide.

"My back was to the river itself as I was tending traps. He's minding his business, and I'm minding mine. We're paralleling each other. The stream bed is necking down and he's getting a little closer than comfort accommodated. I was spending too much time watching him rather than what I was doing, so I picked up a rock and threw it at him. Unfortunately, I hit him with it, stung him, and he turned and came at me like an express train.

"He was only 50, 60 feet away at the time I threw the rock. There was no place for me to go but in the river or shoot him. The river was one that I'd never have gotten out of — it was very rough and rampaging. I had this old Springfield I used to carry with me on the trapline, but it didn't chamber cartridges too well. I could get one shot off, but I never knew if I could get two. I would have fired over his head or tried to divert him if I'd had time and if the distance between us permitted; but, unfortunately, it didn't.

"I hit him in the sticking point and he turned and started in the other direction, which is not uncommon. He collapsed maybe a hundred feet from me. I was at that stage one of those who was contemptuous and critical of all the charging bear stories I'd heard. I'd been out with a number of bear hunters and had seen the alleged charging bear which were usually just trying to get out of the country, were running bluffs or what have you. This guy seemingly meant business, and I had no way to get out of there to find out whether or not he'd turn, so I did shoot him.

"I went over and took a look at him. One of his tusks had been knocked out. In his jaw was lodged a hunk of lead from an old bullet wound. He had in his hide three different sizes of birdshot that he'd been 'peppered' by. He had as well an ulcerating mass on his shoulder where he had apparently been in a fight with another bear. He was a very unhappy and uncomfortable critter that appeared to be just looking for somebody to avenge himself on. I happened to be the most appropriate target. There was a good cause for him to hate everybody. I didn't particularly hold that against him.

"There was a peculiar spin-off to that story. As I say, I was working for Fish & Wildlife at that time as a professional government hunter and trapper. I went into town, and some woman newspaper reporter got wind of that story and interviewed me.

"Her story was really something. I had been described as kind of a large, burly guy who dressed in hairy Canadian-type sweaters. Since I was trapping wolves, I probably didn't smell much like a human. Somebody had given her the details of this story and she'd written this article.

"The event occurred during the mating season of the big brown bear. Bears have notoriously poor eyesight, and the punch line of the story was perhaps the bear was bent on amorous dalliance when he saw this rather hairy looking creature standing on the other side of the stream bank. In order to protect myself from a fate worse than death, I had to dispatch it.

"That is not true, and I want to set the record straight. But, that's in essence the way the story came out."

Some men have been closer to bears than they'd like to remember, and others take it right in stride. A story is told about an old-timer named Andrew Berg who had an unusual method of hunting bears. The January 1946 issue of *The ALASKA SPORTS-MAN*® carried an account of his tactics. "Andrew used to go hunting all by himself at times, just for the fun of it. He'd tie a piece of bacon to a rope, and knot the other end of the rope around his leg. Then he'd wrap up in his heavy overcoat and lie down to sleep.

"Pretty soon an old brownie would come along sniffing around for something to eat. He'd find the bacon, and take a bite. That would jerk the rope and wake Andrew. Then Andrew would pull the rope toward him, and the bear would follow the bacon.

"When the bear got up close, Andrew would shoot it. Then he'd come back to Kenai and tell us all about it. He got some mighty big bears that way!"

Some men take the cake. A friend of mine, who wishes to remain anonymous, told me a classic tale about two politicians who came North to hunt Old Ephraim. One of the guides told my friend the story firsthand, and I rewrote it to save the men from embarrassment. The story casts more light on the nature of man than the nature of bruin. It's a story with a lesson for man, and I call it "The Congressman and the Bear."

Threads of truth run through the following story, but the names of the guides have been changed, and the politicians unnamed to protect the bears.

Politicians have an aura about them that commands respect, and such is their magnetism that they usually get what they want. Politicians are so accustomed to getting their way that they would think nothing of dealing with a charging bear in the arena of life.

Plan B Is For Congressmen

Such was the case of two congressmen who wanted to hunt

bears in the Great Land of Alaska. They made the necessary arrangements with a reputable guide and journeyed to America's Last Frontier. A longtime Alaskan pilot and guide named Wade contracted to lead these mighty, congressmen hunters in search of old Ursus. Wade's young assistant, Ben, would help with the guiding.

Years of experience in his profession had taught Wade the necessity of an alternate hunting plan in the event the client did not meet his expectations. Plan A was designed for skookum hunters with lots of energy; Plan B was for that vast array of huntsmen whose strength lies in the area of the index finger on their shooting hand — those whose physical stamina and conditioning vascillates between nil and nonexistent. On this hunt Wade planned a pack trip into country that fairly abounded with bears; his alternate plan was a float trip.

Wade and Ben met the big, silver bird at the airport on the appointed day of arrival, and they switched immediately from Plan A to Plan B. It was obvious that neither client could hike anywhere — one was obese and the other was a hundred pounds beyond excessive fatness.

The hunt got under way. Wade took one hunter in a rubber raft, and Ben took the other. Ben's hunter was shooting a .458 Weatherby magnum with Mr. Roy Weatherby's personally engraved signature on the stock. They were floating along about a quarter-mile ahead of Wade when they rounded a bend in the stream.

A short distance away on shore was a mamma bear and a cub of the grizzly variety. Ben quickly instructed his client not to shoot, "We can't shoot that bear; she has a cub. We'll just float quietly by, easy, no problem."

They were nearly past the bears when the cub began bawling and carrying on, igniting the sow. The bear charged the raft as if the waist-deep water wasn't there. She was rapidly gaining on the raft when Ben shouted, "Open fire! She's legal!"

Now, when it came to splitting molecules, heating gun barrels and slinging lead in general, Mr. Congressman had no equal. *Boom!* A shoreline spruce dropped into the stream. *Ka-boom!* A limb dropped from another tree. Two misses.

The congressman, calling on the reserve and dignity he'd developed during many sessions in the White House, rose calmly to his feet. He held his trusty, and expensive, weapon aloft facing the frothy water and a very angry bear. He spoke softly in his diplomatic tones, "I terminate this hunt." And then, realizing he was totally out of his element and not in the White House, he came unglued, "I TERMINATE THIS HUNT!"

Obviously the bear didn't understand Capitol Hill jargon; it kept coming — the congressman threw his gun overboard and jumped frantically into the stream.

Ben grabbed the fleeing politician by the shirt tail and tried to keep him afloat. At the same time, Ben raised his rifle with one hand and fired at the mad mamma. *Bang.* A miss. He managed to chamber another round one-handed, *Ka-whoom!* A hit.

By this time Wade had come into view upriver, and he commenced barrel-warming, launching salvos toward the bruin. Ben shot again, just as the bear reached the raft and chomped on it. All Ben heard was *sssssssss*, air escaping from the raft; the bear died.

The congressman looked rather ridiculous at this point — standing in water up to his waist and looking at the sinking raft with the strangest expression on his face. But gradually he regained his composure, and the political veneer reappeared. He slowly slipped back into his Never-never Land of debutantes, countrymen and government subsidies. Mr. Congressman stated diplomatically, "That's a fine bear I got."

Ben was understandably dumbfounded and upset, "Wait a minute! Who do you think shot that bear?" The young guide was furious.

At that point Wade came to the rescue and took Ben off to one side saying, "Ben, listen. I know how you feel. I know you shot that bear. You can keep the bear and forget these guys, or let him take the bear and pay us."

Ben cooled down a little, said, "Okay," and gave up the bear.

So the congressman played the game — faced a charging bear, shot and killed it — and won. They never did find that Weatherby rifle, but the congressman got his bear.

Sometimes man's well-meant intentions backfire, and he is left with egg on his face. Fortunately man is capable of reviewing his activities and learning from his unintended harmfulness. The former owner of AAA Taxidermy in Anchorage, Louis Brunner, told me about an experience he had with a bear which was funny, but on reassessing his activities, Lou was a little wiser. Lou called his story "My Pet Brown Bear, Seymour."

Old Seymour

"Every year my friend comes up from Washington, D.C., Al Clark, an old army buddy, colonel, retired. We go fishing and hunting down at Telequana Lake. That's down through Merrill Pass. Last trip we caught some red salmon; and saved quite a few to mount — I'm a taxidermist. We put 'em on the beach and went into the Fish & Game cabin there that we stay in.

"We came back out and they were gone. We thought one of our buddies was playing tricks, so we went back out and got three more and come back and lay them there. While we were in the cabin, we heard a noise and went out. There was about a six-foot brown bear taking off with our salmon.

"We proceeded to feed him about three times a day, and he kept getting tamer and tamer. We had some old syrup and some honey and some other food in the cabin that we weren't using so we put it out, and the bear would come up. He got tamer and tamer. After about four days he would come up to within 15 to 20 feet of us and get the food we laid out for him.

"He'd sneak up, grab the salmon and run. So one day I thought it would be fun if we tied a piece of rope on to the salmon and when he started to grab the salmon we'd jerk it from him (I have some pictures of that here in my album).

"I threw the salmon out there about 40, 50 feet. He snuck up lookin' at us and watchin' the salmon. He acted like he thought something was wrong; and pretty soon he reached down for the salmon, and I jerked it about three feet. He stood there and looked at us for about five minutes; and then he pounced on the salmon, turned around and run. I had a hold of the string, and he toted me right down the beach for about 20 feet on my belly before I let go of the string. Then he and the string and the salmon went back into the woods.

"Bill Aregood, who flew us down there, came in to pick up some of the meat (we killed a caribou or so); and I asked him if he wanted to see my pet brown bear. He wouldn't believe it, all the stories we'd been telling him. So I went out, picked up a big red salmon, sat down on the beach and started hollerin' 'Seymour.'

"Old Seymour came out, walked right up and picked up the salmon and went back into the woods.

"Seymour kept breaking into the meat. We took the meat and put it in a boat about 20, 30 feet offshore. He'd swim out for it, and we'd have to run him off. We took the boat up on the beach and we had an old piece of tin off of the cabin we put on top of it, and several rocks and a bunch of stumps and everything else. He came right up. We heard a noise out there, went out, and he'd just lifted the top off, grabbed a caribou ham and started to run with it.

"We decided to put up one of the tents we had with us, and we put some incense in it that you burn to divert mosquitoes and flies; and from then on he'd stay away. He wouldn't come close. He would go up and look around the tent but he wouldn't go in it.

"We were there for 10 days. We watched him swimming in the lake. He'd go out and swim right in front of the cabin, upside down playing with a stick, washin' himself, rubbin' his belly on the beach. He got relatively tame. We figured we were going to leave and someone might shoot him so we'd scare him away. We shot at him several times, about six or eight feet away from him into the sand. He'd just stand there and look at us. He'd look where the bullet hit, turn around and look at us and go on about his business.

"The last I knew, he was still in the area. I haven't heard of anybody killing him. I haven't heard of anybody staying in that cabin since last fall, but I hope to look him up again this spring when we go down there.

"At night Seymour would come up and roam around the cabin right where we were, all night. He didn't seem to have a bit of fear of us. It's a bad thing, I guess, to feed a bear like that and get him tame because I'm sure that this summer he's going to give some people fishing some trouble."

Some bears get into people-trouble while snooping around man's domain. One cold fall evening an old Russian labored before his stove preparing his evening meal. He lived in a one-room log cabin, and as the heat radiated from the stove and the savory aroma of frying moose steaks permeated the room, he opened the door a couple of inches for ventilation. No sooner had he turned his back to the door when it swung wide several feet. Feeling the cold blast of air and without turning to look, the trapper reached with his left hand and closed the door to the two-inch opening a second time. The door swung wide again.

The third time the man reached for the door and closed it, but before he'd had time to let go, he felt pressure from the opposite side of the door. He looked out the door and spied a hulk of a bear sitting on its haunches, sifting the fragrant air with its rubbery nose, and not the least bit unhappy with the delectable odor emanating from the confines of the little cabin. The man was a bit miffed at the uninvited guest's presence and slammed the door in the bear's face.

The animal took the chef's abrupt behavior as an invitation to force his way inside; but the trapper objected and pushed harder from his side of the slight barricade. By this time the bear had all but lost faith in the good graces of the trapper and attempted to put his paw through the door.

The man was not the slightest pleased with the bear's efforts as he had spent considerable time engineering that door. He latched onto the stove poker and gave bruin a resounding thump on the nose. The bear forgot the door momentarily, giving the Russian time to close and bolt it. Then the man grabbed his rifle and set the lantern at the window. A fraction of a second later bruin's head appeared at the window and the trapper responded on impulse.

The next spring the bear's hide fetched $15. The trapper's total outlay was one cartridge, one small, circular hole in a pane of glass and a couple of burned moose steaks.

Bears become fond of man-food and court disaster in procuring man's tasty morsels. More than one bear has been rescued from a food container. Two such encounters were related in the *ALASKA SPORTSMAN®*: "A yearling black bear who got himself in a terrible predicament is out of the can now. Literally. And he owes a heap of thanks to Doc Hall of Seward.

"Doc was flying his plane from Anchorage to Seward when he spotted a bear in the Devil's Creek area near Mile 32 of the Seward Highway who was acting very strangely. Closer inspection showed that the bear was plodding around and around in small circles with a 20-pound coffee can on his head. Doc flew on to Seward, enlisted the aid of two policemen, and with a tranquilizer gun borrowed from the dog catcher, a length of rope and some tin snips, flew back to the scene.

"The bear was still there, still canned, and still walking around in circles. 'In fact,' Doc reported, 'there were five or six smooth circular paths worn in the mat of leaves that covered the ground. That bear must have walked 500 miles.'

"Three light dog loads of tranquilizers were shot into the bear cub but they didn't faze him. So the men got the rope around his neck and hind legs and went to work with the tin snips anyway. By the time they got the can off, the dope, fortunately, had taken effect and the bear lay on the ground snoozing it off. When he finally came to he looked his benefactors over with a rather dazed expression, then pulled himself together and made tracks for the timber — straight as an arrow." (*ALASKA SPORTSMAN®*, January 1966)

A similar incident was in the January 1973 issue: "What do you do with a healthy, wild black bear who has his head stuck in a coffee can? Workers at a construction camp near Cordova were faced with that dilemma recently, when the garbage dump-raiding blackie became too inquisitive about a 10-pound can filled with kitchen grease. Taking pity on the slowly-suffocating, panic-stricken animal, the men lassoed each of the bear's paws and began to cut the can. To avoid being mauled, they had a pickup truck handy so that they could jump into the back of it as they freed the young bear. That plan was working fine, until the last critical moment, when one of the men toppled off the getaway truck and fell smack on top of the confused bruin. Luckily, the bear was intent only on getting away, and didn't even pause to say 'thank you.' "

Some of the stories involving man and bear have evolved into tales of the far-fetched variety. No Alaskan with any grain of decency would stoop so low as to deceive a visitor or a newcomer. It just wouldn't be right. I have long maintained that the residents of the South 48 states should be told the truth about Alaska — that they should be informed that we *do* live in ice houses, travel only by dog team and that in areas where the snow is deep we build caches (houses on stilts) to avoid the danger of the deep snows.

Evidently Dick Willoughby shares my views because for years he told visitors the story of a huge bear he was forced to shoot. The tourists often suggested the bears were slow, but Dick reassured them of the bear's true speed. He awoke one morning, threw his door open wide for a breath of fresh Alaskan air and observed a monster brown bear, 14 feet long, strolling up the path Dick used regularly to go to the lake to fish for salmon. Dick reached down his old buffalo gun from above his door and fired a missile toward the animal that had stopped in front of his cabin with its mouth open wide.

The bullet struck the brute just above the tongue and ranged straight down its spine and exited just below the tail. The animal was so surprised that it swapped ends and lit out down the trail. The creature was so fast in its movement that while the bullet was still in its body, the bear turned almost 180 degrees; and the exiting bullet struck the door jam next to Dick's head. He always explained that he was thankful for the bear's advancing age which slowed it down just enough so that it didn't get turned the full 180 degrees or the bullet might have seriously injured him.

Malcolm S. Roberts reported a story to *ALASKA*® magazine that was strikingly similar to Dick's. In the January 1973 edition he said, "Eight years ago I came home from ANS hospital in July. It was hard for me to get around using a brace and crutch.

"In September it got dark nights. Lucky we still had a screen door up. About 9:00 p.m. my wife and I were playing cards and the screen door rattled. I told wife take the light, see who is outdoors. She went out and came back said, 'Bear out there.'

"She took .30-30 rifle, and I went out with light in one hand and crutch in other. I turned light on bear about six feet away. My wife just behind me pointed gun at bear. Poor bear didn't know any better and opened his mouth as she pulled the trigger and let the bear have it right in the mouth.

"The bear turned around so fast the bullet came out right below the tail. Poor old bear almost killed herself."

Some men have a way with bears and are able to tame and gentle them for suitable companions. A true story is told about an old prospector on Kodiak by the name of Nels Peterson who gentled a brown bear. Friends of Nels say he is the only sourdough who believes the story. It seems as though one day he was hiking the three miles that separate his mine from his cabin when he discovered an orphaned little cub which was famished. The gentle man took the little critter home with him and fed it some food and went to bed.

The next morning when Nels started to the mine, the cub was sitting on his front porch. Time passed and Nelson continued to feed the cub which made itself right at home, polishing off bushels of food quicker than any growing, teen-age boy. It got to the point that Nels decided to make the fast-growing animal earn its keep.

Nelson bought an old, used saddle and began riding the bear to and from his mine. Each day the man unsaddled the bear at the mine and sent him looking for berries in the vicinity. As Nelson's work day ended, he would whistle for the bear, saddle it and ride home. This routine persisted for weeks. One day Nels whistled for the bear while he put his tools away. The bear didn't show.

The prospector figured the bear would arrive shortly and smoked passively on his pipe. After several minutes of reflection Nels decided the bear had finally reached adolescence and wandered off to mature on its own. That was fine with him. He shouldered his saddle and headed for home.

Not far from the mine the prospector's attention was drawn to the top of a tree, and there sat his pet. Nelson had grown fond of the bear and was very proud of its well-mannered behavior. He called the bear which reacted in a surprised fashion. The bear made no effort to move which angered Nels. He lost his temper, called to the bear and threw rocks at it. In due time the brute sulked down the tree and over to Nels.

The man decided it was time to teach his pet a lesson and punished it with a strap. The bear was submissive but reacted in a bewildered manner to his whipping. Nels had no hard feelings and decided to forgive the bear. He saddled the animal, rubbed its ears, fetched some sugar cubes from his pocket and offered them to the bear as a concession. They then continued their journey home.

The prospector approached his cabin and departed his pet's back with haste, for there on his porch was another bear sound asleep. It lay on the porch with a can of maple syrup between its paws and the same old leather collar around its neck that Nels had fashioned for his pet several weeks before.

The old sourdoughs were a hardy lot. Their imaginations never dimmed for something exciting to do, and their stories matched their mountains for size and color. A bunch of the boys were trading tales one night, trying to outdo each other, when one of them told about a bear that he had outrun. Not to be outdone, another bewhiskered chap piped up and told about out-jumping a bear.

Seems he'd put in a good day on the creek pannin' for colors. He was looking forward to getting back to his cabin and some rib ticklin' vittles when he noticed a bear following him across the tundra. He knew of only one tree between him and his cabin, but that was quite a distance ahead. Well, the prospector made for the tree, the bear gaining with every leap. The miner reached the tree just ahead of the bear, but the man was frazzled from the run.

The lowest limb was 20 feet from the ground, and the man couldn't climb that distance before the bear overhauled him. With every ounce of energy that he had left, the man gathered his strength for a herculean effort. He sprang for the limb just as the bear reached him.

One of the eager sourdoughs asked the prospector, "Did you make it?"

A thin smile pierced the miner's lips, and he replied with a twinkle in his eye, "Wal, I missed it on my way up; but I caught it comin' down."

Many of the stories told about bears are really preposterous. It's gotten to the point where all you have to do is talk about bears and people turn a silent ear. But Frank Wooton shared a story with me that is a credit to his profession. He called his story "Trained Bear."

Smart Bears

"My name is Frank Wooton. I've been a registered guide in Southeastern Alaska for 25 years or more and had quite a bit of experience with bears. People's always wantin' me to tell narrow escape stories. Even the fishermen and the hunters have all got bear stories. Some of 'em are true; some you got to take with a grain of salt. But this one I'm gonna tell happened to me, and you can just judge for yourself whether it's true or not. You can easily see it could happen.

"It seems like we were out on my brother's boat *Radar,* that's a 50-foot yacht, and the hunting party lived on board the boat. And then we'd go ashore in a skiff to hunt. It was in the fall of the year, and we do all the huntin' in the fall on the salmon streams, that's where the bears are feedin' on salmon. And we went into Rodman Bay one evening, that's out in Peril Strait between Chatham Strait and Sitka. That was before there was any loggin' done there; there was nobody in there at all.

"But I started up to hunt with this hunter I had, he was a fairly old guy, couldn't walk very fast. So, we put the skiff ashore and then I saw that the wind was blowin' up the creek where we wanted to hunt. Well, it would be absolutely useless to hunt bear with the wind. But I had another idea.

"There was an old railroad quite a ways back from the stream and goin' up the same canyon; so I decided we'd walk up that old railroad for half-mile or so. Then we'd cut down to the creek and come down against the wind and have a good chance of gettin' a bear.

"But we started up the railroad which was a little higher elevation than the creek, and there wasn't any wind at all. We got just about where I was goin' to turn down to the creek, and here comes a big bear, walkin' across this track, just takin' it easy and not lookin' from side to side at all. He didn't even see us, and I told the hunter, 'There's your chance. He's a good one, and it'll be a lot easier than goin' down to the creek after one.'

"And the bear, it kinda hesitated and stopped there before he crossed the track, and the hunter got down on one knee and let drive at him. He got the bear right in the neck, the first shot. And the bear just folded, all four feet went in the air.

"We waited a while to make sure he was dead 'fore we went up to him. We got up there, 'n I threw off my packsack and set my gun down by a little jack pine tree and proceeded to sharpen my knife a little bit to skin the bear.

"Well, it takes quite a while to skin a bear, and the hunter wanted to bring the head back to the boat so his wife could see it (that weighed about 70 pounds). The hunter says, 'Well, you know, you're gonna have quite a load of bear hide. I'll take some of this stuff and go on down the track, and you'll probably catch me. I don't walk so fast as you do anyway.'

"I thought that was a good idea and told him to go ahead. I went on skinning the bear. Finally I got him all skinned, got him on the packboard, and I started pickin' up my tools, knives 'n ax. I looked around at the tree where my gun was standing and saw no gun. Well, I looked all over the place for it and the only thing I could figure out was this hunter had wanted to help me out so he carried my gun for me too. There was nothin' I could do but start on down the track and thought maybe I'd catch up to him.

"I had gone quite a little ways down the track, and I sense somethin' behind me. I looked back and here was another bear coming. And he was coming pretty fast. I started going a little bit faster, and the bear started going a little bit faster. And he was gaining on me. And holy smokes, I had no gun! I thought I'd catch up with the hunter, but I didn't see him.

"I just kept on a goin' a little bit faster, and I got to makin' about six ties to the step. And that bear was doin' the same thing. Finally I got down to a spot where I figured I might get out of it, if I worked things right. I knew he'd catch me before I got there, and I threw the packboard off. That slowed him down; he stopped and sniffed at it a little bit.

"I thought maybe he was after that smell of the bear hide; but it was me he wanted it seemed like, here he come. But there was a side track there, going up another little canyon. I got a little bit ahead of the bear when he stopped to sniff at the packsack. I jumped to one side just before he got there; and I threw the switch. And that old bear went lopin' up that side track, and as far as I know, he's still going."

For those of you who find Frank's story too much of a tale, perhaps the following story will convince you of our Alaskan desire for total honesty and integrity. Its veracity is further founded because it was printed in the internationally famous *The ALASKA SPORTSMAN®* in August 1937. George R. O'Neil went to shore to try his luck on rainbow trout with a fly rod. George caught several trout then decided to take a rest. Sometime later a brown bear appeared and began eating George's trout. The fisherman decided to shoot the bear.

A slight dilemma faced George as he was too far from the yacht in the bay for anyone to hear his shot and his camera was on board. George was in luck, however, as he found a rowboat. He decided to row the bear to the yacht.

"I tried to get the boat close enough to the bank so I could roll the bear into it, but could not keep the round-bottomed boat there. Then I noticed a long rope that the boat owner used to tie up his boat. It was curled in the bow. I took it out, tied the loose end around the bear's neck, and, standing in the water, kept the boat close to the bank. I then gave a quick jerk on the rope. The bear rolled into the boat.

"I managed to sit in the stern of the boat and, with one oar, paddled and steered the boat to the mouth of the creek. It was then time for the tide to go out. I was carried out into the bay by the tide.

"Just when I was worrying about whether or not I could handle the boat with one oar, I heard a grunt. It was then I discovered that my bear was not dead, but evidently only stunned. He was in the boat with his head toward the bow. He finally pulled himself up so he had his rump on the bottom of the boat and his front paws on the front seat.

"To say I was scared would put it mildly.

"I thought maybe I should shoot him again, but I gave up that idea when I looked around for my gun. I learned it was in the bow of the boat. The bear was between me and my trusted firearm! I had a .45 revolver in my pack that I had brought along on the trip for a side arm, but the packsack was on the fishing boat. It did not do me any good to wish I had taken it along.

"In my hunting experiences I have found myself in many tight spots, but this was the first time I ever found myself out in the bay in an open boat with only one oar and a live bear for a companion.

"The bear turned his head. When he spied me he let out a roar that chilled me to the bone.

"He then stood up full length. As he did so, a wave struck the boat and Mr. Bear lost his balance and fell overboard.

"He almost upset the boat and I had to get busy bailing out water we took in when the bear fell out.

"While I was busy bailing out, the boat took a quick turn which almost threw me out. I then remembered the rope that was tied about the bear's neck. He had started swimming for shore with the boat in tow; and while I was pleased to be rid of what might have been a disagreeable companion, I congratulated myself that he was swimming toward shore.

"When the bear reached shallow water where it was no longer necessary for him to swim, I took out my pocket knife and cut the painter and let him go. He ambled off toward the woods. I did not have the nerve to shoot him as he had been kind enough to tow me all the way across the bay.

"I looked over to the fishing boat which was within a hundred yards of where I landed, expecting to hear a lot of loud laughs from the guide and the fishermen. But they had been below, icing fish, and had not witnessed my exciting trip across the bay.

"I did not mention my experience to the gang on the boat, and when they read this they will know for the first time why I returned to the boat in the middle of the day instead of fishing all day for trout as originally planned . . .

"It is only fair to inform the readers that the writer of this story has twice had his picture in *The ALASKA SPORTSMAN®*, both times in connection with the Liar's Club. In fact, records show that I am a charter member of Alaska Sportsmen's Liars Association."

Many tall tales are overshadowed by true but humorous stories. One such incident involved a tree. An old Scandinavian prospector amused readers of *The ALASKA SPORTSMAN®* in January 1939 with this story about his friend Ole.

Ole and Mama Bear

"It was one summer when Ole was working for a grubstake," Hans wrote, "and Ole had taken a job as ax-man on a survey party up the Susitna River. He was working with several other fellows, clearing out the brush ahead of the line so the rod man and chain men could get set. The brush had to be cleared away so the transit man could see the marks on the rod.

"Ole was working a little ways ahead of the rest of the gang when he ran into a black bear, an old she-bear, with cubs. She looked at Ole and he looked at her — both startled, but not for long.

"Well, sir, that old gal swung a fast right to the backside of both the cubs and shooed them toward the trees, then turned and made straight for Ole, a-spittin' and a growlin' like all get-out. Ole was so surprised that he dropped his ax and, as he had no time to look for it, and no other weapon, he started running for a tree.

"It wasn't exactly the best thing he could have done, for black bears are good climbers, but Ole knew that he was no match for the old mother bear in a straight race across broken ground, and his first idea was to put as much distance between himself and her as he could. Naturally, he picked out a nice, close tree.

"Now it happened that Ole was so busy watching what the she-bear was doing that he didn't see where the cubs went. When he reached the first tree handy, he grabbed himself an armful of tree-trunk and bark and started up, like a monkey up a string.

"Old Mama Bear reached the base of the tree just one jump behind Ole, and started right up after him, keeping him humping to try to stay out of reach. As he climbed higher, the old gal redoubled the terrific growls she was letting out, and he heard a whimper above him. He looked up and his hair stood right up on end!

"About three feet above him was the lower of the two cubs, with the other just above. Below him was the mother, coming up a little slower now because the tree was small.

"Ole shooed the cubs up, and climbed after them until the tree began to bend with the combined weight of the man, two cubs, and the enraged mother bear. Ole let out a yell for help that could be heard halfway to Anchorage.

"Not daring to go any higher for fear the tree would break and deposit the whole party in one mix-up on the ground, Ole was finally forced to stop. The old lady made an overhead swipe with her paw and fastened one of her long, curving, needle-pointed claws in the heel of his rubber boot. That started a tug-of-war.

"The bear tried to pull Ole's foot down within reach of her jaws, while Ole let out another roar and tried to park his feet behind his ears. Finally the bear got her jaws on the boot heel and chewed it off, but fortunately could not reach high enough to include a portion of Ole's anatomy in the bite.

"When the heel tore free, Ole tucked his feet up out of the way as high as possible, and just out of reach of the searching claws of the bear. Ole sweated, cursed, and yelled for help. The cubs hung tight, looked down on the scene with a somewhat bored attitude, and whimpered for their mother. Mother answered the whimpers with roars of rage, and struggled mightily to get higher. The tree top drooped threateningly, and now and then an ominous creak could be heard as the straining wood endeavored to support its shifting burden.

"Down below, someone shouted to Ole. He looked down, and saw that three or four of his fellow ax-men had come in response to his roars for help. Armed only with axes, they stood around the tree helplessly, their only contribution to the situation being a considerable quantity of unneeded advice.

"Ole was getting cramped, and his foothold on the small limbs was slipping a little. Furthermore, the old she-bear seemed to be inching a little higher. Ole had a bright idea.

"Hanging on with one hand, he fished in his pocket for the ever-present can of 'snoose,' brought it forth, and pried off the lid. Then leaning back a little, he dumped the entire contents of the nearly-full can in the bear's face, hoping to blind her and discourage her from further climbing efforts. The maneuver was not blessed with any marked success. The old gal just let out an extra-big snort, shook her head, slipped down a few inches, and gave the tree trunk a terrific left-handed wallop of rage.

"The group below continued to shout encouragement and advice to Ole, but also continued to do nothing to relieve the situation. Ole was getting desperate.

"At last the old lady took notice of the men below, and did not seem too pleased with the attention she was getting. While watching the men on the ground, she slipped down a few inches, and was unsuccessful in an attempt to climb back. Ole let out a very small sigh of relief and stretched a little, very cautiously.

"Evidently the mother bear finally became tired of being in the limelight, and decided to leave the cubs where they were for the time being. She started back down the tree towards the ground while Ole, still sweating profusely, began to breathe more easily, and the men on the ground began to find points of vantage more to their liking.

"Upon reaching the ground, Mother Bruin headed straight into the woods, looking neither to right nor left, and seemed intent only on getting out of the country. Ole slid to the ground, shook a vengeful fist in the direction of the departed bear, found his ax, and limped off on one heelless boot with his fellows . . . Ole still has that boot. He doesn't like she-bears — especially if they are black, and have cubs!"

In November 1949 *The ALASKA SPORTSMAN*® carried an interesting account that was quite similar to Ole's 12 years earlier. "Carl Ling, who operates a sawmill near Seward, might have had a spectacular career if he had gone in for track. Ling was out last summer blazing trees he intended to fell when, hearing a noise behind him, he turned and found himself facing an enraged she-bear. It seems her cubs were up a tree — the very tree Ling was blazing. Mrs. Ling came up in time to see her husband tearing off down the hill with the bear at his heels. It was a close race, but Ling won."

In August 1976 a black bear was creating a little havoc near the Harrel Crawford residence five miles west of Wasilla on Knik

Road. The bear had been in the Crawford yard a couple of times and harrassed the bird feeders. Mr. Crawford decided it was time to take action against the beast and lassoed it. The bear scampered right up a tree, and the legal authorities were called.

No tranquilizer gun was available for darting the bear and relocating it, so an alternative was sought. The wildlife man considered shooting it, but the locals didn't want to kill the critter. Finally it was decided that Mr. Crawford would hold the rope taut while the wildlifer went up the tree and cut the rope from the bear's neck.

After the rope was cut, the bear came down the tree; and it showed a lot of smarts for its mere one and a half years of age, bounding off into the forest.

There's a Moral Here

Bears don't confine themselves to the forest; they frequent man's dwellings if the opportunity presents itself. Two stories involve man's outbuilding with the crescent moon on the door. Early in the morning on July 25, 1953, two young daughters of Erwin Miller stole quietly from their house to use the outdoor plumbing. Mission accomplished, they scrambled back to their house, running into a bear which rummaged in their garbage.

They ran back to the privy and locked the door behind them. After considerable screaming, they managed to awaken their sleeping parents who came to the rescue.

The outhouse was the meeting place for another man and a bear some years back. A logger was having some back trouble and decided to knock off for a while. As he rested beside the trail to the outhouse, a bear ambled down the path and into that building. Just moments later another logger buzzed by the resting lumberjack, rushed up to the outhouse in great haste and slammed the door.

Pandemonium broke loose inside the confines of the man-made rest room. A great noise and shuffling of feet gave way to an explosion from the "water closet." The man burst from the outhouse followed instantly by the bruin, each running for his life — in opposite directions!

Several years ago another man had the daylights scared out of him by a mammoth brown bear. Andy Simons was guiding the man on a photographic mission. They were surrounded by the hairy giants on the Alaska Peninsula, filming from a flimsy blind of brush. Many of the animals were within 40 feet of the men and ignored them for a while.

Suddenly one of the monsters rushed the blind full bore, skidded to a stop, reared on his hind legs and thundered a *WOOF!* Andy noticed the clicking of the movie camera had ceased. He dared not take his gun's sights from the bear at that moment, but shortly it dropped and returned to its business. Only then did Andy lower his rifle and glance toward his cameraman to ask if he was scared.

The man had a hand over his mouth and stood with a greenish hue on his face. He gasped out a reply to Andy that he *wasn't* scared — he'd only swallowed his wad of tobacco.

Bears are clowns and have their humorous moments. Several years ago Kodiak guide Alf Madsen was on a filming trip with writer-photographer Jim Bond when they encountered a real belly-buster. In the October 1955 issue of *The ALASKA SPORTS-MAN®*, Alf told readers about the bear they dubbed Elmer. One day they started up the shore of a salmon stream. They rounded a bend and heard a loud splash.

"A few yards away was a large pool about six feet deep where the sockeyes were concentrated. Suddenly a head so unlike a bear's emerged from the depth, dripping, black and snorting like a hog. He looked to the right and to the left, as if hoping that no one saw him without a fish.

"We set up our camera equipment behind a large willow on the gravel bar and settled down to watch this fellow continue his fishing. His habits and methods of fishing were unlike any we had observed on the entire trip.

"He climbed up the bank again and looked around as if trying to get a long, running jump. He backed up to a distance of 30 feet from the pool and looked around once more. Suddenly, with a great rush, he headed for the fish hole at full speed. With a loud splash he landed in the middle of it and went completely out of sight.

"Again this peculiar head appeared looking more like a prehistoric oddity than a bear — and without a fish again. This performance was repeated a number of times until, finally becoming frustrated with fishing, Elmer went along the stream and picked up the remains of fish that some more fortunate fisherman had left.

"One day Elmer spotted us before we saw him. He took a couple of quick looks over his shoulder and started at a full gallop toward the cottonwoods, running and looking back at us. Suddenly he smacked head-first into a 12-inch tree. His progress was stopped very abruptly, and he sat down on his haunches for a moment as if to contemplate how the tree happened to be in the way."

Many men have crossed trails in the field with the men of the Fish and Feathers. Not all such meetings are pleasant. Jim Van Buskirk told me about his most unusual encounter with a wildlife man. Jim sent me his story which he called "My First Bear."

"We went out specifically looking for a bear because moose hunting was all over with, so there wouldn't be any pressure. We went out toward the end of the Swanson River Road on the Kenai Peninsula. It was about 6:45 A.M. when we came near a gate, and I didn't know it at the time, but there was a road that went out several miles, up towards the moose pens that Fish & Game had fenced off for research.

"We started hiking down this road when it was just getting light. We had been walking quietly, and had walked about 45 minutes, when the road made a left bank and started going down a small hill. Halfway down the hill, we saw a sign about 25 yards up on the right. There was brush on both sides of the road, so you couldn't see very well. As I got down near the bottom, the bank dropped and put me down on level ground. At that point I had crossed the road to go read the sign, when out of the corner of my eye I saw a black bear.

"Actually it looked like a black hole. I looked at it, and I couldn't believe it was only 15 to 20 yards away. The bear and I startled each other. The bear acted queer, hunching down like it was stunned or hoped I would pass. Sensing it wasn't going to run, I swung my rifle around and shot the bear through the head. The bear felt no pain.

"We walked over to the bear, and I was sure glad to see it. Dead, and it was mine. The bear looked like it had its arms wrapped around a tree, like it was hugging it. I walked around, behind the bear, and then I saw it. *It* was a snare, on the bear's left front paw. Let me tell you, this fellow was heartbroken. My first thought was, 'Oh, no!' I was appalled.

"I said, 'Can you believe it, some guy is out there snaring bears illegally.' Naturally Fish & Game didn't snare animals, they darted them for research. I really felt terrible. There went all the feelings of the mighty great white hunter, almost become poacher.

"If it had tried to run when it saw me, I would have noticed it was tugging; but it hunched right down.

"Then I went across the road to read the sign that we had seen when we'd spotted the bear. It said, 'ATTENTION! BLACK BEAR TRAPPING GOING ON! PLEASE DO NOT GO NEAR AREAS WITH RED TAPE! FISH & GAME, FOR RESEARCH PURPOSES, IS TRAPPING BEAR.'

"I thought, 'I've had it, here I go shooting one of Fish & Game's bears right in the trap.' Then I thought the sign's location was ridiculous. I had walked down the road and the sign was 25 yards ahead on my right. The bear had been 15 yards on my left. It was either go read the sign or shoot the bear.

"Then I realized that Fish & Game did trap bears. 'What am I going to do?' I said. Instead of leaving the bear there to go to waste, we thought that the best thing to do was dress it out. I was pretty sure that Fish & Game would take the bear away, but I didn't want to leave it there to rot.

"We put the bear on a pole and had gotten about 200 yards when we heard a truck. It stopped around the bend at the trap, so I walked back. A game biologist was sitting there scratching his head when I said, 'I did it!'

"He looked at me and said, 'You did what?' I told him I'd shot the bear, and you should have heard him curse a blue streak. He had thought a brown bear had come along, killed and eaten the trapped bear, leaving the gut pile.

"About 20 days prior the federal government had started a program for trapping bears. It was the first time they had ever done it, and the Fish & Game had received a grant, hoping to catch an adult female specimen to tag, weigh, take blood samples and a tooth, and put a radio collar on it to monitor it in hibernation. They had succeeded, finally; but so had I!"

The officials excused Jim from the incident although he was greatly disappointed to have shot his first bear in such poor circumstances. I was equally disturbed but for a different reason when I found myself in a situation where I was without a weapon and only yards from a black bear. It was a spur of the moment decision, like many I make.

"Lake Creek? Yeh. How soon? Right away? Okay, I'll meet you at the strip," I told Ralph Ertz over the phone. He and his wife LaVonne were going to fly over and inspect some land a few miles upstream from Lake Creek Lodge on the Yentna River in hopes of staking land under the Limited Entry Program. This was the summer of 1974.

We landed and left Ralph's PA-12 on a sand bar near the confluence of the Yentna and Lake Creek, waded a slough and started hiking leisurely up Lake Creek. Our destination was a distant clearing, and we alternately walked the bank and the stream bed, wading across and recrossing the waist-deep water at random.

Bear tracks seemed as abundant as the spawning salmon, so we kept on our toes. I felt a certain security when Ralph was in the lead, even though our only weapon was his folding Gerber belt knife. When it was my turn to lead, I talked loudly and whistled with much vigor, especially in the head-high grass.

Fortunately we saw only where they had been. Big tracks, little tracks, brown bear, black. Fish with blood still dripping from their silver scales.

We finally reached the clearing and left LaVonne on an island while we investigated the area. Ralph immediately spotted a black bear lazing in the warm sunlight, and two quick thoughts popped into my head: 1) "Wow, just what I need!" and 2) "Where's the nearest tall tree?"

We hollered a little and the bear melted into the low brush, then we continued through the bunches of grass in an old, dry beaver pond. I kept looking back nervously, and tried to stay out of Ralph's rear pocket. It wasn't long until I spotted the bear again, following us. He was a hundred yards back and strolling right along our trail, head down, seemingly asleep.

I wasted no time drawing Ralph's attention to the critter, and he said, "Let's lie down in the grass and see if we can scare him."

"You've got to be kidding," I thought to myself, "all we've got for protection is a pocket knife, and you want to scare it!" Timidly I replied, "Okay."

"Let me know when it's 15 yards away, and we'll jump up and holler," Ralph oozed confidence and was not the least bit worried. He flopped onto the ground in the tall grass. Ralph folded his hands behind his neck and closed his eyes, but The Kid kept his eyes glued on old *Ursus.* "No way am I gonna let a bear get me!" I determined weakly.

The bear walked along nonchalantly sniffing at our trail like a friendly mutt, stopping occasionally to rise on his hind legs and look about. *He* didn't see us, but I observed his every move through the grass between us. I nervously told Ralph *he* was getting closer, but Ralph just said, "Let me know when he's 15 yards away." I kept telling myself that 15 yards was pretty close.

Finally I could wait no longer. "Okay, Ralph," I whispered, "it's about 12 yards."

We jumped to our feet and hollered. I gave the best rendition of a wounded air horn ever heard.

The bear came unglued. I never realized an animal could spring five feet into the air, reverse fields and land 12 feet down the trail all at once. That bear hit the ground running, and *she* released fear every time *she* hit the ground. I never thought I'd come so close to drowning on dry land! ☐

BOWS, SLINGSHOTS
AND BOOMSTICKS

"I say he literally whipped that bear. I don't know how he missed the brain, but he probably was behind it the first time and on the side, maybe below it, the second time. He just whipped that bear bad enough that she took off." (Keith Johnson, Master Guide, commenting on Guy George's ice ax bear encounter, personal interview, Anchorage, June 1977)

"I started towards the bear and shot him with my sling shot. Then I picked a stick up and began to hit him on the head." (Mike Moerlein, mauling victim-rescuer)

The advent of modern weaponry ended man's dependence upon traditional methods of hunting. Whereas he once relied upon spears, and/or bow and arrows, he now uses the boomstick. For the vast majority of American sportsmen the rifle or shotgun is their means of obtaining big game. However, there are some who still seek the challenge of procuring game with handgun or archery tackle.

The Tree Blind
One of these men is an archery enthusiast and a friend of mine, Ralph Ertz. In October 1975 Ralph flew across Cook Inlet from

Anchorage to hunt brown bear in the Alaska Range. A mutual friend of ours, Dan Hollingsworth, who is now Ralph's son-in-law, went along with Ralph. They hunted from tree blinds two miles apart, and both men experienced the thrill of a lifetime the same night. They returned, and Ralph had quite a story. He called it "Big Bear, little Bow."

"Using this old rocking chair for my tree blind was a good idea. It's comfortable, and I can shoot easily from it. I wonder if he'll come tonight, and if so, when. Last night I had four opportunities. I'd waited, not knowing when to shoot . . . waiting for the best shot; then he was gone.

"Tonight I'll wait for the good shot. It's 6:45 P.M. The earliest I've seen him was 7:00 P.M. and the latest, 7:40 P.M. This is prime time. I won't make a sound or move for one hour. Tonight I'll take the step.

"A distant guttural sound. Movement. The bear. He's here, a hundred yards out. Easy now, take it easy. Don't get excited. His low, rhythmic breathing is louder. He's popping his teeth — a loud, hollow sound. His head sways from side to side. Continuous popping; and the breathing is louder. He's telling the world, 'I'm king here!'

"He's going downwind. This is the acid test. Will my chlorophyll, stinky sack and beaver scent work? The chlorophyll tablets I've been taking will cover my scent; the sack of rotting salmon hanging by me will throw out a strong odor; and everything in the woods is familiar with beaver.

"The wind is really blowing. I guess I'll have to hold the arrow on my rest. It keeps falling from the rest to the arrow shelf. Glad I've got a hair silencer on the shelf, every noise is critical.

"My left hand tightens on the grip, and my arm straightens as I slowly raise the bow. Almost before I know it my bowstring rests on my chin, and my right hand fights an urge to release the shaft. One shot is all I have.

"I've rehearsed this night in my mind many times since last spring when bears destroyed my bear camp at this same spot. They tore up my tent and all my gear. When I returned to camp and found all the bear sign, I decided to seek Old Ursus with my Carroll 70-pound compound bow. Since last spring the stage has been set. He found a bonanza last year, and will no doubt return this year looking for more booty.

"I built a frame up in a spruce tree then nailed plywood to the frame. My tree blind is two feet by five feet and 12 feet above the ground. I hauled an old stuffed rocking chair from Anchorage in my PA-12 and set it up on the platform — the chair was well lined with comfortable cushions. This blind was like none I've used since beginning bowhunting in 1956.

"Since my initiation in Montana to this demanding sport, I have taken deer, black bear, coyote, caribou and small game. Because of my interest in the ultimate challenge archery offers, I established a guiding service in Anchorage specializing in bowhunting.

"My desire to offer this challenge prompted me to attend the Pope and Young Awards Convention in Boulder, Colorado, in July 1975, where I met many of the greats of the sport. I have always wanted an animal that is worthy of the Pope and Young Record Book, but I never had anything measured. The interest at the convention was so high in out-of-state hunts I determined to get a representative trophy which led me to start with the brown bear. I knew just the spot, my bear camp 100 miles west of Anchorage in the Alaska Range.

"Now here I am, and here he is, downwind and coming my way. My heart begins an incessant pounding. My adrenalin begins to flow. He's at the bait, seven yards away below the aspen. He grabs a bite and hurriedly leaves.

"Should I have shot? His rear end was to me. It has never been right. The wind is blowing, but he couldn't have smelled me. My heart stops pounding.

"Again he grunts. He's coming. No downwind swing this time. Straight to the bait pile. What's he going to do? Will I have a shot this time? If he goes back and returns, it'll be too dark. Should I shoot? I'll have to hold a little into the wind. It takes only a second to draw, anchor . . . release.

"My arrow's on its way . . . *shhhhhunk!* An indescribable beller shatters the stillness. Whatever led me to hunt a brown bear with this piddley equipment? Gravel, leaves and twigs fly as he swaps ends and digs out into the darkness, leaving me paralyzed and breathless from his horrendous roar.

"Now the doubt. I hit him, but where? A hundred yards away he showed no sign of injury. Wind's blowing to the left; bear faced right. I tend to shoot to the left of target. I don't remember aiming to compensate for the wind. Maybe I shot too far back. Comforting thought, years of practice and wind couldn't have caused more than a two-inch difference at this range. Regardless of where I hit him, he won't be back.

"No need to spend another night in my tree blind. Might as well get back to camp where it's warm. It's only a half-mile to the plane.

"How many times have I looked back over my shoulder

nervously as I hurry toward the plane in the waning twilight? I wonder how Dan's doing in his blind up river? Maybe he got a shot at the bear we scared off his bait. [Use of bait was legal at the time. It is prohibited now.]

"What a wonderful sunset. If Dan doesn't make it back tonight, I'll go looking for him tomorrow. Look at the northern lights.

"Hours spent in my down bag were completely devoid of sleep as my mind continually relived the final moments of my shooting. All through the night as the wind rocked my plane in an effort to blow it away, I thought about the shot, the point of impact and the penetration. Haunting questions, and yet the reassurance... hours of practice and fundamentals stand me in good stead. Tomorrow I'll track him down.

"A quick search in the morning around the stand revealed no arrow. Footprints and hip-high blood smears on trees traced the path of the big brownie. The first hundred yards across the sand was easy to follow, but once inside the thick brush, the spoor was weak, and the deck was stacked in brownie's favor. At that time Big Bertha's presence in my hand was a great solace.

"Fifty yards inside the brush I found half of the fletching end of the 2117 Easton Swift on the ground. I knew then that the razors of the six-bladed Wasp were doing their job inside the bear. Fifty yards beyond the fletching lay the big brownie in his death bed.

"His 22⅞-inch skull will place him fifth in the book, but if I had trailed him too soon last night as he lay on his backtrail, I'm sure I would have made his record book.

"The full mount eight-and-one-half-foot brown bear now decorates my hunting room. Having guided and taken most of America's big game, I have never had a more rewarding experience or a greater thrill than the night I hunted the great brown bear with my bow.

"And maybe next time I'll tell you about Dan's number seven brownie he got the same night I nailed mine."

Many men have taken bears with archery equipment and trembled with the thrill of the hunt. In the spring of 1958 two men killed polar bears which were believed to be the first ever taken by sports hunters. A bush pilot out of Fairbanks, Dick McIntyre, landed and was charged by the bear which bumped its head on a wing strut. The bear fled with McIntyre in pursuit. Dick shot the animal which wore a hide ten feet, one inch long and a 27½-inch skull score.

George Thiele killed the other polar bear with a bow and arrow. It was a nine-footer and was taken 90 miles north of Point Barrow. Thiele contemplated taking an ice bear in the same tradition of his ancestors, with a spear.

Spears In The Old Days

When my wife Pam and I first came to Alaska in 1966, I was all ears for any bear stories, and I still remember first hearing that the old-time natives used to hunt bears with spears. They'd get the bear angry enough to attack, stick the butt end of a seven- or eight-foot spear in the ground, hold the point at the level where the bear could impale himself and fight the bear with the embedded spear. It was a great story to tell a cheechako; and I believed it. I looked forward to hearing more about native spear hunting, hoping some day to speak to someone who had hunted in this primitive manner; but I never did.

I did speak with Gust Jensen, Athabascan Indian from Lake Iliamna country, about hunting this way, and he said, "When I started hunting, all they ever used was a .30-30. They used spears before my time. I was born in 1917, and when I was growing up, I never saw a spear. It must have been 1900, maybe in the 1800s sometime. That's the only way they used to get their meat, with a spear.

"My grandfather used to use a spear. He'd go out and wait in a bear trail and spear the bear. He went with a couple of guys, maybe one or two. They'd wait along a bear trail for a bear and spear him in the heart.

"When he started fighting, they just kept spearing him. They had to let go of the spear — you can't hang onto it when the bear is fighting, he would throw you. You had extra spears. The bear might have two or three spears sticking in him before they killed him.

"Sometimes the old-timers got the bear mad, then when that bear charged, they just stuck the spear in the ground and let the bear spear himself on the point."

When I talked with Charlie Evans of Galena, veteran of the Nome serum run, he agreed with Gust's comments. He said the natives used spears before his time and that it was common for natives to look for hibernating dens, cut a hole in the top of the den and kill the bear with a hand ax by striking it in the head. Charlie jokingly said of those who hunted with ax or spear, "You've got to be crazy to do that."

The Nunamiut, Alaska's northern Eskimos, killed grizzlies in a number of ways. Their favorite method was for three or four men to locate a bear, shoot it with arrows then spear it several times. They also dug bears from their dens and speared them. On some occasions the bears were caught in caribou snares, and it was a common practice to set a snare of bearded seal rawhide, attach it to a heavy log which was used as a counterweight or drag, then hunt down the bear.

Eskimos used dogs to hunt the ice bear. They would track the animal by dog team until it "bayed" then turn the dogs loose (if they hadn't already — sometimes they had hunting dogs used separately from the dog team). The men approached the bear with spears and hurled them at the animal. It was risky, but with good dogs, the bear was kept busy fighting them and paid little attention to his two-legged tormentor(s).

More than one Eskimo has pulled a dead seal along behind him only to have it pounced upon by a hungry ice bear. In a dispute of this nature sometimes the Eskimo won, but more often the native chose discretion as the better part of valor and let the bear have the seal.

Some of the real old-time Eskimos had their challenges with the ancient black powder weapons they used. One old-timer stalked a sow polar bear with a cub using such a weapon. He tried to find a round stone to use for the bullet. Unable to find one, he tried shoving his ivory pipe stem into the barrel. He settled on half a dozen shells which he filled with shot from other shells; then he killed the bears.

The set rifle became popular with Eskimos and required no one to fire it. The gun was anchored with the baited line attached to the trigger. When the animal tried to retrieve the food, the bear shot itself.

A Classic Simple Bear Story

The late Simon Paneak was living at Anaktuvuk Pass when he told the March 1960 *ALASKA SPORTSMAN®* ("We Hunt to Live") about the grizzly he killed with his .22 Hornet. "I go by myself on my trap lines, pick few marmots from my stone deadfalls and I saw more marmots but I cannot shoot them. I have only six shells and I am quit shooting marmots any more. I save for grizzly bear and wolfs.

"When I come near to our home camp pretty soon I see grizzly bear on my caribou meat. After he buried it with ground and dirt he sleep on top of it. He laying like a man laying on his back. Distance about two miles.

"I know I only have six shells before but I counted them again and never different. It was only six shells. I was thinking and sit down and smoke and bear was sleep on top of caribou carcasses.'

"Finally I think I have enough shells to kill the bear and I walk right up to him but I did not went very close, 100 yards away close enough for little .22 Hornet. And I hollered to him and wake him up before I took a shots. But at first holler he do not wake at all just stretching out his forearm. Almost wake up. And I hollered once more and when he wake and head up he look at me while I aimed in his neck and after I almost pull my trigger the bear beginning to get up.

"I pull my trigger anyway and hit the bear in his ear and he almost drop dead, rolled and roaring hollering and shooking his head. Little 46 grain .22 Hornet bullets make him mad. Just soon rolled and roaring were finished he begin to run after me and I fired another little bullet while he was running toward me and little bullet drop him again, but he got up again and running sideway. I aimed in shoulder blade while bear running and shoot. Bear fell down and can not get up any more. Dead there. And I only have three shot left and the grizzly bear was pretty good size bear (male)."

The Dive-Bombed Bear

With man's creative genius it was inevitable that somewhere down the road a bear would be chased away with one of man's most daring technological and gravity defying creations — the airplane. Men have lived dangerously in their time, but none ever entertained a thought which could have made an eternal pilot of him quicker than the reflexive impulse taken by fishing guide Bill Martin in 1973. I heard the story from David Weir, one of my students, and Bill confirmed it.

"In September 1973 Bill Talley, a client who had fished at my Royal Coachman Lodge, wanted to go moose and caribou hunting with me on the Alaska Peninsula. Not being a guide, I had Joe Delia of Skwentna, a very well-known and very professional person, book Bill; and I went along on the hunt as an assistant guide for Joe.

"We hunted the Alaska Peninsula. Bill Talley and Bill Talley, Jr. were both real good hunters. Bill Sr. was aged somewhat and his eyesight was poor (we had him on nine separate caribou stalks and he never popped a cap). Bill Jr. filled out on moose and caribou, and we flew his dad into the Kerjulik River area, which is the main tributary into Becharof Lake on the Alaska Peninsula.

"We spotted a fairly good-sized bull moose in kind of a hummock outcropping in this swamp on the left-hand side of the Kerjulik River going upstream. I landed the floatplane (this being back during the days when landing on game and shooting the day airborne was legal), and we proceeded to make a stalk on the moose.

"Bill Talley weighed about 275 pounds, and with bad eyes, going half a mile was a pretty hard stalk. We finally got on the outskirts of the hummock, around 30 to 40 feet away from the moose; and Joe waited until Bill had got his breath, which was two or three minutes. Then we all stood up straight, Bill in the center. Joe made a couple of grunts like a moose; the moose stood up; Bill from almost a hip position, shot the moose right in the neck.

"We went over and gutted the moose out and quartered it up. It was starting to get towards the latter part of the afternoon. Joe and I agreed that I would take Bill and a load of moose meat back to King Salmon and then return and pick up Joe with the rest of the meat plus the other hunting paraphernalia.

"Joe and I took a load of meat to the airplane; Bill followed along. We loaded up the gear and took off. Joe in turn was going to walk back to the hill and finish off the meat. Joe had left his rifle at the kill site while I had packed mine back to the airplane so that I'd have it when we took the meat and the hunter back to King Salmon. Joe's leaving his rifle was a mistake.

"I took off and I was climbing so I could get over the ridge between Becharof Lake and King Salmon River. I had an altitude of probably a thousand to twelve hundred feet, and I looked back. I could see Joe walking back from the river with a packboard in one hand and a meat saw in the other.

"As I looked towards the moose kill to orientate myself so that I could fly directly back to it, I saw what first gave me the impression of two ravens on the meat sacks and on the hide of the moose. The second thing that went through my mind was that ravens very seldom land on hot blood or a freshly killed animal. I took a second look and realized that they were larger than ravens. It appeared to be a larger bear and a smaller bear, which naturally told me it was a sow and a cub.

"Knowing Joe, he was whistling and walking right into this hummock that was loaded with half the remains of a moose and a sow brown bear and a cub.

"I turned my Cessna 185 hoping that I could get back to where Joe was intercepting the location of the bears to try at least to warn him or, if nothing else, run the bears off the kill. I started a long dive, about two or three miles from Joe.

"I had a panoramic view of a lot of sequences that are now hard to put in my mind. I could see the entire ongoing circumstances, it looked like from a hundredth of an inch. As he approached the hummock and got right to the perimeter of the hummock, the sow stood up on her hind legs. That's when Joe and the sow came eye to eye.

"Joe started to walk backwards. He was waving his arms, the packboard and the saw, and walking backwards towards an ox-bow lake about 150 to 200 yards from where the moose kill was located. The bear walked out of the hummock-brush outcropping to the edge of it where the bear had full sight of Joe, and Joe had full sight of the bear. Joe continued walking backwards into the ox-bow or the old river channel. As he got into the water, he started to splash, and we could see Joe making motions and waving his arms, trying to scare the bear off. The cub had stayed on the kill.

"As we approached closer, I looked at my airspeed indicator, and it registered 190 to 195 miles per hour. I had exceeded redline. I remember that I was carrying about 75% power. I was at about 2,400 RPMs and 24 inches squared, trying to get more speed. As I continued to dive, I was approximately a half-mile away and an altitude of about 300 to 400 feet. The bear dropped on all fours and started an absolute dead run directly in line for Joe.

"The bear was at a full run 20 yards from Joe when my plane separated them. I could see out of my side vision on the left the bear stop and start to stand up; and I could see Joe out of the right window 20 or 30 feet off of the right wing.

"The bear stood up as I made the first pass. I went on past and tried to turn as fast as I could to get back to see if the bear had continued on. I think it's the first successful wing-over that I'd made in two or three thousand hours of flying in Alaska. I did make the turn after I'd flattened the prop. I'd shoved the prop pitch to the dash to allow myself full RPM for the climb, and in doing so, I know I over-revved the engine. I discovered later that when I firewalled it, I didn't flatten the pitch of the prop. I went into full power, and I blew the right two jugs, just built up too much pressure. That one dive cost $1,700. Flying back I had 80, 85% power.

"But I did make a successful wing-over and turned around and went back down. The bear was still standing up on its hind haunches. Joe was still splashing water with his packboard and waving his Knapp saw.

"As I was making the second pass, Bill, who was in the right seat of the plane said, 'Where's Joe. Where's Joe?'

"I said, 'Bill Talley, shut up and hang on!'

"We went back down again very, very low between the bear and Joe. Then the bear was out of our view. The second pass made the bear turn and run to its cub. I swung over Joe again the third time and noticed the sow had picked up the cub and had started running up the Kerjulik River. I made another pass over the bear to make sure it wasn't going to change its direction, and the last I saw of the sow, it was probably 400 or 500 yards out in front of the cub running at full hilt.

"The biggest thing that I was thinking about the fourth time was how would I tell Carleen, Joe's wife, that Joe got ate up by a bear. If that bear, on the second pass, had continued on toward Joe, I had placed it in my mind that I was going to clip it with a float or a cross member. It was the only defense I had. I've never had an occasion to hit the ground or any object with a float while in flight. I didn't know what it would do. I'm sure it wouldn't do my float nor my flying speed any good; and if I'd hit that bear pretty solid (those bear probably weigh 700 or 800 pounds), I'm sure I'd have dented my float. I don't know if it would have knocked me out of the air, turned me sideways or what.

"After everything was said and done, Joe believed that the bear was going to get him. He firmly believes that the bear wouldn't have stopped if it hadn't been for the airplane. I wouldn't have left after watching Joe go over and pick up his rifle at the kill if it had been anybody else other than Joe Delia. I would have landed and made other arrangements to leave the moose meat and take Joe and the hunter back to King Salmon. Knowing Joe, he waved me on with the packboard and his rifle showing me that he had reached his rifle. I made several more passes and then left.

"I dropped off Bill and the meat at King Salmon and returned through deteriorating weather to pick up Joe. When I got there, Joe had everything down on the beach and was all ready to load up. We made a couple of passing comments about getting close to the brown bears. Joe asked, 'How close do you figure you were to the ground?'

"I said, 'I don't know, you were in a better position to tell than I was.'

"He said, 'You were down below the alders. The alders right there are only two or three feet high, so you were pretty close to the ground.'

"I never thought I'd rescue someone from a bear with an airplane; but then, I guess a bear never thought he'd get chased off a moose kill by a big, loud bird either. What a surprise that bear must have had!"

Secret Weapon

Some men have used unusual methods indeed to scare bears away, but none was ever so efficient, humiliating or humorous as the one employed by Ray Machen who was working on the Swanson River oil fields on the Kenai Moose Range in May 1975. Here is what happened in Ray's words:

"On this particular spring day when the ground was still covered in patches with snow, I spotted a foraging black bear across a swampy area a half-mile away. Several oil wells were scattered over three or four miles, and every day I'd go out from work, count the nesting geese, calving caribou and watch for the moose at Beaver Creek.

"The wind was blowing across my shoulders right toward the bear. I wanted to get his attention so I made a sound like a dying rabbit. The bear looked up and started ambling over my way. He had a long way to come, and I could tell he would come out on a little, low, dry hogback.

"I thought I'd ease over and try to head him off. I found an old windblown cottonwood stump. A sliver of the tree was leaning against the stump which was only 15 feet high. I waited on the ground for the bear, thinking I could go up the sliver to the top of the stump if need be. Pretty soon I could hear him popping some brush over the rim of the hogback and coming my way about 150 feet away. He didn't act like he had noticed me; he just kept on coming.

"He got about 70 or 80 feet away, and I started hollering at him and waving my arms so that he'd know that I was there. I was hoping he'd stand up, look at me, turn around and leave. 'Hey, this is me over here!' He didn't go for that. By the time he got about 40 feet away, I decided it was time to run up that slab. The slab, which was attached to the stump, was eight inches wide and one and a half inches thick. I shinnied up the sliver, and the bear came right up to it. When I got to the top, he was right at the bottom of it. I kicked it down.

"He started up the stump, but the dead bark kept falling down with his weight. I kept pulling bark off the stump and throwing it at him. I had three or four nuts and bolts in my coveralls, so I took them out of my pocket and pitched them at him. I ran out of ammunition, and he kind of lost interest; but he wouldn't go away. He walked off about 10 or 15 feet, sat down and scratched his ears. He never did growl once, just looked at me. He was probably 250 pounds, a full-grown adult bear.

"He kept walking to and from the tree whenever I tried to move. It had been at least an hour since I'd first spotted the bear, and I was tired. I figured, 'When he comes back over here, I'm going to try something new.' The next time he came over and started looking up the tree, I unzipped my pants and showered him down. I got him right between the eyes, full in the face.

"He took off running like a bat just as fast as he could go for 100 feet, stopped, sat up on his back legs, turned around and looked at me real funny and got down on all fours and eased off like nothing had ever happened. He saved his dignity."

More Old Eskimo Tales

It is astounding to think that man has been able to subdue or deter bears in some of the means he has employed. Stories of Eskimo ingenuity abound regarding his close calls with polar bears. One old Eskimo was surprised by a bear as the man cut the tusks from a slain walrus. The bear approached the man with mouth agape, and the Eskimo swung his ax at the bear, splitting its skull open.

Another Eskimo was attacked by a sow polar bear. She was quite a distance away, and the man produced a stone the size of a hen's egg and tied it to the end of his 70-foot dog whip. The man snapped the whip toward the bear which was a hundred yards away. The bear dropped dead. Upon examination the rock was found embedded in the bear's skull.

A common practice of the Eskimos was to kill bears by inserting sharp bone into blubber then allowing it to freeze. They baited the bear with these frozen chunks of blubber which thawed and killed the bears. Such a story was related in *ALASKA SPORTSMAN®*, January 1962.

"A thick and strong piece of whalebone, about four inches broad and two feet long, is bent double. While in this state, some pieces of blubber are wrapped around it, and the contrivance placed in the open air, where a low temperature renders it hard and compact; it is now ready for use. The natives being armed with bows and arrows, and taking the frozen mass with them, depart in quest of their prey, and, as soon as the animal is seen, one of them deliberately discharges an arrow at it. The bear, feeling the insult, pursues the party, now in full retreat; but, meeting with the frozen blubber dropped expressly for it, swallows the lump. The chase, the exercise of running, and the natural heat of the inside, soon cause the dissolution of the blubber; the whalebone, thus freed from encumbrance, springs back to its old position, and makes such havoc with his intestines that the beast discontinues the chase and soon dies."

The Eskimos are a hardy, courageous breed. And the men are not the only ones who have killed bears. One woman named Nayume was in her igloo at Akpatok Island prior to 1932. She was alone with her baby when a polar bear came calling. Her husband Akpek was hunting with Lowell Thomas, and no one could help the lady when Nanook came up the entrance to the domeshaped tunnel and thrust his head into the room itself.

She had just laid the child down to sleep and was placing a caribou skin blanket on the baby. The woman grabbed the blanket and covered the bear's head with it. The animal jammed its body in the narrow tunnel and was unable to turn around or to use its paws. The woman had only a knife for a weapon, but she hurriedly dug her way through the snow wall.

She took her infant outside with her and placed him on the snow. Then she turned her attention to the struggling bear and jabbed repeatedly with the knife into its side, hoping to hit the heart. After a time, the animal died.

One of the most unusual bear escapes and deaths I've heard about took place near Wainwright. A woman was walking along the beach across the bay from Wainwright. She was gathering coal when she saw a bear approaching. She searched her brain for some means of escape realizing that she couldn't outrun Nanook. It seemed futile, and as the bear shuffled up to her, it opened its mouth just inches from her. As a last resort, she shoved her fur-mittened fist down its throat and withdrew her arm before it could bite her, leaving the mitten in its throat. The bear instantly started choking, and forgot about its victim. Within minutes it lay suffocated at her feet.

It seems as though all kinds of bears have been faced with all kinds of weapons. Pete Williams suffered a close call and was called upon to use his knife when he faced a black bear. *The ALASKA SPORTSMAN®* in August 1949 carried a brief account of his experience: "Pete Williams of Marshall, on the Yukon River, has a breath-taking bear story, and eye-witnesses to corroborate it. Williams was hunting with some friends along the river when he shot a black bear close to its winter hide-out. 'Poke a stick in its den and see if there's any more,' one of his companions suggested. Williams did, and sure enough, out came another blackie. 'I'd put my gun down where I couldn't reach it,' said Williams, 'so I just jumped on its back and stuck it several times with my hunting knife. It fell over dead.' The stabbed bear weighed 250 pounds."

More than one bear has come to grips with a desperate man, and the September 1942 *The ALASKA SPORTSMAN®* told a most unusual story. A man "From the town of Nelson, far up in the wilds of British Columbia" tangled with a bear. Bert Bennett was a Canadian woodsman. "Bennett met the bear on a lonely forest trail near Nelson last May. Unarmed, he picked up a small boulder in a desperate attempt to protect himself. A lucky, solid blow with the rock crushed the bear's skull and killed it. Bennett went on his way, with the distinction of being probably the only modern man alive who has ever killed a bear in so primitive a manner."

Often the only weapon available to man was his fists. A strange account in *The ALASKA SPORTSMAN®* appeared in October 1943: "An Army sergeant, stationed in Alaska, had an encounter with a black bear which ended in an unexpected manner. The sergeant had gone for a swim in a river when a black bear spotted him, came out into the water, and started making passes at him. Because there wasn't much else to do, the soldier traded blow for blow with the bear, and caught him on the nose two or three times. A few smacks in the kisser sent the black bear back into the woods, while the soldier went to the station hospital for treatment of chest lacerations."

Joe Beaty had an encounter with a brown bear on his ranch, and the experience was out of the ordinary. He told me, "The brown bear I clubbed to death had his front foot in the trap and the trap chain was wrapped around a bunch of alders, so he was tied pretty hard and fast. I stretched him out with a rope tied to his hind leg and wrapped around the horn on my horse's saddle.

"I'd been haying. I'd been going up every day looking at this trap by a carcass; and I went over that morning. It had been raining, and I was going to wait for the hay to dry a little before raking it with a team of horses.

"I rode up there and I could see the trap was gone. I had a 60-

pound sea anchor on a cable to trace where the bear went. I saw him in the brush, but couldn't see how hard he was fastened. My rifle was at the house, and my only weapon was a machete; so I cut an alder club about the size of a baseball bat.

"I was using a large bear trap with about a 15-inch opening that weighed about 65 pounds. I lassoed his hind foot and stretched it tight, with my horse doing the pulling. The bear was spread out pretty good. I walked up behind him with the club and caved in his skull. He was about a six-foot, 500-pound bear."

Flares May Be An Answer

Amidst all the cries of high powered weapons and means of staving off a bear attack, it is uncommon to hear about a peaceful, harmless method of self-defense. In my probings I came across the name of R.W. Griffith. I contacted him, and he wove a very interesting theory about his experience with bears and highly recommended it because of its efficiency and harmlessness.

Griffith, a civil engineer who builds runways for the Federal Aviation Administration, spoke about using a flare gun and said, "There are many different methods used by Alaskan outdoorsmen to ward off an attacking bear. Some are effective and others are very marginal.

"Perhaps the most used deterrent against an attacking bear is a large caliber rifle or shotgun. Carrying such a weapon is cumbersome to the average person who has no intention of hunting. There are many recorded instances of people being mauled who were carrying a rifle, which leads one to suspect that perhaps a rifle is not all that effective.

"A rifle weighs eight pounds and to a backpacker this additional weight could represent many days of extra food. Also a rifle is always in the way and usually ends up being strapped to a packboard where it is of doubtful value.

"A large pistol is often carried by people venturing into the Alaskan wilds. One very often sees people carrying a rifle and a pistol. This type person is overreacting to a very remote possible attack by a bear. These people are usually cheechakos. They take their first paycheck and buy a big pistol and rifle because they actually believe that there is a bear behind every bush. Fortunately these people are not seen very far off the beaten path.

"A pistol may stop a bear and it may not. The average person is very inept with a pistol.

"Like the rifle, the pistol is difficult to carry. A pistol carried on your waist is a real pain in the rear when you are carrying a modern tubular pack frame. The metal frame of the packboard is forever banging against the pistol butt. One has a tendency to shift the pistol holster around so that the pack frame does not mar the pistol grips, then he finds out that his leg movement is hampered. Pistols usually end up in the bottom of the packsack where they are useless.

"I have walked thousands of miles through bear country in Alaska. On some of the longer trips I carried a rifle and on the shorter trips I carried a pistol. There have been several instances where I would have gladly traded my eight-pound rifle and scope for an eight-pound bag of oatmeal. I have been charged by bears twice and both instances were avoidable.

"My only loss so far is one chewed up Kelty pack frame and a day pack which was ripped to shreds. I believe that one will eventually have an encounter with a bear if he is exposed for a long period of time.

"There is absolutely no reason that a charging bear should be killed since 95% of the charges are merely feints. I have found that a 25mm flare gun will provide one with the necessary confidence to repel a charging bear. A flare discharged 10 feet in front of you on the ground lays out a lot of fire and smoke.

"I once discharged a flare gun at close range at two grizzlies feeding upon a moose. These two bears literally tore up the alders trying to escape the flare charge. At close range it is doubtful that a bear would keep advancing after a flare has been discharged into its fur.

"A flare gun with three charges weighs slightly less than one and a quarter pounds and can easily be carried like a pistol about the waist. I keep my flare gun at my waist at all times and at night when I sleep, I very carefully lay the flare pistol next to my sleeping bag. A flare discharged at night on the ground lights up the entire camp area which is a decided advantage."

As remarkable as they sound, these unusual methods of killing and deterring bears seem to work. Most raise the question of efficiency and workability; but they worked for those who lived to tell about them.   □

YOU DO A LOT
OF THINKING

"When I first heard the bear charging, I turned and saw him only a few seconds before he grabbed me. The only thought I had at first was, 'God, please don't let him kill me.' " (Creig Sharp, mauling victim, taped interview)

"I don't think I ever went into shock, but of course, I cried a bit. I mainly thought about how I would handle the situation. Was he mauled beyond recognition or was he even alive? I was prepared for the worst." (Mrs. Creig Sharp, wife of Creig Sharp, taped interview)

At first the sow just sat on the far stream bank with her cubs. She was a picture of brute strength and beauty. She got up and paced along the bank, her muscles rippling under her chocolate-brown coat. She stood up a couple of times on her hind legs and sifted the air with that rubbery, black nose of hers. The hair on her neck stood up; she dropped to all fours; and then she came. Seven hundred pounds of bone-chilling fury roared across the gravel bar. Her head was slung low, ears pinned back, eyes red, teeth chomping and froth flying.

Will she stop? What is it like to be mauled? Will she kill me? Should I fight to the finish or play dead?

What goes through a person's mind when a bear is ripping and chewing him? What are the thoughts of his rescuer? And how is a loved one affected?

These are many questions that I've wondered about. Often a mauling victim tells his story about the actual attack but doesn't really go into what his thoughts were at the time or his recuperatory experience. Richard Bennett was attacked by a sow grizzly with cubs on a stream, and he told *ALASKA*® magazine in October 1974: "I didn't think she'd keep coming, but she never stopped. I could hear my own skull being raked like an animal rakes a rock with its teeth. I got past the point of terror and started figuring how to survive."

It's interesting to note the thoughts different people had when they were attacked. Forest Young had considerable experience with bears and, even though he saw two grizzlies a hundred yards away, he didn't expect them to attack. And even after one mounted an all-out charge, he still believed it was only a bluff. If he'd climbed a tree when the bear first charged, he'd surely have escaped.

Cynthia Dusel-Bacon was concerned that she do the right thing when she saw the black bear that attacked her. She was relieved that it was "only a black bear" and, assuming that it would leave if she shouted, Cynthia clapped her hands and told it to go away. Once the bear knocked her down and began dragging her toward the brush, she determined to live . . . but after she finally managed to radio for help and her second arm was mangled, she knew she had done all she could to save herself and her only hope lay in the hands of others.

Cynthia had thought about her husband of less than six months. Al Thompson also thought of his spouse. He rallied himself with fresh confidence and determination as he remembered his wife Joyce who said later, "As Al was being carried by the bear, he thought, 'What a hell of a way to die,' then he thought of me, faced with the shock of me having a dead husband, miles from anywhere or anyone, and having to hike out of there alone. He became very angry and a strong fight for survival overcame him. Al realized his only chance was to convince the bear he was dead."

Another man who was severely mauled and called upon thoughts of his loved ones was Dan Ludington. In October 1949 Dan had gone in search of a grizzly that had been scrounging for food around human habitations in the neighborhood of his Alaska Range Summit Lake Lodge. The berry crop had been bad that year, and food was scarce. The bear surprised Dan along a ridge in the falling snow. She knocked him down, and as she tore at him, he kicked and screamed at her. He kept thinking that it was a lousy way to die. He thought of his pregnant wife and his kids. The more he thought about them, the harder he kicked. Eventually he was able to get in a killing shot and stumble to the highway where he was picked up by a passing trucker friend.

When Creig Sharp was attacked his first thought was, "God, please don't let him kill me." Creig told me later, "Then my thoughts changed to fighting him. As the bear flipped me over on my back, I didn't want him to bite me in the face or privates, and when he started to, I stuck my rifle in his mouth; and he tried to pull it away.

"He bit the stock and tore the sling off it. I wouldn't let go of the gun. I must have had a death grip on it. Then he started to run down the hill and I knew I didn't want him to come back so I sat up and shot him in the rump.

"Gary (Grinde, who was with Creig) told me right after it happened that at first he was afraid to shoot for fear of hitting me. Then when he started shooting, he was sure the first shot had struck me in the head. He had nightmares for several days after the accident, all pertaining to the fact that he had killed me with that first shot. Had he not fired at the bear I surely would be dead now."

Creig Sharp credits Gary Grinde for rendering him life saving first aid also. "Gary had a thorough knowledge of first-aid training that he obtained in the Army. I'm sure that if he hadn't had it, I would have died in the mountains. He was able to slow the bleeding of the bear bites and he also left my boots on so the bleeding and swelling on my right foot and leg was minimal.

"When we arrived at the cabin, he dressed my wounds with pressure bandages and kept me warm by placing me in a goose down sleeping bag. Both Gary and I had extensive combat experiences in Vietnam; Gary for three years, part of the time as a corpsman and the rest of the time as a combat squad leader. I was a member of the Underwater Demolition's/Seal Team, an unconventional warfare group.

"I feel that with this experience we remained level-headed enough to get out of the mountains alive, and attribute this to our survival of the initial bear attack."

When Ron Cole was mauled on Lake Creek by the sow and boar brown bear, it was his wife who went for help. Ron managed to get to his cabin and call for Darci who was inside doing her spring house cleaning; and she responded to his plea for help. *ALASKA*®

magazine printed the Coles' story in June 1976. Darci related her thoughts, "When I saw his face, I screamed. And I felt instant panic. I ran down to Ron, telling myself, 'No, you can't panic,' and all the time I'm calculating what I have to do. I really didn't know what had happened, but I knew he had to have a doctor and that I would have to go down to the lodge before I could reach anybody.

"When Ron asked me how bad it was, he recalls I said, 'You need a couple of stitches.'

"He told me a couple of bears had gotten him and I didn't really think I should ask any more questions right then. I told him I had to get him into the house, up to the cabin. Ron said, 'Well, I can't walk any more.' And I told him I would carry him because I wasn't going to leave him out there.

"He said he wanted some water first. I could tell that he really couldn't drink water but I figured I had better get him the water. So I ran up to the cabin and I got a big thing of water and I started to run out again when I thought of something.

"When you first walk into our cabin, you enter the kitchen. Then you go down two steps into the living room and there is a mirror hanging right there, and I knew I would have to take him past the mirror and lay him on the couch. I took the mirror down and hid it under the couch because I was afraid that if he saw himself he would panic.

"I went back down the hill and gave him the water which he couldn't swallow. I got him up on his feet then pulled and tugged him up the rest of the hill. I noticed that his bleeding had practically stopped and knew no arteries had been cut. I got him into the cabin and laid him on the couch. When somebody is in shock I had heard that you should prop their feet up and cover them. But I couldn't prop up his feet because if he lay down flat he couldn't breathe, so I propped up his head and covered him up."

For the seriously mauled victim time is of the essence. Some people have survived for several hours with near fatal injuries and pulled through. Others have had the good fortune to be accessible to immediate medical attention because they were close enough to a major roadway or a partner could get them to a hospital by such means as a small plane or helicopter. Such was the case with Ron.

Darci ran for Lake Creek Lodge three miles downstream from their cabin. She had to cross two streams on the way. She ran up the beach towards the lodge where they had a radiophone; ". . . when I hit the beach I started screaming for them to call a helicopter with a paramedic quick. They had gotten the message through by the time I reached the lodge door."

First Lt. James C. Woolworth piloted an HH-3E helicopter the day Darci's emergency message crackled across the airways. I contacted him in Florida, and he responded with a letter explaining his crew's part in the Ron Cole rescue.

"We were nearing the end of a two-hour training flight at Elmendorf Air Force Base when we were notified by the Rescue Coordination Center of a bear mauling at Lake Creek. We had an hour and one half of fuel left . . . enough to fly to Lake Creek and back providing we didn't have to search when we got there. We didn't know how bad the mauling was but we had to assume the worst so we picked up a flight surgeon at the Elmendorf Hospital Helipad and proceeded direct without refueling.

"We landed on a sand bar at Lake Creek Lodge where Dulcina Cole boarded our aircraft to direct us upstream to Ron's cabin. She was amazingly well composed considering what she had just been through. She had run miles through the woods to reach the lodge where she could radio Anchorage. We flew up Lake Creek and eventually located the cabin on top of a hill surrounded by tall trees. We landed in the only available spot, a rock bar on the creek, and shut down to conserve fuel.

"Our flight surgeon, along with TSgt. Ewton, TSgt. Mulhall and Dulcina then made their way across the creek and up to the cabin with medical equipment and a Stokes litter. It was about 30 minutes before TSgt. Ewton came back and said Cole was in bad shape and the doctor didn't want to chance bringing him down the steep embankment in the litter.

"We decided on a rescue hoist recovery and a few minutes later we were in a hover over the trees near the cabin. We made several attempts to lift Cole off the ground but the litter would start spinning and a blanket protecting Cole's severely lacerated face kept blowing off and exposing Cole to the severe force of our rotor downwash. The litter eventually stabilized and with Cole's face protected we hoisted him into the helicopter. We then recovered the rest of our crew and Dulcina and returned to Anchorage.

"When I first saw Cole lying in the litter in the back of the helicopter, I was concerned for his life. He was covered with blankets with only his head exposed. His facial features were indistinguishable because of dried blood from the massive amount of bleeding. It appeared as if he had lost one eye. Our flight surgeon assured us that his condition was stable and he would eventually recover.

"Since that mission I have had one other mission involving a bear mauling. We recovered the body of a man who was killed when he was struck once in the head by a wounded black bear. Ron Cole had obviously taken more than one blow during his encounter and he survived.

"I talked with Ron several months after the incident during his recovery and he confided that while he was lying at his cabin before our chopper arrived, he had every intention of shooting himself but due to severe shock he couldn't move a muscle to reach his rifle."

Ron Cole was not the first bear mauling victim to want to die. Some hoped the bear would finish the job quickly. Others contemplated suicide. It seems that they felt they were so far gone that their chances were hopeless; they didn't want their loved ones to see them in that condition or they couldn't stand the pain. Whatever the reason, some men have actually tried to finish the job which the bear started.

After the grizzly's initial attack on Forest H. Young, Jr., he was convinced he was going to die. He didn't know how long he would have to await rescue or even if his partner would find him. The pain was intense. Somehow he managed to retrieve his small jackknife from his pocket, open it and slash his left wrist. He cut deeply hoping to cut the main artery, but there was no blood. He saw tendons after the third cut, and decided he didn't want to go through life crippled should he survive; so he gave up on the wrist.

Forest then decided to try for the jugular vein. It was all he could do to find his pulse. He was so tired he had to stop to rest. As Young resumed the second time, his partner called from a distance, giving Forest new hope.

Henry Knackstedt and Knut Peterson shared similar experiences as Young's. After the angry sow left Knackstedt lying in a pool of his own blood, he regained consciousness, breathing was difficult and the pain excruciating. Henry wasn't sure whether the bear was present or not; but at that point he didn't much care.

Knut Peterson felt the same way. He had had all a man can take when he discovered that the bear had left him. His condition was such that he figured it didn't matter anyway; but since he still had life in him, he decided to try to make it to his friend's cabin. Ole was home and helped Knut into his cabin and to the hospital.

One mauling victim who was beyond medical help was King D. Thurmond. His Kenai Peninsula travels took Thurmond from Seward to the Chickaloon Flats. The title page of his diary reads, "King D. Thurmond, Seward, Alaska, May 14, 1914." The other entries in his diary indicate that he spent the summer of 1914 working on his boat, making a forge, planting a garden, shooting both a brown and a black bear, prospecting, cutting wood and visiting. The last entry was made Saturday, July 25, 1914, and stated, "Came to Flat Cabin."

King wrote a note on regular sized paper and dated July 26, 1914, which read, "To whom it may concern, this camp outfit belongs to the undersigned. Please do not take it and disapoint [sic] the owner. King D. Thurmond."

As far as we know, that was the last thing he wrote prior to being mauled by a bear.

After the bear had mauled Thurmond, he realized he was too far from immediate medical attention, his pain was more than he could endure, and he chose to end his suffering.

Nobody knows when Thurmond was mauled, but sometime after the first of January, 1915, John F. Rowell and George R. Ament discovered the grisly remains of Thurmond. They notified authorities in Seward, and United States Commissioner M.J. Conroy appointed James Kalles as guardian of Thurmond's estate with authority to collect personal property and to satisfy the deceased's debts.

Rowell and Ament assisted Kalles in his task, and upon its completion Kalles wrote the commissioner a letter, part of which is quoted below:

Kenai River, Alaska
March 12, 1915

Hon. M.J. Conroy, U.S. Commissioner Seward Ak.
Dear Sir:

Having just returned from the Chickaloon River where with the assistance of John F. Rowell and George R. Ament I cremated the remains of King Thurman [sic] who was found dead in his cabin by Rowell a few weeks ago I herewith submit my report with full details concerning the manner and causes of death of the deceased.

Thurman [sic], as his clothing and marks on the body showed had been attacked by a brown bear a short distance from his cabin and was unarmed at the time. There were teeth and claw marks in the left thigh, the right calf, right shoulder and the back and a bullet hole in the left temple, his colt revolver lay on his breast and the position of the body and condition of the right shoulder showed plainly that he fired the shot with his left hand.

It is quite evident that finding his condition hopeless he killed himself rather than suffer and his cabin being situated in an isolated spot thirty miles from the nearest camp and unknown to any of the prospectors or trappers here about, he knew that to get help was out of the question.

His rifle stood in a corner of the cabin, the magazine was full and the Colt found on the deceased's breast contained five cartriges [sic] and one empty shell under the hammer. His water pale [sic] was missing and not to be found so that it may be that he was after water when attacked.

The body was badly decomposed and although we cut the clothing from it, could find no papers or any description.

In cremating the remains we filled the cabin with dry wood and set fire to it, after it burned for three hours we went back, knocked down the walls and burned the whole thing to the ground.

Interestingly enough the men who left King Thurmond's remains behind discovered the note telling of his camp outfit which he'd dated July 26, 1914. But sometime between his writing that note and his death he had printed the following note on the same paper in capital letters and in two columns: "Have ben [sic] tore up by a brown bear. No show to get out. Goodby. I'm sane but have to sufering [sic] the . . . of death."

And so, beyond hope, King D. Thurmond ended his mortal life.

I asked several people their reaction to the mauling of a friend or loved one. At the time of Creig Sharp's mauling his bride-to-be, Kathy Tebow, was completing plans for their upcoming wedding. When I first heard of Creig's mauling, I spoke with Kathy's brother Stan, who was in one of my classes. I then contacted Kathy who had also been a student of mine, and she made arrangements for me to talk with her and Creig.

Kathy was crowned Miss Alaska on March 28, 1976, and during her next year in that capacity she met, was courted by and became engaged to Chief Petty Officer Creig Sharp of the United States Navy. Creig had planned a hunt for April, two weeks preceding their May 14, 1977, wedding date. On April 28 Kathy received news that Creig had been mauled.

She told me later, "I knew he was a very good hunter. Something must have gone terribly wrong. I don't think I ever went into shock, but of course, I cried a bit. I mainly thought about how I would handle the situation. Was he mauled beyond recognition or was he even alive? I was prepared for the worst.

"The phone rang and I finally found out that Creig was in Kodiak and doing fine.

"He had two bites on his left thigh and a broken right ankle and leg. Thank God he was alive!

"A Coast Guard airplane flew Creig in from Kodiak to the MAC terminal on base outside of Anchorage. My father and I drove out to meet the plane and I rode in the ambulance with Creig to Elmendorf Air Force Base Hospital. I'll never forget what he looked like when I got in the ambulance. He was extremely pale and had a four days' growth of beard on his face. He was strapped on the stretcher and wrapped in a sleeping bag. All I could do was cry and put my arms around him.

"Creig was admitted at the hospital and prepared for surgery that night. I stayed and waited to hear the results. The doctor came out later and told me Creig's right ankle had a bullet wound but no one was sure how it happened at that time. I went into the recovery room to see Creig after the surgery and he was still under sedation. I sat with him awhile and then got up, kissed him on the forehead and drove home where I knew a sleepless night awaited me.

"In the days that followed, we decided to keep our May 14 wedding date. Now we are Mr. and Mrs. Creig M. Sharp and we've had some rough times, but have managed to keep our sense of humor. We've been through an awful lot for this first part of our marriage. It's certainly different to spend the first part of your married life sitting next to your husband's hospital bed knowing it will take many months for him to recover completely. Ours has been a very unique situation and I know we will have a very interesting and enjoyable life together."

Creig told me, "I was in the hospital for four months. During that time I went to the operating room 23 times. They had to pack the bullet hole in my right foot with five and a half yards of two-inch gauze packing and plaster cast my leg every other day. It was a very slow healing process as the hole had to heal from the inside out. They were very concerned about infection setting in.

"When I was admitted to the hospital the doctors felt they would have to amputate my right leg below the knee, and I had constant fear that this would happen. My foot was completely numb and the swelling was tremendous. They decided to wait at least three days and check it for feeling.

"Thank God some feeling returned and no infection started. They left my leg on and it is fine now. I am able to walk with only a slight limp. In a few more months it should be back to normal.

"The bear had bitten my left upper thigh several times and the doctors had sewn the bites up with wire sutures. They were in for two weeks and when they were removed, I was able to move my leg, and the doctors kept me on i.v. for 33 days. I did get an infection in the bites after two months of hospitalization. It lasted about two weeks and wasn't very serious."

Hospitalization and the healing process take time. Knut Peterson was told by his attending doctors and nurses that he was the most torn up man they'd ever worked on that survived. His recuperation, like most, was extremely painful.

Knut said the worst suffering of all was four months of intense headaches. He was given two pain killers every four hours, which worked for two hours, then he suffered two hours of pain. Knut was so impressed and thankful for the tender loving care he received from the hospital personnel that he said he was determined to live.

Having a positive medical staff that cares works wonders on a patient's healing, both physically and mentally. And having the support of spouses and other loved ones is a tremendous catalyst for the mauling victim's healing and eventual recovery.

Cynthia Dusel-Bacon wrote that "I was amazed by the way my husband dealt with the sudden change in our marriage. All at once he went from being a bridegroom of several months to a real husband, called upon to give his maximum support. I doubt I'll ever see anything as beautiful as he looked to me as he came down the aisle of the plane that brought me to San Francisco. For at least an hour, while I was being mauled, I never thought I'd see Charlie, or any other human being again."

Another person who thought about his spouse was Al Thompson.

I had heard a lot about the game warden Al Thompson and the terrific beating he had taken from the brown bear when he punched it in the face with his fists. I expected to see all kinds of scars when he brought his story by our home. I welcomed him in and noticed right away that he had a bubbling smile, ruddy complexion and a cheerfulness about him. I thought, "This guy couldn't have been mauled. He doesn't have any scars!" But when Pam asked for his coat and hat, I discovered I'd been wrong.

Scar tissue covered his upper left forehead, and a good part of the top left side of his head was hairless. It didn't bother Al in the least, and we treated it in the same manner.

Al told me, "Joyce saved my life by her quick action. She had remarkable courage. Four doctors worked on me. Dr. Joe Sangster of Soldotna Hospital is the surgeon that did the most work (not only a good doctor but also a good friend, a fine man and a really good outdoorsman). I couldn't have been treated better. All the staff was great.

"My oil was a little low on the dipstick, and I was starting to knock but they gave me a good tune up and I'm doing okay now. I have adjusted to my mauling pretty good. It took six months to get back to normal (as good as I got), about one year to completely recover. Wounds always give some problem, but the doctor did a remarkable job on me; and I learned to live with the wound problems. I feel that I've lost one third of my stamina since the mauling. I used to be able to hike all day and stay up 22 hours without tiring, but I can't do that anymore."

I asked Al if he had any reservations about going into bear country or any advice for a mauling victim, and he replied, "I approach my wilderness outings no different than I did. I don't worry about anything. Each day is a free one. I had no nightmares after the first few weeks. I won't ever try bluffing any bears off again. I'll shoot while I have the chance.

"Never give up. It would have been easy to give up and pass out after the attack. If you arc handicapped a little, you just have to try harder. I experienced no fear during the attack; I had no time — I was too busy staying alive. Fear came afterward when I really realized what could have happened."

Concern for the victim is always great when we first hear about a mauling. But as time goes on we often forget and/or assume "the guy's gonna make it, he's doin' fine." We often fail to realize the loss of use of certain body functions the victim has suffered. Sometimes it is a minor thing like the loss of coordination in a finger (Al Johnson jokingly told me that one or two of his fingers flopped down as he shot a basketball and seriously affected his shooting ability on the court). But frequently it is much greater like the loss of sight in one eye or as in Al Thompson's case, the loss of one third of his stamina. That is a tremendous loss.

Often adjustment is a lifelong ordeal. After Alexie Pitka was mauled on the Yukon in 1950, left faceless, crawled one-half mile to his boat during the next 55 hours and spent months in the hospital before returning to his home, he questioned his condition and thought maybe he would have been better off dead.

One of the greatest adjustments known to man is the adjustment that one makes with the loss of limb. When Cynthia Dusel-Bacon was in the Stanford University Medical Hospital, she developed a high fever, and her life was in jeopardy. She could keep the one arm the doctors were trying to save and chance losing her life; or she could undergo amputation to improve her chances of survival. The limb came off.

Cynthia underwent excruciating physical pain during and after

ALASKA BEAR TALES

the mauling, which will in all likelihood be forgotten in its extremity with time; but the mental anguish she suffered will remain with her forever. Lest you consider a mauling something slight, please consider very carefully the words she wrote me. "Every day of the six weeks I was in the hospital seemed to drag by. I was able to sleep very little at night. Every six hours I was given a large dose of morphine prior to dressing changes. During those periods I had to instruct the nurses just how to hold my badly torn and tenuously attached right arm so that it wouldn't fall off. I never really felt that my arm would be the same. This made it easier for me when it, too, had to be amputated.

"The hardest adjustment I had to make after I left the hospital was to suddenly be different from everyone I came across. There was no way I could hide or forget my disability. Every time I saw a young woman, walking around with two arms, I remembered my old self, and my beautiful and strong, long arms.

"My emotional state was like a roller coaster. Only my husband was, and still is, aware of my periods of deep depression and sadness. Now the span of time between my up and down moments is much greater. I don't think I'll ever completely get over being without arms. Most people are amazed by my quick rehabilitation and adjustment. Funny how one can deal with something when one has no choice.

"I have managed to devise a way to do most things for myself, using either my hooks (such as driving, eating, writing, typing, putting on make-up, or turning pages) or my feet (cooking, washing dishes, opening doors, or rolling down windows). In many activities I use a combination of hooks, feet, and teeth. One year after my accident I can cope with things when my husband is gone on trips. It's the emotional, not the practical adjustment that's the hardest."

At a time when a man's world comes tumbling down on him, the reassurance, care and love of his fellowman makes all the difference. Interestingly enough when Creig Sharp and Al Johnson were mauled, their fiancees came to their bedsides. Kathy Tebow and Cleta Robbins cared for and loved their men back to health and recovery.

I talked with Cleta Johnson, and she told me her feelings and experience during the critical days of Al's hospitalization. She was aghast when she saw Al in the hospital. "He looked awful, just terrible. When I first saw Al, I even asked the nurse if that was him. Ninety percent of his face was covered with bandages and large blood blisters. He had all these scratches from either being pulled out of the tree or from being pushed into the brush. There were these tiny little scratches all over his skin.

"I was there four days and went back Sunday; and the little scabs had already come off. Some of the swelling had gone down. He could see out of his right eye by the day I left.

"They were worried whether he was going to lose the vision in his left eye. They were pretty sure his right eye was going to be all right. It was so bloodshot that all you could see was the pupil.

"They never did let me stay in the room with him when they changed his bandages, which was fine with me. He had several packs on his elbow, and he had a tube into the elbow to let it drain; it seemed like it was just running out. Two i.v.s infiltrated into his hands and feet."

When Cleta first learned of Al's mauling, the state trooper told her he had hopes that Al would make it. She told me, "That didn't give me much to go on. He said he would call someone to have them be with me, but I said no, I could call. I called June Johnson, my friend in Oceanview, and I told her I really felt like I didn't need anybody, so she said she'd pray.

"Then I called Jim Gourley, who is kind of a grandpa to us. He came right over. He prayed with me — he's a real genuine Christian; when he talks to God, it's like he just spoke with Him. After he prayed, a confidence came over me. It seemed like all of a sudden I could think; but I didn't sleep that night."

Cleta left her bank job and went to McKinley Park to get Al's car and then on to Fairbanks to see him. She said, "The next morning I remember brushing his teeth. All they had given him was ice chips. There were blood clots all through his teeth; and he had two huge ones about eight or nine inches long.

"I asked the nurse where he got all this blood in his mouth. She had no idea. His mouth was a mass of blood. I cleaned off his tongue with a toothbrush, and he said that was the best thing that had ever happened to him at the time because it felt like his tongue was about four inches big.

"I read to him quite a bit, the whole book of John from the Bible; but he doesn't remember. The Community Church of God [now Oceanview] and the Jewel Lake Nazarene Church had established prayer chains. Many people felt Al's rapid healing was miraculous, his scabs just seemed to pop off.

"A couple of nurses talked with me about my faith. They stopped me and asked me what faith I was and what church I attended. They wanted to know if I really loved him, and I remember saying, 'Sure, I really think I do.'

"But they said, 'Well, you're smiling and you're so happy all the time. Most people, if they really love somebody, aren't happy when their loved one is hurt.'

"I said, 'I have confidence that the Lord is going to take care of him.'

"And they said, 'That's probably the difference between you and most.' " □

WHAT THE
DOCTORS SAY

"*I looked for spurting blood which would indicate bleeding from an artery . . . I had sewn large game bags from unbleached muslin . . . I tore the bags into long strips to use for bandages which were quickly soaked with blood. His left arm was badly chewed, and the pain was very severe. He instructed me to take my knife and cut off the shredded piece of flesh that was hanging from the largest wound. There appeared to be a great deal of muscle and nerve damage . . . All I could do was to squeeze a tube of first-aid cream on the wounds as far as it would go and wrap up his arm. I had placed some strong tea in the fire and gave it to him to drink, along with some aspirins.*" (Joyce Thompson, wife-rescuer of maulee)

"*He removed his jacket and shirt, bent over and pushed his scalp back over his head and tied his shirt around his head to hold it. Then with much pain, because the initial shock was wearing off, he put his jacket back on, picked up his rifle, and headed the mile and a half down the mountain to the highway.*" (Don Hess, son of mauling victim, "We Weren't Afraid of Bears," ALASKA® magazine, August 1970)

"*Dangerously weak, blood gushing from his wounds, Dahl managed somehow to crawl back to his skiff, launch it and paddle with one arm back to his homestead.*" (Niska Elwell, "At Your Peril," The ALASKA SPORTSMAN®, August 1951)

When I hear about a bear-man confrontation, I am always curious as to the severity of the injuries. So much of the victim's well-being is contingent upon the nature of his injuries and the availability of medical attention.

In the past many mauling victims had little opportunity for immediate evacuation to a medical facility; they were at the mercy of whatever help they could get in the bush. They were often miles from the proper medical help with only a slow or rough means of travel to take them to help. In such cases the victim's treatment in the field was of ultimate importance to assure his recovery.

Nowadays most mauling victims can be airlifted to help within hours of the mauling, thus improving their chances for survival and recovery. It is still crucial to administer the best available first aid.

I've wondered about the types of injuries a man normally incurs in a bear mauling. I also wanted to know 1) the amount of injuries a man could receive and still live and 2) the first aid and medical attention he would need to survive. I pursued the subject while researching the mauling of Dick Jensen. Dick was treated by a cannery doctor in Naknek after his bout with the sow, and later Jensen was attended by a team of five medical specialists, two of whom were Dr. Milo Fritz and Dr. Donald Addington. Both doctors agreed to comment on medical aspects of mauling victims.

I queried Dr. Addington about the types of injuries inflicted by a bear, the amount a person could withstand and the medical treatment he would need. Dr. Addington replied with the following letter:

3 July 1977

Dear Mr. Kaniut:

Re: Your letter of 21 April 1977

I read your letter with a great deal of interest and I will try to answer your questions.

Basically, the type of wound sustained is usually a rip made by the bear claw, tearing into anything which happens to be in the way. The level of injury is dependent on what is hit. If it happens to be a vital organ, then the victim is in serious trouble. If the wound does not involve a vital organ the victim can usually get to medical help.

If the victim is mauled, i.e., where the bear actually "squeezes" the victim, in all likelihood he or she will never make the trip to the emergency medical facility. This type of crushing wound is the most severe, encompassing broken limbs and organs.

The emergency treatment is in reality no different from that of most other areas of emergency medical treatment, i.e., the ABC's of emergency care:

A. Airways — Secure and open airway;

B. Breathing — make the person breathe. Either spontaneously or by mouth-to-mouth;

C. Cardiac — Keep the heart beating, by itself or by external cardiac massage;

D. Treatment — Care of the specific wounds.

In Mr. Jensen's case, the airway was extremely important in that he sustained a laceration of his trachea in addition to his other wounds.

In all honesty, I have treated only about three or four victims of bear attacks and then mostly of lacerations of varying degrees of seriousness. Some have been extensive. As to the initial reaction to a bear attack victim . . . surprise, since considering the amount of people foraging about in the wild there are really very few cases of attacks. Most of these occur when the victim places himself between the mother and her cub as you well know.

I hope that this information will be of some help to you. If I can be of any further service, please don't hesitate to contact me.

Cordially,
Donald B. Addington, M.D.

I found myself wondering why some maulees live and others die. I wanted to know why, when two victims received essentially the same type of injuries, one died and the other lived. I wrote Dr. Milo Fritz of Anchor Point, and he invited our family to his residence for an interview. Much of our conversation centered on Dick Jensen and his treatment, but Dr. Fritz also made some timely comments on the will to live and the modernization of medical technology. I am indebted to Dr. Fritz for his courtesy in allowing me his time and comments.

"Dick Jensen has been a friend of mine for many years, ever since I first learned to fly in 1951; and I received many helpful suggestions and much help from Dick through our relationship in King Salmon over those years.

"I was called early in the morning July 21, 1973, by the cannery doctor down in Naknek saying that Dick — I could not hear the last name, connection not being the best — had something wrong with his eye and that he had been clawed by a bear.

"Having been mixed up with things like this before, the first thing I did was to alert the people I would possibly need to have on hand at the hospital, not after the patient got there and these people began their day's routine or scheduled chores, but *right now.*

"I called up Don Addington, a plastic surgeon; John Smith, an orthopedic surgeon; Dr. Chei Mei Chao, an anesthesiologist; and Jack Smith, who's a younger chap in my line of work and whose training is more intensive and more recent than mine. I very anxiously wanted him to consult with me and took off for Anchorage International Airport in time to pick up Dick. The ambulance got there when I did, and meanwhile I'd also alerted the tower so I wouldn't get shot by the guards if I dared to go through the gates.

"Everything went like clockwork. We went in; the airplane taxied up. We opened up the ambulance and shoved Dick in. The doctor who had come along with him climbed in too. Dick was breathing through a little slit of a wound in his neck. Most of the damage had been done across his throat. He had some marks on his shoulder (possible fracture) and on his fingers.

"Having mobilized the team, one is prepared as he can be. One should always remember the O.R. (operating room) crews and the hospital admitting office.

"When I got out of medical school, I would have had to do it all myself. But now we have people who specialize in the different fields of medicine and surgery. John Smith, all he does is fix people's bones. All that Jack Smith does, as much as possible, is work with the ears, throat and nose. Addington tries to make people look respectable.

"There was no such thing as an anesthesiologist in the olden days. But here we had a woman doctor, Dr. Chao, who's absolutely terrific — she just plays on that person's vital signs, so to speak, the way an organist plays a concerto or a fugue — monitoring heart rate, blood pressure, respiratory rate, etc. The patient is plugged in so his heartbeat and his respiration can be seen by all in the operating room. Blood gases are analyzed to see that he gets enough oxygen.

"It so happened that Smith, the orthopedist, wasn't needed at all because there was no fracture; but he sutured the shoulder and hand wounds.

"I alerted the surgical crews; I said, 'Look, we've got a patient coming in with a badly injured eye; he's been mauled by a bear. He will have other injuries too.'

"When we got to the hospital, we started an intravenous flow of sugar and salt solution right away. I immediately cut the stitches on his throat (if the doctor had put in one more stitch, Dick would have died of suffocation). When I opened up the wound, the front half of his upper windpipe and the cricoid bone underneath his Adam's apple had been torn loose, all but just a little sliver of soft tissue holding it there. A neophyte might have cut that off and thrown it away; but I've been in this work a long time and save everything. If the tissue dies, it will be sloughed. If it lives as it did here, the airway or windpipe will heal.

"When Smith came, I said, 'I'll assist you now.' He's younger. He's had more extensive experience and more recent training than I. The two of us patched up what was left of the important cricoid bone. Below the upper three tracheal rings, like signet rings, which makes the windpipe flexible, had been torn loose. We put a tracheotomy tube through the fourth tracheal ring. We tied it around the patient's neck with ribbons to secure it. He breathed through that easily and his color improved. Every once in a while the anesthetist would say, 'Would you suction him out; a little blood has gotten down there.'

"When he stabilized, because he'd been so brave, having had only a quarter-grain shot of morphine since four o'clock in the morning and this was maybe eight, nine or ten o'clock (when the airway was clear and the tracheotomy in place), we put him to sleep and then continued the repair work without hurting him.

"Every minute anesthesia is prolonged, the danger of complications increases. So here we had the orthopedist, poor Addington trying to work between Smith and me, and I was helping Smith. Our patient spent as little time in the operating room as it was possible to spend and get the job done. Blood for transfusion was ready too. That's another difference between now and 40 years ago.

"I might have saved him 40 years ago without help because it happened that the main thing was the airway; and I'd already laid that open. He was pink and the oxygen carrying ability of the blood was unimpaired as soon as I laid open the upper part of the trachea by opening up the wound. We could look right down into his lungs through his windpipe below the vocal cords.

"In case of cardiac arrest, we were all trained and know what to do. I was trained to make a slit in the fourth interspace between the ribs and spread it and massage the heart by hand. But now we do cardiac massage through a closed chest. A defibrillator, an electric device with electrodes, is also available. A controlled shock is given the heart to restart it beating or correct its rhythm.

"We have two excellent vascular surgeons and a cardiac surgeon in Anchorage. If anything had made us suspicious that all was not well with his heart, we'd have called one of them in.

"Dick's big problem was his airway — no shock, no extensive blood loss. He was young, in good shape, and our problem was well localized.

"This is the fourth bear case I've had experience with, and the most recent. If his airway had been okay, it would have been Addington's job alone to sew him up so he'd look respectable.

"This was a real emergency; and we were all ready for it. There's nothing we couldn't have done for him. He did not have time to go into shock.

"I wasn't at the cannery when they brought Dick in. I didn't have the equipment that the poor doctor had at hand which was probably nothing. It's very easy to criticize when surrounded by a galaxy of all the specialists, the best in Alaska, with the best equipment, and with a forewarning of several hours versus a doctor who's jerked out of bed in the wee small hours of a summer day to face a patient spurting blood out of a hole in his neck and only a handful of old instruments to work with. The doctor at the cannery stopped the bleeding that could easily have killed Dick, and left enough airway for survival.

"I think the doctor's caring and easing Dick so that he could breathe through this little slit that he left in his neck was probably instrumental in saving his life. How many more minutes could he have gone? I don't know. But because I was specifically trained, I realized those stitches had to be cut and the neck laid open down to the breathing hole and then reconstruct what was left into what we hoped would be a functional airway. We were lucky. His wounds healed and he soon had his breathing tube removed.

"Jensen is an indomitable sort of man. He threw himself between the charging bear and his wife. Could one do anything braver than that? 'I say unto you, nothing is greater than a man giving up his life for another.' He had many troubles, and he surmounted them all. When we said, 'This is going to hurt and we can't put you to sleep,' he croaked, 'Go ahead and do what has to be done.'

"There was no flinching or groaning or complaining. I infiltrated the area with local anesthetic to ease the pain further; and he had the *will* to live. I've seen people that I've felt in my own heart, 'You're never going to make it, Old Soldier;' but they made it. Then I've seen others and thought, 'This is going to be a cinch,' and they die. It's their motivation I guess.

"The will to survive applies to everything, as well as mauling by bear. For instance you approach a 220-pound hockey player with a 30-gauge needle (about the size of a draftsman's compass point). He can lick his weight in wildcats; and yet he faints. Then you care for a little Norwegian woman who'd just been run over by a railroad car and had her leg almost cut off; and you ask her, 'Does it hurt, Mrs. Svensen?' and she says, 'A little, vot you expect; I yust almost lost my leg!' It's the difference between people.

"What's a fatal injury to one man might be not fatal to another. You can get two people that are apparently exactly alike except for one thing, the will to live. The patient without the will to live dies even though his blood gases and his heart and all vital functions seem normal; and the other one pulls through. In Dick Jensen's case there was no doubt. He was determined to *live.*

"My first bear victim was the mayor of Wrangell in 1940. He was mauled by a bear, and they brought him down to Ketchikan where I was in practice, just out of my residency. He had most of his back torn away into his thoracic cavity where the lungs and heart are. He had an eye torn out and a whole lot of other injuries that I don't remember.

"He was on a steamer, which was the only way one could get from Alaska to the South 48 in those days. I patched him up the best I could, made him as comfortable as possible consulting with the two general surgeons who were there and sent him on his way. He looked pretty hopeless. We supplied the accompanying person with medicine that would at least keep him free of pain; but he didn't make it.

"The primary difference between medical treatment for mauling victims now and in the old days is the ability now to monitor the living heart, to monitor respiration, to determine minute by minute, if necessary, the blood gases among other things — all very important. We monitor urine which shows certain things happening within the human body. We have electronic measurements of temperature; and we also have blood banks now which we didn't have 40 years ago.

"And the instruments, what a change in the needles and sutures! We used to have just plain old cat gut which was like the kind of stuff you used to tie a light cruiser to a dock. Now sutures are made out of various plastic materials that are very, very smooth — so smooth, in fact, that you sometimes have to make four knots instead of two because of the tendency to slip; and sometimes you've got to wrap the fine sutures with another suture to tie it so the knot won't come untied. That makes the plastic surgery so beautiful because sutures are finer than a human hair.

"The first sutures were so thick and the needles were so dull that one would have to force till our hands trembled and yet check oneself so the wound edges would not be torn. But now the instrument makers have developed needles that are surgical instruments. They go through tissue and no resistance is felt; control is by vision, not feeling.

"Also we have micro-surgery available for most specialties. It is possible now to unite the ends of a vessel 1 mm in diameter.

"Blood types, instruments, sutures, technique, the availability of banks for certain replacements — cartilage banks, bone banks, kidney banks — these are the major differences between now and the olden days.

"The men and women that are now finishing residencies, that's graduate training in medicine, are much better trained than we were. That's the reason that maybe the mayor of Wrangell could have been saved today. Now we do lobectomies or take out an entire lung; but we couldn't in those days.

"Three of the four mauling victims I worked on (and checked) had something that I think is not usually appreciated. These three people were between 40 and 60 years of age, and they were all men. They had one thing in common — they had high tone hearing loss. A person who's been around diesel engines or unmuffled snow machines or doesn't wear his earmuffs when he's a ramp boy (one servicing arriving and departing aircraft) or he's working in a boiler factory as a riveter, he has a hearing curve which shows he can't hear high tones.

"When a bear steps on a twig, it cracks — a high pitched, soft sound. These chaps didn't hear it. They don't hear the bear until the bear is on top of them or, as one man said, the ground vibrates under the weight of the charging bear and that made him turn in time to defend himself.

"A person with normal hearing would hear the bear and get his magnum out and be ready, or maybe he would shout at the bear and wave his arms. Often the bear would turn and go wandering off if the hunter weren't between a bear and her cubs.

"Most of the men who hunt have to be fairly affluent. Most affluent people are usually 40, 50, 60, around there, just at the time when we begin to lose everything — not only hearing but a whole lot of other things equally important. People are never reluctant to discuss their arthritis, but they all hate to have people think that they're deaf.

"When a patient calls, one takes their history, finds out what they do for a living, what they do for a hobby.

" 'Do you do a lot of hunting? With a hearing curve like this, don't go alone.'

" 'What do you mean, Doc?'

" 'By the time you know the bear's there, it's too late.'

"Anybody who goes out in the woods alone better be very sure that he can hear! The sportsman should have a hearing test. I'm not suggesting this to make money. Most states have hearing and vision conservation programs paid for out of tax funds. Anyone can get his hearing tested for nothing.

"The logical thing to do in any first-aid situation is to do the best one can with what one has. If a nice Johnson and Johnson First-Aid Kit with thick, fluffy dressings and a bandage is available, put the bandage on if it's a place that can be bandaged. Stop the bleeding.

"If a radio is available, call for help as the cannery doctor did. Don't keep it a secret and burst in on some poor doctor somewhere with someone like Dick. Raise someone on your CB or the single side band radio in your boat and say, 'I'm comin' in and my partner's been mauled by a bear.' Give the doc as much of an estimate of what you think the trouble is as you can . . . 'Looks like he's broken his right arm; looks like his stomach is open, I see his guts sticking out . . .' or whatever you see. Give the doctor some warning so he can get ready with whatever he has or summon whatever help he needs or get an airplane in there to take the patient to a place where he can be helped."

After talking with Dr. Fritz, I made a list of additional first-aid considerations.

Obviously immediate attention to the victim's medical needs is critical. It is of extreme importance to check for breathing and pulse immediately, stop the flow of blood and administer whatever form of first aid possible.

A person who ventures into an isolated area without a thorough knowledge of first aid is taking his life in his own hands. He may very well be endangering the lives of others. You owe it to yourself and any others who may be dependent upon you for their safety to take the first-aid course from a qualified medical person.

The number one rule for the first-aider to follow is, always remain calm. Don't panic or project panic to the victim.

The primary "injuries" that a first-aider could expect and deal with in bear maulings are: 1) airways, 2) cardio-pulmonary resuscitation (CPR), 3) bleeding, 4) shock and 5) broken bones.

First, an airway is essential to the victim's survival, so make sure he can breathe — check his mouth for obstructions to the airway. Clean out any obstructions. Elevate the head by gently rotating his head (toward the top of his head and back). You may need to place the victim's head on its side rather than have him lying on the back of his head.

Second, it is critical to get the victim's heart going immediately if it has stopped. You need to be familiar with the proper steps of cardio-pulmonary resuscitation.

Third, bleeding can usually be stopped or slowed down by applying direct pressure to the wound. Try to keep the wound as clean as possible (without endangering the victim).

Fourth, constantly observe the victim for shock. You should always treat a mauling victim for shock. Keep him as warm, calm and comfortable as possible. Reassure him as much as necessary without alarming him. Try not to let him see himself; and tell him that he looks and will be fine, be encouraging and give him hope.

Fifth, broken bones should be splinted — even if you only suspect a broken bone. Immobilize the limb and use whatever is handy to construct a splint, again making it as comfortable as possible (padding it with soft items). Tie it securely without making it too tight.

Have morphine syrettes of quarter-grain for pain — except in head (cranial) injuries.

Do not give the victim fluids unless it is going to be several hours or days until he gets to help. A full belly is the worst thing for general anesthesia.

The main thing is for you to become familiar with the best methods of aiding a bear maulee. Learn the steps for applying dressings and treating a victim for the types of injuries he could sustain. A good working knowledge of first aid is advantageous to us all.

Below is a recommended check list of essential items for your back country first-aid kit. I carry a water-tight plastic, zip-lock container with a minimum of items:

1. Matches — waterproof
2. Antiseptic — Iodine, hydrogen peroxide
3. Tape
4. Gauze pads
5. Bandage(s)

6. Pain killer — morphine sulfate quarter-grain syrettes
   (they have needles attached)
7. Thread
8. Ace bandage
9. Band-Aids
10. Emergency space blanket

If you have to leave the victim alone, consider the situation. Do you leave matches, firewood, weapon, water, food, etc.?

Another critical aspect of treating a mauling victim is to be prepared. I am convinced that the number one reason Al Thompson survived his ordeal with the bear is because the Thompsons were prepared. Their camp was in tip-top shape, with firewood previously gathered. They had medical materials with the knowledge of first aid. They were able to utilize their clean game bags for bandages. And one thing which most would overlook, they were in good physical condition.

The Lord was good to the Thompsons. Many mauling victims credit God with their rescue and/or recovery, and well they should.

Anyone who goes into the woods owes it to himself to get into condition long before the outing and to acquaint himself with first aid and other means of preventing injury.   □

A FEW RULES —
PLENTY OF CAUTION
AND COMMON SENSE

"I know many people have been curious as to whether women pose any attraction to bears that is unique to their sex. One of the first questions several people asked me was whether or not I had been menstruating at the time of my accident. I had not been, nor do I feel that this poses a special attraction to bears." (Cynthia Dusel-Bacon, mauling victim, tape-recorded story, December 1977)

"Trees suitable for climbing are found on a small fraction of the vegetated lands of the park. Approximately 70% of the human injuries inflicted by bears in the park have been inflicted in places where suitable trees were not available for climbing." (Steve Buskirk, biologist, Mt. McKinley National Park, personal letter, June 1977)

"I can give one hint, look out for grizzlies when the berry crop is poor. Sometimes the berry blossoms freeze and the crop is almost nil. The old grizzly gets mean, and look out. By the way, there was hardly any berries in the fall I got beat up." (Knut Peterson, mauling victim, personal correspondence, November 1977)

"The victim camped next to a stream frequented by many bears and had food in his tent. These two factors made the odds of

encounters with bears a certainty." (John Sarvis, official U.S. Fish & Wildlife Service report, August 1974)

He was wearing hip waders, carried a light spinning rod in one hand, wore a .44 magnum revolver on his hip and had two sockeye salmon on a stringer in the swirling, glacial water. She walked along carrying a rock hammer and whistling a tune to warn any bears of her approach. He stalked silently, his .30-'06 clasped tightly in his right hand, his eyes scouring the clearing ahead. They laughed loudly as they set up their tents, and they shared plans for the days ahead. He rested on the limb, adjusting the lens and checking the available light before aiming his 35 mm SLR camera at the sow and cubs.

These people were all attacked by bears. They were fisherman, cartographer, hunter, backpackers and photographer. They all had two things in common: 1) they were outdoors and 2) they were in bear country. There is no profile of a bear mauling victim. Anyone in bear country is eligible. You don't have to be male, small, single or registered to vote. Bear mauling victims come in different sizes, shapes, sexes and colors (though Caucasians predominate), and usually they don't expect to be attacked.

When Knut Peterson was walking the trail from his friend's cabin to his car in 1949, he never dreamed a bear would attack him. He wrote me, "I guess we're all much the same. I know I never did trust any bear, but I always told myself, 'Oh it will never happen to me.' But it did." And Knut never did find out why the bear attacked.

Generally speaking, bears attack man for four reasons: 1) protection, 2) surprise, 3) pain or 4) hunger. A bear may attack if man represents a threat to its cubs, mate, territory, den or privacy. Many bears have attacked spontaneously because they were surprised. A good many bears have been injured at man's hands, and that is cause enough for some of them to attack. And still others are driven to attacking man because of hunger.

Probably the greatest single cause for bear attacks is the mother bear protecting her cubs. A national park employee and biologist, Steve Buskirk, spoke with me in May of 1977 in Mt. McKinley Park and later wrote me, "There appear to be no concentrations of bear attacks within the park although the area between Igloo Creek and the Toklat River is well represented in the human injury statistics. Most injuries have been inflicted by sows accompanied by cubs and most have occurred within two miles of the park road."

Most of the time when a sow attacks man in defense of her cubs, she stops the mauling when the cubs are safe or the man stops moving. Most of the sow maulings are not fatal, but the victim is often seriously injured and often crippled for life.

Bears often charge in defense of a mate, and as Alf Madsen wrote in *The ALASKA SPORTSMAN®* in October 1955: "Probably the most dangerous time to meet any bear is during the mating season. A large male will go completely berserk if he is disturbed."

Bears frequently protect their kill or territory, and they do not like outsiders getting too close. *The ALASKA SPORTSMAN®* carried an interesting account in February 1951 about Al Lysher who was looking for trap bait and came across a pair of bear tracks. He pursued them only to discover that one of the bears was unalterably opposed to his presence. "He followed the tracks into some willow brush, then froze suddenly at the sound of a bear growling. Lysher couldn't tell what direction the sounds were coming from, though he could hear the bear 'licking its chops.' Finally, having to do something definite, he released the safety on his rifle and took one step backward. Out came the bear from the brush not 15 feet away, no black bear but an eight-foot grizzly in a furious charge. It reared up on its hind feet before him, he fired from the hip, and it fell so close to him he was able to touch its head with his rifle without taking a step to fire a finishing bullet. The grizzly had been feeding on a black bear it had evidently killed after chasing it to exhaustion. There were no signs of struggle near the partly-eaten carcass, but the grizzly had hidden the remains under a heap of moss. Lysher believes the grizzly took him for some animal trying to sneak in and steal the kill, and that its rearing up in front of him was caused by its surprise at seeing a human being. That split-second hesitation gave him his one chance to save his life."

More than one man has been attacked near a bear's den. In the old days when natives hunted bears with hand axes at the den site, it was common for bears to charge their assailants. It was theorized that Lloyd Pennington and Everett Kendall were trying to drive from its den the grizzly that killed them in the spring of 1956.

Another common cause for bears to charge is the person who gets too close while trying to get good pictures. It is unfortunate that men do not use the long lenses that were manufactured for close ups, as guide Clark Engle told me, "God and Nikon make long lenses to get away from bears." In many cases the bears react to man's aggressiveness much as a person would who is harrassed by media people — be they reporters or cameramen. It seems as though the bear would go to almost any lengths to avoid a fight — bears have bluffed and tried to warn man that he was getting too close, but there seems to be something in man that keeps him pressing for a better shot; and when the bear finally does attack, it becomes the villain (I'm not saying that all men push their luck nor that all bears give a warning, but there are many cases where man's persistence has triggered attacks).

Bears also attack when they are in pain. The most common type of pain bears experience is that of a bullet wound. As Frank Dufresne wrote in *ALASKA SPORTSMAN®* in December 1963: " . . . another reason many grizzlies are grouchy is that they carry hunters' bullets in their bodies or suffer the agony of festering wounds. Take the case of 'Old Groaner.' This huge boar who patrolled the Unuk River in Southeastern Alaska gave vent to such menacing moans and bawls that few anglers dared visit the wild valley for its wonderfully primitive salmon and trout fishing. At the first taint of human odor the bear would redouble its outbursts. The forest would echo with blood-curdling roars.

"Word spread around that 'Old Groaner' was a maniac bear, a man-killer, and through the seasons it became a challenge among local hunters to see who among them could slay the dreaded monster. Finally, the deed was accomplished and the massive skull placed in a Ketchikan sporting goods store window for all to admire. But onlookers were strangely silent as they noted that the cranium was grotesquely misshapen, fractured and knit in a hideous deformation. The secret of the man-hating grizzly was out at last: 'Old Groaner' had been living for years with a rifle slug."

And another wounded bear was noted in *The ALASKA SPORTS-MAN®* of August 1958: "He was an old animal, with teeth all worn down. His nose had been broken in some violent encounter of long ago. Once, perhaps in his youth, he had been caught in a snare which had left a scar an inch wide from ear to ear across his throat. And, he was packing lead from no less than three old bullet wounds long since healed.

No wonder this old bear had it in for all mankind! No wonder the sight of a man made him boil out of the brush full of hate and fury and murder!"

Bears suffer physical injury or health problems which also cause attacks. Bears not infrequently take out their anger or frustration on man. If a bear has recently lost a battle to another and a man just happened to stumble onto the defeated animal (or the victor), an attack could result. Bears with poor eyesight or painful mouths (abscessed teeth) may attack man.

Sometimes the bear which attacks man is a bear that has been conditioned by another human. Perhaps a bear that has suffered pain in a snare associates a trapper as his enemy. Perhaps a bear that bites into a can of insect repellent attacks another person who happened to have that repellent on. Or as in the case of some bears, they associate people in boats as enemies. *The ALASKA SPORTSMAN*® carried such an account in September 1941: "As a party of sport fishermen from Bert Hanson's roadhouse at Big Delta were heading up the Tanana River toward Clearwater Creek, a huge grizzly bear appeared on the river bank. Apparently angered by the noise of the outboard motor, it pawed the bank, then waded out into the river and tried to intercept the boat. There were no guns aboard, so the boat dodged the bear and went on upstream. The bear disappeared into the brush, only to reappear a short time later farther upstream for another try at intercepting the noisy boat."

It is common and unfortunate that bears too often become the target of thoughtless people in boats. Many bears have been shot at as they walked the beach by people offshore who had no intention of killing the animal or of pursuing a wounded bear, but ended up in mortal confrontation.

Hunger often drives a bear to attack man. Sometimes it is because the animal has poor teeth. One polar bear pulled a radio operator named Gibbon from his cabin at Resolute Bay and probably would have killed him had his partner not been able to shoot it. The bear had badly worn teeth and claws.

Another polar bear killed a man and started eating him during an expedition by Barents. The man's colleagues tried to scare the animal off, but it continued eating.

In some areas of the Far North after severe winters polar bears have been known to attack people in their huts or igloos.

One bear attacked a man who killed her then examined her. He wrote in *The ALASKA SPORTSMAN*® in August 1938 that "The big female's forepaws and hams were also full of quills. There was only a field mouse and a few berries in her stomach. Right there I knew why she had attacked me. She had been desperately hungry and driven almost insane with the pain of those quills."

Some people claim that bears will attack man when there are few berries. In 1963 there were numerous "unprovoked" bear attacks in the Fairbanks area. Some folks theorized that it was due to the scarcity of berries, but others laughed off that explanation. Knut Peterson wrote me that "I've seen big grizzlies in heavy patches of blueberries all blue around the snout and looking so well contented that I am almost sure you could have gone right over to them and scratched them behind the ears." And Knut pointed out that there were very few berries the fall the bear attacked him.

There may be other reasons for bear attacks upon man, but there is a great deal of uncertainty in some of these instances. It appears that some men are mistaken for other animals in some cases. A bear may detect a sound and mount a charge only to discover at the last moment the sound was made by man. Sometimes an odor sets a bear off.

Guide Clark Engle told me about a time when a grizzly attacked. "I know of one case at my place that a young fellow who was working for me guiding a hunter had to shoot a bear. They were stalking a black bear; and the only thing I can come up with is that possibly the grizzly smelled the black bear because the wind was right for him to smell the black bear and saw them and thought that they were black bears. It took off after them, and Ronnie finally shot the grizzly about 15, 20 feet away, right between the running lights.

"It was a nice bear. The hunter didn't want it, he'd already shot a bear; but that wouldn't stop him from shooting in defense of life. Ronnie tried everything else — yelled, hollered, jumped up and down, fired his gun in the air — but nothing could stop him. The bear was coming full tilt."

Unprovoked attacks are a subject of uncertainty. Many people do not know the reason they were attacked — maybe there was a reason, maybe there wasn't.

During the compilation of material for this book I have contemplated the idea that there is no such thing as an unprovoked attack. That people are attacked without knowing the reason, yes. A person is walking along a trail when a bear boils out of the brush toward him in an all-out attack; he certainly did not provoke it. However, it appears to me that every bear has a reason for attacking, whatever the bear's reason, thus making that attack a provoked attack.

A bear may have been formerly conditioned by man to the point that it attacks this particular one. The animal may have a toothache. Perhaps it has just lost a fight. Maybe this particular bruin is a grouch and takes on anything that happens to cross its path. In that sense I do not believe there is such a thing as an "unprovoked" attack; but in the sense that someone is minding his own business when a bear charges him, then I can go along with the idea of an "unprovoked" (by that person) attack.

Another serious question centers around human menstruation and its effect upon bears. Some people swear that bears attack women who are going through their menstrual cycle; while others vehemently disagree, stating there is no scientific evidence.

One story told of an old native in Southeastern Alaska who suggested that men who have had sexual intercourse recently with their wives not go into the woods. Perhaps it was a native custom.

An old-timer who wished to remain anonymous told me that "It's been proven to me that menstruation of women can cause bear attacks. It's a natural scent. When the bears got into our cabin on the trapline, they didn't disturb my winter, down clothes at all; but they tore the devil out of my wife's. They don't publish this enough because people in the park go to visit the park. That's the problem with the park system; they won't tell the public the truth about these animals and this danger because if the public knew the danger, they wouldn't go to visit the park."

Clark Engle told me "Most people don't know about the problem a woman can run into in the wilderness during the wrong time of the month for them. This has been proven beyond a shadow of a doubt, that there have been maulings because of this. The two girls that got mauled the same night in Glacier National Park in Montana in 1967; I found out about a year later from the head of the fish and game department in Colorado that both of those girls had been in their periods. And they were killed by two bears."

In reviewing the mauling deaths of the two young ladies in Glacier National Park in 1967, I wrote the park superintendent and received a reply dated May 31, 1977, from Clifford J. Martinka, research biologist who permitted me to use his letter. I asked if there was any evidence to indicate that bears do attack women under circumstances involving their menstrual cycle, and Mr. Martinka responded, "My judgement is that human female menstruation cannot be discounted as a possible contributor to certain attacks. I realize that supporting data are lacking but, at the same time, I am not aware of data which will permit complete rejection of the hypothesis. The effects of various human odors on wildlife are poorly understood, and the subject holds promise for productive research."

I received another letter from Martinka dated December 1, 1977, part of which stated, "Several that I have talked to have quite strong feelings about the potential contributing influence of female menstruation. Also, I've talked with a primate behaviorist that echoed the same sentiments."

Bruce S. Cushing of the Department of Zoology at the University of Montana, wrote me, "As far as I know I am the only one who has done any experimental research in this area. I do my work in Canada. My work is an experimental analysis of the bears' response to menstrual odors.

"You must realize that the question you are asking is a difficult one to answer yes or no. However, I think that it can be answered more satisfactorily than 'maybe.' For the last year I have been working with polar bears in Churchill, Manitoba. I know this question is asked more of the other North American bears, but polar bears are a more practical experimental animal. Because of the relationship of polar bears and seals it is possible to have a definite attractant with which to compare other responses. This is not possible with the other bears.

"My study is conducted in the laboratory and the field. My results give a strong indication that menstrual odors are capable of acting as an attractant. I feel that it is safe to say that a woman in the back country during her period is more likely to attract bears, not just may. As far as leading to attacks I would not want to comment.

"I am in the middle of my research and feel that until I have completed my next season that I can't state it much stronger than that. There is experimental data available which lends support to the theory that bears are attracted by menstrual odors.

"The preliminary results of my study indicate that menstrual odors of the human female may act as an attractant to polar bears. Used tampons elicited a stronger response than any other test stimuli except for seal oil and seal blubber."

Mr. Steve Herrero, Associate Professor of Environmental Science and Biology at the University of Calgary, has done extensive studies in the area of bear-man encounters, primarily in Canadian and U.S. national parks. I queried Mr. Herrero about the subject of female human menstrual effects on bears, and he wrote me that "I am ... currently preparing additional information on this topic for publication but it will be at least a year before it is available ... I do not wish to distort it until I have had a full chance to properly analyze it."

Until some substantial documentation is made on the subject of human menstruation and its effects upon bears, this subject will remain unsolved and a matter of opinion by those experiencing bear behavior regarding it.

In researching materials for this book it became one of my number one goals to be able to advise the reader of ways to prevent a bear attack. It is crucial to: 1) have a knowledge of and respect for bear nature; 2) be alert; 3) use precautions; 4) practice common sense; 5) eliminate temptations or lures; 6) utilize possible means of escape; and 7) understand your physical condition.

The bears in Alaska's outdoors are not zoo bears. They are wilderness creatures. With few exceptions they grew up learning the ways of Ma Nature, schooled in the philosophy of the survival of the fittest. They are not partial to humans unless they have previously crossed paths. If it comes to a showdown between man and bruin, the bear instinctively fights to save face or to kill his adversary.

The bear race is not in the habit of losing, and everything in his nature has taught him that he is to be feared. Unless some conditioned reflex tells him otherwise, he will enter the battle with victory in mind — whatever the cost.

Make sure you know your bears.

Dr. Will Chase of Cordova was so impressed with the mild-mannered nature of brown bears that he stated they do not attack without provocation; the injured men were usually victims of an attack due to an injury they'd inflicted on the bear, and that many a man sought the giant brown only to go home empty-handed because he couldn't find one of these shy monsters.

Jim Allen of Anchorage spent many years in Southeastern Alaska where bears congregate on salmon streams, and he told me, "My experience is that if you go into the woods and make noise, you're not going to see the bear. They'll usually clear out ahead of you, whether you're hunting, fishing, logging or whatever. God only knows how many bears you've walked by."

You seldom have to worry about seeing a bear if they don't want you to see them — they melt into the brush. It is most common to see them if they're fishing a stream (if you are on a salmon spawning stream), if they're on an open hillside or if they're in an area where bears are indifferent to man. Jim Allen confirmed the salmon spawning situation: "When you go out into the woods in Southeast Alaska, you are always bear conscious because you always see bear. You either see the bear sign or you see the bear or you hear them; and if it's the time salmon are running up the streams, you're always going to see bear."

Alaska's park bears are not tame. Steve Buskirk commented on McKinley Park bears saying, "Since recreational use of the park is heavy by Alaskan standards, the assumption is often made that park bears are tame, solicitous or otherwise habituated to the presence of humans. Such is not the case! A few bears may be found which have had repeated contacts with humans, but most have not. Even those which have, should not be considered any less of a risk to back-country travelers."

It is, of course, against the law to carry firearms in the national parks. This is a law which protects bears, and it is meant to. It becomes man's part, then, to recognize his limitations in associating with these park creatures and to answer some questions before stepping into bear country.

To what extent do you want to pursue a photograph? Are you adequately prepared to prevent a bear mauling? Will you enter a park armed or unarmed; and if you are armed, are you prepared to face the consequences of your illegality? Do you carry the minimal first-aid equipment to help a mauling victim?

In all likelihood bears will not bother man, but you need to be alert — don't take bears for granted. Every year people are injured — ranging from superficial wounds to severe maulings, and sometimes death. This doesn't have to happen. Be on the lookout for bears or situations which could be dangerous — fresh tracks, bear kills, more than one bear traveling together. Develop an awareness for bruin, like you would for poison oak or snakes if you lived in their environments.

One of the ingredients for success in any endeavor is anticipation. Often we become apathetic to our environment because of familiarity. We develop bad habits and forget to be alert. We need to expect the unexpected and be prepared to handle "bear situations."

In October 1976 a large brown/grizzly was killed a short distance from Anchorage. At the approach to the Eagle River bridge a motorist, Dave Dickey, hit the bear one early morning. The bear was in the ditch, injured, when it was shot and put out of its misery. A few years before that two men encountered a good-sized brown/grizzly on the railroad tracks near the Eklutna Flats a few miles south of Palmer, and they killed it. Bears, as well as being unpredictable in their behavior, are unpredictable in where you might encounter them.

Winter is not a guarantee against seeing bears either.

You don't know when you will encounter a bear, what kind it will be or what kind of mood it will be in.

It is of utmost importance to use every precaution in bear country. Guide Clark Engle told me, "If people would just back off from bear and leave them be, they wouldn't bother them. You push a bear, you got problems." Usually they will not bother you if you don't bother them, but remember this is not always the case.

Everyone knows that bears won't bother you if you don't bother them. So if I take my family on a camp-out up Resurrection Creek Trail, we're safe. And another thing, even if a bear does charge, all I have to do is rattle a few pebbles in a can to frighten it away. These two facts are well known by everyone. In the event we run into an especially cantankerous bear that doesn't know or follow the rules, I can get everyone up a tree.

Okay, here we go. I'm walking along beneath my load, Pam is carrying a light pack and each of our children, Ginger, Jill and Ben, has his sleeping bag. We're enjoying our little nature voyage along the trail when out of the brush boils Mr. Bruin.

"Oh, hi, Mr. Bear. How ya doin'?"

"I'm fine, but a tadly hungry."

"Oh, my. Well, as you know, if you don't bother us, we won't bother you. See ya. Hey! You're not playin' fair — you're not supposed to bother us. I'm shaking these pebbles; go away now!"

The bear isn't the slightest distracted by the fact that he's not supposed to bother us, and the pebbles theory doesn't hold sway either. He's coming, and it isn't likely he'll stop.

Let's see, now, I can get the gang up a tree. No, not enough time. We can run — that's silly, he'd catch us. I know, I'll feed him one of the kids. Wait! Pam's bigger, maybe he'll let the kids and me go. Or, I could just take him on with my bare hands.

When people tell me "Bears won't bother you if you don't bother them," I reply, "Fine, do they know that?"

William H. Berry wrote in *The ALASKA SPORTSMAN®* of an experience in September 1943 when he hiked into Cordova, shooing bears away all the way. The more he rattled his can of pebbles the more bears he saw. He said he " . . . decided 30 years ago that if you don't bother a bear, he won't bother you," and he's "been having trouble ever since. The best way to do is just not to take any chances."

One of the best ways to prevent a bear mauling is to use common sense. Tony James and Dan Hollingsworth, two former students and young men I coached at Dimond, told me about a bear that they strangled with their belts about 1970. I told them I'd like to use their story to show people a good way to get mauled.

They had spent most of the day hunting on the Kenai Peninsula when they decided to return to their car; and on the way they spotted a bear. They shot and wounded bruin, lost then found it in the alders, still full of zip. It took off when they got close, but they shot it again. Tony told me what happened next in the tale they called "Bear Stranglin'."

"Real careful we sneak up behind him to find out that he's still alive and mashing his teeth together real hard and growling.

"Dan's about ready to put another bullet into him when I yell, 'Don't shoot him anymore! I don't want another hole in his pelt. I'm going to mount him.'

"Dan said, 'This is crazy, but maybe I'm crazy. I've got an idea.' Dan thought that we could join our belts together and strangle the bear. We took off our belts and put them together. I had a bead on the bear's head while Dan took the belts and leaned around the alders. He put the belt under the bear's neck. The bear started really thrashing and growling as Dan started to tighten up the belt as tight as he could get it, strangling the bear in the end.

"The bear turned out to be a six-footer, a real fine trophy. But now that it's over, I know we would never do it again. Learning what we have up to now, we could have very easily been killed or carried scars for the rest of our lives doing the crazy thing we did then."

Tony and Dan were in high school when they had the experience with the bear, and they would never think of doing such a risky thing again. Their approach now is strictly that of common sense, the same approach you should use. Don't get too close at any time to a wild bear — unless you know for a fact that it is dead.

Master Guide Keith Johnson of Anchorage shed some light on tracking down wounded bears. "When you go after a wounded bear in the brush, the number one thing is to locate the bear. You go in the brush a little ways and get out of there. You never go in and keep going.

"A hunter shot and wounded a brown bear once, and I had to go in and dig him out. I went in and out of this brush pile and went almost all the way around it; but I didn't give him the wind. I could not locate that bear, just couldn't do it.

"I had to come back and follow his trail in from the beginning. The bear did just what they say they'll do. He went in the brush, made a big circle and came right back to his back trail and laid down and watched his back trail. When I got in there, I ended up almost face-to-face with that bear. He was lying down, crouched down just like he was ready to lunge right on me.

"When I saw him, I was 15 yards from him. I just knew I was ate up. I was in the wrong place. It was a bad scene. I was in real thick brush. You couldn't see more than 15 yards; and he was lying there with his head straight forward. I threw snow and sticks at him until I could see his eyes were glassy. I punched him and found he was dead."

Some men seem to think they can protect their kill by camping next to it, and some have even stayed under Visqueen or tarps in the rain to protect the meat and themselves from the weather. This is risky. Bears that get the fresh scent of bloody meat commonly seek out its source. Any man in the vicinity is jeopardizing his health.

It makes good sense to have a partner along when you are hunting. It would be comforting for you to have faith in your partner's woods savvy and marksmanship.

Another consideration is the one of the location of your tent. Don't pitch it in a bear trail; and it is not recommended to park your tent close to a bear stream either.

Another critical issue regarding common sense is that of a bear's food source. If you stumble onto a kill site — a mound of earth or vegetation piled up around an unearthed or scraped area, start looking for a bear, and move from that area. In all likelihood the bear is in the vicinity, probably watching you. Birds often will warn you of the kill — ravens, magpies or Canada jays may be squawking, flying or perched on trees in the area.

If you're in an area where you can make out tracks and spoor, use it to your advantage. I've only seen two really big tracks; but when I saw them, I made a few of my own — the other way! The first track measured 14⅝ inches long and nine inches wide (hind paw).

I saw the second track in early winter.

A few years ago my family and I drove a mile or so up Bird Creek from the Seward Highway in late November. My wife pointed out a track beside the road, near the garbage dump. I reminded Pam that bears were in hibernation and got out to look at the track.

I couldn't believe what I saw. It looked like a snowshoe print! The snow around the actual print was melted, giving a larger appearance to the track; nevertheless, it was the largest track I've ever seen. It looked to be at least 18 by 12 inches. I didn't bother measuring it — splotches of blood showed in the tracks and it was fresh! All I did was bounce into the car and skedaddle!

In bear country, listen for "bear" noises. A bawling cub sounds like a baby crying. If you hear any strange sounds, anticipate bear.

Eliminating temptations or lures will decrease your chances of man-bear encounters. It is a good idea to have a clean camp. Do not have food in your tent or close to it.

Another unproven "lure" could be a female during her menstrual cycle. The utmost care must be taken to consider your safety in the woods at this time when it is essential to practice the best sanitary measures.

A debatable subject regarding the prevention of bear maulings is the item of trees. The general public believes that a man can escape a bear by climbing a tree. This is usually true in the cases of brown/grizzlies; however, black bears can climb; and brown/grizzlies can also if the limbs on the tree are so spaced and low enough to the ground to allow the animal to pull itself up (like climbing a ladder). One of the chief difficulties in using a tree for an escape route is the tree's availability.

In discussing some of the questions about bears and Mount McKinley National Park, Steve Buskirk wrote me that, "Trees suitable for climbing are found on a small fraction of the vegetated lands of the park. Approximately 70% of the human injuries inflicted by bears in the park have been inflicted in places where suitable trees were not available for climbing."

I was interested in Joyce Thompson's comment in her narration of her husband's mauling on the Kenai Peninsula also. When she first contemplated the gravity of their situation, she considered climbing a tree, then she realized ". . . The trees were large with no limbs low enough for me to reach."

The best way to avoid a bear encounter or mauling, obviously, is to be in a safe place out of his reach. The most logical place in bear habitat to escape their reach is a level above, below or beyond them. Such a "bear proof" sanctuary would be a tree, a ledge on a cliff, the opposite side of a canyon or a jumble of trees.

But it is not always possible to get out of their reach. Time does not permit. In the previously described maulings, man did not have enough time — time to unjam a rifle, get in a(nother) shot, climb a tree or reach safety.

And often man suffers because a "bear proof" sanctuary is not available. Many maulees had time but no place to go. How does a man escape a brown bear in an area where there are no trees?

And even where there are trees, many are not "climbable trees." Many trees are too small, have limbs that are too far from the ground to reach easily or the limbs are too small to support a man's weight.

Since climbing a tree seems to be one of the best ways of escaping from a bear (when trees are available), I wanted to determine how long it would take to climb a tree to a height of 12 feet. I wanted also to consider the feasibility of this escape route in lieu of the time element. I asked two young men from Dimond High School in Anchorage to help me with my experiment in May of

1977. Both Calvin Lauwers and Dale Steele were well-conditioned athletes; Lauwers a basketball player and Steele a wrestler. They were both 16 years old and juniors. Calvin was 5'11" tall and weighed 150 pounds whereas Steele was 5'6" tall and weighed 135 pounds.

I was 35 years old, 5'11" tall and weighed 185 pounds.

We timed both our climbing without packs and then shedding packs prior to climbing. I chose a well-limbed evergreen tree about 35 feet tall and 20 to 25 inches in diameter at the base. I was primarily interested in 1) the time elapsed from base to 12 feet up the tree (what I consider the minimal safe height) and 2) the time needed to cover 30 yards, then climb the tree.

We took turns climbing and timing each other, imagining we were being chased by a bear in a life and death situation. Before we started, we cleared a few branches and brush out of the way to ease our ascent, and we studied the terrain between the tree and the starting point 30 yards away. On the 30-yard run we came down a slight hill over dead grass and a couple of logs. The hill was about 15 feet higher than the base of the tree.

We made some startling discoveries. First we timed ourselves climbing the tree free of our packs; then we started the stop watch, peeled the pack and climbed; and last we went up the hill and timed our run and ascent without a pack, then with a pack (having to peel it off as we ran to the tree). The fastest we made it from the ground up 12 feet was exactly 5.1 seconds. It took us a minimum of 7.3 seconds to peel the pack from the base and climb the 12 feet. From 30 yards without a pack the quickest we made it to "safety" was 12.7 seconds. We covered the same route, peeling a pack on the way, in a minimum time of 13.5 seconds. People have told me in a real-life situation the times would be faster; try it!

After the climbing experiment I went home and timed our one-year-old black Labrador retriever. I went out to the back yard, called him, had our six-year-old daughter Jill let him out of his kennel and timed him from the time he left the kennel until he reached me, a measured 25 yards. He came like a shot, 3.3 seconds (later I opened the kennel door, turned and sprinted for the house to see how far I could get before he overtook me. He caught me in seven yards).

We were programmed for *that* tree. What would happen if someone walking through the woods was suddenly confronted by a bear at 30 yards? Next time you're out driving the friendly roads of Alaska, see how many trees are readily climbable.

According to our experiment, a man's chances of climbing a

tree to escape from a charging bear within 30 yards are pretty grim (I refer you to the Ron Cole and Forest Young maulings). If you surprise a bear in the woods, it would probably take at least one second to recover from the shock and another second to pick a tree. You would then have a couple of seconds at best to get to a tree and up it to safety. And what if your family were with you?

One other aspect of prevention of bear attacks or maulings which is seldom considered was brought to my attention by Dr. Milo Fritz. In discussing treatment of victims and preventive measures in the field he told me about the number of men who hunt at an older age (over 40) and brought up the subject of high tone hearing loss. As stated earlier, three of the four mauling victims he treated had hearing that would not detect sharp, crisp snapping noises (one of these victims didn't even know the bear was near until he felt the ground shaking). It would be to the outdoorsman's advantage to ascertain his hearing levels before embarking into bear country.

In situations where you cannot prevent a bear attack or mauling there are some diversions that may work. A number of things may divert the bear's attention long enough for you to make a getaway — dog, food, pack or clothing.

There is a controversy over the value of a dog. Many believe he will save your life, while others maintain that a dog will antagonize a bear and bring the bear to you. There are ample cases to substantiate both claims. Bruce Johnstone's dog Slasher almost assuredly saved him from a serious mauling from Old Groaner when the dog lunged at the bear; but many men have had their dogs disturb a bear to the point of endangering the men or their party. Many a man has spent several hours on the branch of some tree (often overnight) while an angry bear sat below; meanwhile, man's best friend, which brought the bear on the run in the first place, either went home or slunk off into the brush.

More than one man has been able to slow down a charging bear by throwing it his lunch. A fisherman can try placating a bear with his catch. Sometimes a bear will attack a dropped pack, swatting it about. Clothes often serve as a diversion. A hunter had wounded a grizzly, and the guide approached the animal prior to determining it was dead. "The infuriated bear had reared up and lunged at him, clawing and biting viciously, while the frantic hunter tried to get in a telling shot. Then, by some freakish luck, the bear got its teeth tangled in the guide's old felt hat. When the brute stood up on its hind legs to get rid of the hat it gave the hunter a chance at last." *(The ALASKA SPORTSMAN®*, October 1950)

Hip waders have saved many men, often enabling them time to escape up a tree. The pursuing bear would grab hold of the sole or heel, pull at the boot, frequently pulling it off and fighting it, and the man could climb out of reach.

A final diversion is one I suggest with tongue in cheek. I have a standard joke with my students about carrying a honey-scented hand grenade or having a hunting partner along that you can outrun. I tell them that I don't hunt with Mr. Roumagoux (cross-country coach) or Mr. Muehlhausen (counselor) anymore because I can't outrun them.

A number of deterrents have been used in stopping bear maulings; some of which are fire, flare gun, noise and some weapon. Fire may keep a bear at bay though a couple of instances show that it did not in these cases. An old-timer went ashore to film bears, armed with two whiskey bottles of gasoline. He spied a brown bear cub and poured the contents of one bottle between them. The bear, a 200-pounder, walked up to the blaze and looked around one end of it then began squalling. Instantly the mother charged from behind the man, who dumped the other bottle's contents between him and the mamma and lit it. The sow didn't even slow down, but ran around the two-foot wall of flame toward the man who legged it past the cub. The cub quit crying, and the mother stopped.

Another case of using fire as a deterrent involved the mauling deaths of the two college girls in Montana in 1967. It may be that the fires died down during the night, but they had little effect on discouraging those bears from attacking. In many bear-garbage areas where garbage is burned, fire is no stranger to bears; they seem accustomed to it.

Gust Jensen told me that "At night if a bear sees the light from a fire, he'll come to it. Different guys have told me if a bear sees flame on a beach, they come for it. Some people tell me a bear will go for a campfire."

Fire worked for one old-timer who was chased up a tree. A sow brownie stood below his tree snorting and raising cain while her cubs watched from another tree close by. The old-timer grew weary from waiting when an idea struck him. He dropped his jacket into her chomping mouth, and she ripped it to shreds. Then he procured some matches and torched his shirt which he had wadded up. When the shirt got to blazing pretty good, he dropped it into her open jaws. He described the bear as leaving instantly, with her cubs, like a Roman candle.

Mr. Griffith felt confident with a flare gun (as described on pages

221-222). In talking with my neighbor Carl Snyder he told me that surveyors working for the Cadastral Survey have successfully used regular road flares to discourage bears from bothering them, "bears that have actually started to charge have immediately back-tracked. Normal road flares seem to be a definite deterrent, and have kept the bears at bay once they are lit."

Lighted lanterns seem to be effective to a degree in keeping bears at bay.

Another rather unusual deterrent is that of human urine, or at least it worked for Ray Machen when he was treed by the black bear.

Noise qualifies for both preventive measures and deterrent. Nearly always a bear will fade into the brush if he hears your approach. One of the safest and most successful ways to prevent an attack is to let the bear know that you are in the area — unless, however, you are trying to get close. Making the bear aware of your presence can be done by talking, whistling or as is recommended by most people having experience in bear country, by rattling pebbles in a can or using bells, which some people tie to their packs.

There is some controversy as to whether rattling pebbles or talking causes bears to leave or attracts them, however.

A whistle will frequently deter a bear. John Vania, once Regional Supervisor for Southcentral Alaska, of the Alaska Department of Fish & Game shared with me some of his experiences using whistles and similar devices. "During the summers of 1961 and 1962, I supervised a salmon tagging program in the northern end of Southeast Alaska. As part of the program I had two- and three-men crews walking salmon streams in July and August looking for salmon we had tagged earlier in salt water. During the two summers more than 100 salmon streams were walked on Admiralty, Baranof and Chichagof islands as well as a few streams on the mainland between Juneau and Petersburg. Records were kept of all bear sightings. Nearly 200 bears were recorded sighted during the two-year study. Most of them were brown bear.

"The crews were made up of college students who were majoring in fisheries or wildlife. All had little or no experience with bears. When we first started the project, I was concerned about the possibility of crew members getting mauled by bear. Most people I'd talked to said that the 'danger was in surprising a bear; to avoid that, make lots of noise.' As a result I equipped each crew with a small horn purchased in a boat shop and powered with a small cannister of gas (believe it was freon). The gas cans were replaceable. The horn and gas can measured about six inches and weighed less than a pound.

"Crews would walk up a stream and toot the horns occasionally, especially when the brush around the stream was dense. When the crews did this, they never encountered a bear, even though there was a great deal of bear sign along the streams. After walking a number of streams and not seeing any bear at all, some of the crew decided they would like to at least see a bear. So they stopped tooting their horns. They immediately began to run into bears along the stream.

"For people who really are afraid of bear, who are in brushy country and want to avoid running into them, I highly recommend a gas powered boat horn or some similar device. When walking along streams that are noisy (lots of rapids, etc.), you need something that makes a loud noise. In my opinion bears do not have very acute hearing.

"I tried police-type whistles on bear, blowing both the police whistle and the silent dog whistle. These whistles had no effect, but the boat horn really got the bears' attention! The police whistle is better than the human voice or a can of rocks but not as good as the air horn."

Guide Clark Engle told me about an efficient bear scarer he used. "We used to have a cure for bears that are bothering our camps — we'd put a Raid can or an Off can out and maybe cover it with a little bacon fat, or throw it out on the trail away from camp. And if a bear came close, he'd bite into this and usually they'd take off."

On the other hand, Bob Brown told me about a bear that "ate" an entire case of Off (insect repellent), showing me one of the chewed cans.

Naturally the most effective deterrent to use in a bear encounter — one that has the capabilities of eliminating the problem entirely — is a firearm. Over the years I have talked with people who represent a myriad of philosophies regarding an adequate deterrent for bears. A few photographer friends cling to the belief that if you are filming without a firearm, your chances are greater for surviving because the bear can sense your situation — it is able to smell the metallic odor of a firearm as well as the smell of gunpowder. Others have told me that they will carry nothing in the woods but a lightweight, high-powered rifle of .300 caliber or larger. Some believe that a sawed-off shotgun is the best means of defense, and still others rely upon a magnum handgun in the .357 or .44 calibers.

It is, of course, against the law to carry firearms in the national parks, so you need to determine a plan of action or consider an alternative if you plan to enter bear country in a park.

If you are carrying a weapon and plan to use it for protection, it is imperative to heed Al Johnson's suggestion: "I realize that in many situations a person committed no avoidable error in judgment and yet got mauled. And that, in many cases, the victim had a weapon but was unable to use it or used it but ineffectively so."

Al went a step further in his choice of weapons and said, "My bout with the sow . . . did cause me to add weight to my pack, for I exchanged a .44 magnum pistol (which I had left in my VW bug) for a sawed-off 12-gauge shotgun. The shotgun is not so much a safety device to me but more of a comforter. Though a bear may get to me, I'll still be struggling, and I won't have to lay there helpless as I once did."

In the summer of 1967 I worked for Mike Nelson and Darwin Biwer, Jr., out of the Dillingham office of the Alaska Department of Fish & Game. Darwin wrote me that I'd be an office flunkey for the most part, but that I might be going into the field to count salmon on streams. Naturally I wanted a weapon that would stop a bear if it came to a showdown.

I considered the rifle-shotgun-pistol controversy and settled on a 12-gauge Browning autoload. The scattergun had a long barrel and a sling already attached when I purchased it. I practiced "fast drawing" from my left shoulder and experimented with both slugs and buckshot before leaving for Dillingham with my wife.

During one experiment I shot three rounds of 00 buckshot with magnum loads (12 pellets to the shell). My target was a cardboard box two by three feet. The distances I fired from were 10, 15 and 25 yards. I aimed at the center of the two-foot circle I had drawn on the box to represent the head of a brown bear. Of the 36 pellets discharged, all hit the box, 27 were within the circle, and 18 were in a double fist-sized area in the center of the circle, about where the bear's nose and eyes meet (I alternated slugs and buckshot).

I felt very comfortable with these results and figured that shotgun would be adequate in stopping a charging bear, though I hoped I'd not have to use it.

The last area of deterrents is that of self-defense. There are a number of things you can do if none of the previously mentioned methods work, or if you do not have time to consider the above methods. You may escape an attack by talking down a bear, shouting at it, playing dead, fighting the bear or actually attacking it.

The "Bear-Man" of Admiralty Island, Allen Hasselborg, advocated talking bears down. He believed that it didn't do any good to bluff a bear because it was too intelligent. Hasselborg advocated getting firm with the animal and telling it to back off; and others witnessed him telling bears to go away, which they did.

The late Master Guide Hal Waugh also suggested speaking to alerted bears. "Hal also told us how bears respond to subtle changes in the human voice, and that if one would remain calm and speak softly with the Alaskan brown bear, at least, one could often talk them out of a charge or other aggressive action by standing one's ground — while the bear stood in front ripping up the earth and telling the speaker all the things he was going to do to him in the next few moments." *(Alaska Game Trails with a Master Guide,* Alaska Northwest Publishing Company, 1977)

Some people yell loudly at the bear, trying to turn him, but others disagree, saying this approach is comparable to cussing out a stranger — it might do more harm than good.

Most people who have been mauled and played dead have survived. Playing dead seems to be one of the most successful means of escaping alive from a bear mauling, however, it is also an action that not many people could endure. Gust Jensen told me about a friend of his who saved his life by playing dead. "I know a guy that went out duck hunting, old Alex Flyum; he lived on Iliamna Lake. He went out with a double-barreled shotgun. This bear come up with a cub bear which started hollerin', and he heard this mother bear get after him. He musta shot and missed. That bear just took that gun and bent it and took him and start wrestling. He didn't know what to do. First he start hollering at her when she was coming, waving. She kept coming.

"She took the old guy and started maulin' him, so he just played dead, fell down; and the bear walked away. If you play dead, he ain't gonna bother ya. He might try to cover you up, lots of times a bear'll do that. But make sure you don't move; he's going to go a ways and look back. If he sees you movin', then he's going to shake you up some more."

Some men have survived bear attacks by fighting the bear. I talked with Leo Beeks who was mauled in Southeastern Alaska in 1970 (he was on his way out of town to go back to work but encouraged me contact his sister Cheri Taylor who gave me his story).

"I was cutting trees on Admiralty Island for Pat Soderberg of Clear Creek Logging Company.

"Two buddies and I had been working about a quarter of a mile from the landing and had to quit for lunch. We left our saws where they were and went down to a ravine by a creek to eat.

"I don't remember much except hearing an odd noise and looking up to see a big brownie crashing brush and roaring down on me. She must have had her sights on me from the top of the hill for she ran over my buddies to get me.

"I'm not a small man — at the time I probably weighed 250 pounds. She was a big one though for she bit into my thigh and stood up with me like I was a rabbit or something. When she finally dropped me all I could do was curl into a ball to protect my stomach and clasp my hands behind my neck to keep her from snapping my spine. I knew she'd try to disembowel me or break my neck and I figured if I could keep her from doing that maybe I'd live through it.

"My buddies had taken off for help as we didn't have any guns with us. I didn't realize they were gone until all of a sudden the brownie took off and I was alone. I guess their leaving was the only thing that saved me because they'd evidently stumbled into her cubs and she left me to see about them.

"I didn't know what to do. I knew I'd have to follow that bear to get back to the landing and I wasn't too eager to do that. I decided to try and hide from her and wait for help so I got behind a big tree and waited for what seemed an eternity. I couldn't hear anything except my own heart pumping so I figured it was safe. I started to come around the tree and when I did, she was staring me in the face! I remember thinking, 'You son of a bitch' and drew back my fist to hit her nose. When I connected with her, she'd opened her mouth and I felt her teeth sink into my elbow.

"I knew my only chance was to keep the tree between me and her and I kept kicking at her nose with my cork boots. I must have connected quite a few times I guess because she finally left.

"I knew if I didn't get help fast I'd bleed to death and I figured the crew probably thought I was dead. So I started out after the bear towards the landing. After what seemed hours I met the crew coming with their guns. They thought for sure I was a goner but they meant to get that bear. I was evacuated by helicopter to Sitka where I spent a few months in the hospital recovering."

A rather unusual means of preventing a bear from mauling you is to attack it. A couple of men did just that and managed to escape with minimal injuries in lieu of the damage they could have suffered. Rade Peckovich and Bill Brody waltzed with brown bears and lived to tell about it.

In March 1940 *The ALASKA SPORTSMAN*® carried a story by

Conrad Puhr which told about Rade's episode. Rade was hunting with a friend whom he had outdistanced when he came to some bushes. "I followed the tracks halfway around a large bush. I had no suspicion of what waited for me on the other side.

"Suddenly, I heard a slight noise and looked straight into the bear's huge face. Less than 10 feet separated us! He rose on his hind legs, towering above me.

"Quickly, I raised my rifle and pulled the trigger within three feet of its wide-open mouth. There was a click as the gun misfired. The bear's swift paws struck out. My rifle went spinning from my hands. Had I had a revolver with me there would not have been time to draw it and fire.

"I didn't stop to reason — to think. The time for that was past. Nor was it instinct that made me act as I did then. To turn now, and run, was to have the bear claw my back.

"I did something which is beyond instinct or reasoning. I sprang forward. I miraculously got past the bear's open claws. With all the strength I had in my body, I seized as much of his hide as I could encircle and hung on.

"I clung tightly to the long fur, pressing upward with my head against its neck and under its wide-open jaws. As I see it now, that act was my salvation, for the bear's claws could rip only at my back, and that without bringing into play its full strength. Also my head, butting tightly against his jaws, prevented him from reaching down and seizing me in his mouth.

"For fully three minutes we struggled in this position; the bear trying to claw me and my own desperate efforts all directed toward keeping as close to him as I could.

"Finally, we fell down — with the bear on top. In the fall, my hold had been broken, and in rising the bear bit into my arm.

"He tried to shake me, but this he was unable to do.

"Then, as quickly as I could, I brought my left hand around and pushed my fingers deep into his nose with all my strength! I felt the pain of his teeth sinking through the flesh and bone of my arm. Then, in a final effort with my fast-ebbing strength, I succeeded in breaking his hold.

"I fell over backward and quickly turned around and tried to rise, but not quick enough. The bear bounded on me and with his jaws he seized me on the hip and flung me 15 feet through the air, back over the trail. He bounded toward me again on all fours.

"Then I heard a shot, next the voice of my companion, a hundred yards down the trail. Halfway toward me, the bear stopped. Turning quickly, he darted into the forest.

"For weeks I lay in bed with an infected arm which swelled to three times its normal size. During the ensuing fever and delirium I fought that battle over a thousand times."

Another bear grabbed Bill Brody, and he grabbed her back. He had gone hunting with a friend in 1955, and they'd split up. Shortly thereafter Bill encountered a sow with cubs a distance of 50 feet from him. Within a few bounds the bear was upon him. "She stood on hind legs," he wrote me, "a picture of brute savagery. Her front paws were outstretched beside her head. Dark, razor sharp claws were poised and ready for action. Her big, ivory teeth glistened below curled lips; and guttural rumblings came from within her.

"My number one thought was that I didn't want her to get me in her jaws. Nor could I let her hit me with those massive paws. I didn't wait for her next move. I jumped right between her outstretched arms, shoved my head into her hairy chest, and she swung her paws over my back. She missed but followed up by trying to bite me. Just then I ducked under a forearm and slid behind her.

"I was behind her only a few moments thinking about escape when she came again. It was like a bad dream. She stood again, paws outstretched and coming. I repeated my first strategy and jumped against her again. She repeated her initial attempts to grab me, but again I slipped under a huge arm and behind her.

"In moments of crisis weird things come to one's memory, and I remember a few things that seem strange. I remember the grass-like odor of her breath. I'd often heard bear attack victims recalled a terrible, rotten smell of foul breath. I remember her clean, white teeth, and their immense size. I remember how easy it would have been to slice into her stomach a number of times had I been able to get my hunting knife out of the sheath. I remember thinking what a beautiful straw-colored hide she had.

"There were at least six times she came for me, each time standing on hind legs, both paws outstretched. Fortunately she never hit me squarely. I continued to jump against her chest and slide behind her, but my strength and speed were waning.

"Once she caught me in an actual bear hug; but before she could squeeze, I slid from her grasp. At this point her claws sliced both my sides from my belt to my shoulders, like hot coals searing into my body — these marks lasted well over a year.

"At one point near the end, she swung a haymaker. I ducked, avoiding the brunt of her blow, but I caught her elbow just over the eye. It knocked me down onto the wet ground. She pounced towards me, and I lashed out with my feet. But she was too fast for me and grabbed my foot in her mouth, rearing up on her hind feet. It looked like curtains. She held me by the foot, my head swinging above the ground; and my body banged against her.

"It is a most terrifying experience to be held above the ground by a monster bear, completely helpless to do anything but pray. She handled me like a man would a youngster, effortlessly; and I weigh 180 pounds and stand six feet tall. Fortunately she was unable to crush my foot since my boot sole acted to keep her jaws apart.

"After shaking me a few times (by rotating her head from side to side), she dropped me. I reached out with my arms to cushion my fall then rolled away from her; but she was on top of me, clawing me across the hip and pulling me towards her. I rolled towards her, freeing myself of her claws, until I lay against her. Somehow I managed to roll away from her and got free.

"Again I got to my feet and jumped against her chest, clutching a handful of hair on either side of her. My injuries were slowing me down. Maybe I was losing my mind, but I felt a crazy impulse to jump onto her back.

"She kept swinging, ripping mostly my clothes. She caught me trying to slip under her forearms and clamped her jaws down between my left elbow and shoulder. My mind spoke to me, but my body was too slow to react. She bit clear to the bone, severing my radial nerve; and the arm slumped useless to my side.

"And again I was on the ground trying to roll away from her. Somehow I got behind her. Just then her cubs left, and she rushed after them in her classic bear gait."

Attacking the bear may not be the recommended thing to do in most cases, but in these two instances it seems to have saved the lives of Peckovich and Brody.

Jamming one's fingers into a bear's nostrils has worked as a self-defensive maneuver for some. This action merely angered the bear John Graybill of Peters Creek told me about; but in some situations it has proved successful.

Man seems incapable of coping with bears in this outside zoo. People tend to think of "park bears" as clowns, models and panhandlers. Bears are cute and harmless. Shutterbugs invade his bailiwick. The bear often receives handouts from well-meaning individuals, almost always to the animal's detriment.

Next time you see a cuddly mamma and her brood, (try to) picture yourself in the hospital, a recipient of four pints of blood and over 200 sutures. Ask yourself which arm you'd rather have handicapped or amputated. Or, better yet, project yourself into an early grave, the result of trying to get some close-ups of a bear on the open tundra.

The most bear-wise men in the state have had close calls with bruin. Allen Hasselborg, the "Bear-Man" of Admiralty Island, who probably knew as much as any man alive about brown/grizzlies, especially on that island, was mauled when he approached a wounded bear, thinking it was dead.

Man should be able to utilize the same terrain as bears without mishap if he practices some precautionary measures. We must consider the nature of the bears — especially speed and power.

A basic problem in preventing a serious bear encounter is attitude. Either because of their experience or lack of it, people assume certain ideas about bears.

Attitudes toward bruin run the gamut. Some people believe they are perfectly safe in bear country — that they will never need a weapon. Some regard bears as cute or cuddly. Some feel that if you don't bother bears, they won't bother you. If you don't show fear, they will leave you alone. The only time man really need be concerned is if he gets between a sow and a cub. Many people do not respect bears and have no concept of a bear's destructive powers.

Others, however, would not venture from their doorsteps without some bear medicine — what old-time Alaskans called "bear insurance" (a rifle of .30-'06 caliber or larger). Their attitude is, if you go into the woods and want to come out of the woods, you'd better have something besides a stick.

When my wife Pam and I first came to Alaska in 1966, we went berry picking a few miles east of Anchorage proper on Upper DeArmoun Road. My mind was programmed after having heard for years stories of the great Kodiak bear, grizzlies and black bears. I had a rifle that went along on this and all subsequent outings for some time to come. My mind was always aware of the notorious bear, and I found myself wishing for a self-defense weapon in the form of a rocket launcher, bazooka, portable tank or mini-flame thrower. In my mind I conjured up inventions like a backpack rocket launcher with a push button release or blueberry flavored hand grenades. I expected to see a bear behind every bush. We never saw a bear!

I carried my rifle everywhere for the first year or two (Pam couldn't understand why I didn't pack it with me when we went to town), then I gradually got out of the habit. Time passed, and it seemed silly to carry a weapon; nobody else did — except cheechakos.

Many people operate the way I did. Perhaps they over-react to the bear-man relationship. The word *bear* has a certain mystique about it and has fueled the fires of man's imagination for centuries. It is common for the newcomer to Alaska to carry a weapon all over and gradually decide it is unnecessary. However, it is extremely important to anticipate and stay alert. Often we become apathetic to our environment because of familiarity. We develop bad habits and forget to be alert. We need to expect the unexpected and be prepared to handle "bear situations."

Otis H. Speer shared his experience about weapons in *The ALASKA SPORTSMAN®* in December 1943: "Never have I forgotten, nor failed to heed, the council of an old sourdough who was watching my preparations for my first adventure. 'Since you are new in these parts,' he said, 'I'm going to tell you the most important thing you should know. No matter what you hear or see that anyone else does, never, never be without your gun along. And always be sure that it's full of cartridges. For you may meet a big one who's in a bad mood, and won't run! That's when you don't want to be helpless.'"

The most sensible thing for you to do in protecting your safety where bears are concerned is to determine for yourself the best plan of action. Time yourself climbing a tree to see how long it takes you. Is your dog the type that will fight a bear to the finish, or would your dog bring an angry bear into the midst of your camp? If you use a firearm for protection, is it adequate? Can you hit a charging bear, and kill it, with a .357 or a .44 magnum? If you plan to shoot a shotgun, can you wait until the animal is within range before shooting?

If you do not wish to carry a weapon into the woods, be sure that you are protected in some way. Bears are bears. They are not toys and should not be treated as such.

Determine the attitude with which you want to approach the bear-man situation. Do you wish to treat them as equals in the outdoors and choose to carry no means of protection, or do you treat them as potentially dangerous and carry an adequate bear "scarer" — firearm, flare, mace, etc.?

Your approach to this problem is of extreme importance, because it could save your life, or someone's you love.

If you could pigeon-hole bears, you could play dead like Cynthia Dusel-Bacon, and a little 175-pound black bear would leave you. Or you could shoot and wound a brown bear like Creig Sharp did, and it would run away and hide. Or you could climb a tree like Al Johnson did, and the bear wouldn't be able to get to you.

But you can't predict what bears will do. That's why Cynthia Dusel-Bacon lost both of her arms. She may have been better off fighting the bear (a black) with her rock hammer. And Creig Sharp's wounded brown bear had him in its mouth. The grizzly sow with three cubs in McKinley never stopped at the foot of Al Johnson's tree but went right up 15 feet and got him.

Weigh your information and decide your best alternatives. Maybe the bear is small enough and you may be able to fight it off. If you want to play dead, you need to get into a fetal position with your legs tucked to your stomach and your chin tucked to your chest tightly with both hands clasped behind your neck to protect it. Determine whether you want to remain on your knees with your head tucked under you on the ground or whether you want to be on your side.

What is the best advice for going into bear country? *No one solution will work at all times,* but the most important things to do are: 1) be prepared and alert; 2) use common sense; 3) have a weapon (or deterrent) that you have confidence in, can effectively use and stay in a position where you can use it; 4) keep your wits about you; and 5) know the reasons bears attack and avoid those situations.

Bears are individuals. Generally speaking they won't do certain things, but there are exceptions. And the same bear will not always react the same way to the same situation. Some things work sometimes, but those things will not work the next time.   □

SOME FINAL ADVICE

"Hopefully the readings in this book will enlighten people to the possibilities that exist when they venture into bear country." (Al Johnson, mauling victim, tape recorded)

"No doubt many bears have gone to bear heaven because someone misinterpreted his false charge, and there are many men who have been chewed on by bears because they assumed the bear was only bluffing." (The author)

There are some sensible things to do in order to avoid serious bear encounters. In the area of using common sense you can place dry brush around your camp area so breaking brush will alert you of a bear's presence. Don't leave a wounded animal. Don't feed bears — when a bear becomes used to man, either around garbage or dwellings, or is attracted by the lure of food (like a moose kill or salmon on a stream bank) the chances of a bear's leaving peacefully are slim. Almost surely man will have a serious confrontation which could be costly for him.

Several persons mauled by bears were in the act of getting nearer for close-up photos. It is wise to prepare yourself for an encounter should you plan for close camera work; it is unwise to push the bear to its limits. One famed Alaskan guide did just that and the encounter ended with the sow's charging (protecting her cub) and ultimate demise — a very disgusting thing for anyone, let alone a guide, to do. Much controversy exists concerning man's ability to photograph bruin at close range — one group believes that a bear won't bother you if you don't bother it and that you don't, therefore, need a weapon; another group believes that a photographer needs to have a reliable weapon while photographing. Believe me, you need to educate yourself in this matter.

At least one old-time guide wanted clients to have memories of charging bears (and to use movies to recruit hunters from hunting clubs), and he had a questionable method of getting them. He either dropped an animal for bait or found one a bear was feeding on, then set up his photographer and hollered at the bear.

Usually the bear charged on a bluff then stopped, which rendered the necessary footage. However, two negative aspects need to be mentioned: 1) some bears didn't stop and "had to be shot," and 2) with this kind of man-conditioning what would be the next man's chances of escaping an incident with this Hollywood bruin if they crossed paths?

While researching maulings, I decided to compile a list of persons and reasons for attacks and to try to draw some conclusions. The number of victims is too small and fragmentary to allow any scientific deductions; however, some trends may be indicated.

Traveling outdoors with a partner has a decided advantage (over 40% of those in groups on the mauling list were saved when a partner shot a bear off them; and many victims would not have been able to get out of their situation alone). While traveling with others, spread out so that an attacking bear is less likely to hurt more than one person.

It is of extreme importance to be prepared to meet a crisis in the woods. While in bear country you need to use every precaution and have the minimal amount of medical supplies to help a mauling victim (three primary reasons for Al Thompson's survival were his physical condition, their preparation and woods savvy and the grace of God).

Bear maulings don't take a whole lot of time. Most maulings last less than 30 seconds. Although Guy George wasn't mauled, his entire encounter lasted but five or six seconds.

Bear maulings are no fun. You can ask anyone who's been chewed on by a bear how much fun it was. I've had people tell me, "Oh, he didn't get mauled badly, he only lost a third of his stamina" or "He still has one good eye." Well, how severe is severe? I figure if you've been in a bear's mouth, you've been mauled; and you can thank the good Lord that you're alive.

Try to avoid surprising a bear. It would be interesting to know how many encounters with bears occur when you're "on the way back" — tired, not really alert or aware of what you're doing; all you can think about is getting back to that boat, back to camp, back to the car or back to the family.

An attacking bear usually gives you a warning; and quite often the "attack" is merely a bluff. Even if a bear gives a warning and attacks, you may not have time to react (58% of those on the mauling list did not have sufficient time to respond).

If a bear does attack, you can try talking it down while backing away slowly — do not turn your back on the bear unless you know for a fact that you can reach safety. You can defend yourself with whatever means is available, or you can play dead. Passivity or playing dead seems to decrease the severity of the mauling (67% of those on the mauling list who moved after the initial attack were mauled worse).

If you are dealing with a bear that considers you a threat, chances are it will leave if you show no hostility or the threatening situation ends. If the animal attacks out of hunger, your chances of survival are minimal. In the case of Cynthia Dusel-Bacon, she may have been better off fighting the bear with her rock hammer.

A black bear will do one of three things when confronted by a human: 1) run, 2) attack, or 3) stand its ground. If the animal gets man's scent or sees man, it will normally run in the opposite direction as fast as possible. However, if it has a cub, is wounded or hungry, there is a good chance it will attack. If you encounter a black bear that neither runs nor attacks, look out. If the animal holds its ground, it has probably chosen to do so out of familiarization with man, curiosity or because of hunger.

There are cases where a black bear may not smell nor see man, consequently it stays where it is. But the greatest danger is that the animal has become accustomed to man and is not afraid of the two-legged critter, or worse yet, the bear may look upon man as a meal. I think that's what happened to Dusel-Bacon. Since she saw no cub, and the black didn't retreat (but rather watched her and circled her for 10 minutes), it appears that the bear was "sizing up" the situation and "closing in for the kill."

It becomes very important for the attack victim to try to ascertain the size, age and motivation of the bear as quickly as possible in order to determine the best plan of action in dealing with the animal. It seems like Cynthia's bear intended to eat her from the beginning, and that's why I say she may have been better off fighting it.

It is difficult to know what to do in these situations, but my recommendation is to carry an adequate weapon — one that will divert or stop a bear attack (consider the fact that 27% of those on the mauling list — one in four — died).

In the past few years a growing concern has been expressed over "park" bears; those animals in juxtaposition with man where man is not allowed to carry a firearm for protection.

One of Alaska's top bear men, Lee Miller, game technician for the Alaska Department of Fish & Game, lives in Indian which borders a state park where bears are protected. Lee has told me of nuisance bears around Indian (within 25 miles of Anchorage), some appearing even in January. He shared some comments about man-bear conflicts around the park.

"Early on a June morning as I was showering, a movement caught my eye out the window of the bathroom. Looking out the window I observed a brown bear walking between my house and the shed about 30 feet away. As I watched, he proceeded to knock down a bird feeder and eat the suet that was in it. I finished showering and the bear polished off my suet simultaneously. Then he started walking around the house.

"Losing sight of him for a few seconds, I went into the kitchen and looked out the window of the back door. There he was, leaning against the back door. If the door had not been latched, he might have rolled into the kitchen. I decided the bear had to go, so I went to get my shotgun and some cracker shells to scare him off (these shells are made to explode and scare animals without hurting them).

"When I returned, the bear was about 25 feet away smelling my picnic table. I stepped out the back door and yelled at him. All he did was look at me. I fired a cracker shell at him; this had no effect on the bear — he just kept walking around the table and looking at me. At this point I picked up several rocks and threw them at him yelling at the same time.

"This had some effect on him as he slowly turned and walked down the trail my kids take to get to the school bus.

"About 15 minutes later I left the house to go to work. As I entered my car I noticed the bear walking up my driveway towards the house. I started the car and drove towards him blowing the horn at the same time. He turned and ran down the drive ahead of me for about 200 yards then off into the woods. This was the last time I saw him.

"This particular bear appeared to be in his third year of life, probably out on his own for the first year (even so his actions were peculiar in that he appeared to have no fear of humans). I feel if you ran into this bear in the woods or on the trail he might give you trouble.

"Late that spring my neighbor observed a female and two yearling brown bears going through my yard. A large boar was seen several times in the valley during the summer. This valley is surrounded by Chugach State Park which allows no brown bear hunting, so as the bear population increases and expands out of the park, I would look to see more bear-people conflicts."

Studies by park officials and others working to alleviate bear-man conflicts in the national parks indicate that bears accustom themselves to man where food is available. These animals often become aggressive and have no fear of man.

Where bears and man are around each other a great deal of the time, each seems to regard the other with less respect than he would if seeing each other less frequently. People and "habituated" bears tend to take each other for granted. (In Churchill, Manitoba, several people have been attacked by polar bears on the annual migration as they await the freezing of Hudson Bay. The bears frequent the dump which is within the townsite, attracting shutterbugs and others who feed and/or harrass Nanook —people have shot the bears just for something to do.) Cities throughout Alaska, as well as "wilderness" areas frequented by people — Russian River, Lake Creek and Denali National Park to name a few — are in or bordered by bear country. If people don't hold these "park" bears with respect, they could pay the price of a mauling.

Steve Herrero, who is preparing a book on human injury inflicted by grizzly bears in the national parks, stated in his study entitled "Conflicts between Man and Grizzly Bears in the National Parks of North America" (1976) that "All species of bears, when repeatedly attracted to people's discarded food, will eventually habituate to people, and even the grizzly bear, symbol of the wilderness, can become a dangerous pest as a result of addiction to garbage."

Mr. Herrero found that a minimum of 79% of "sudden surprise" type attacks in back-country areas were attributable to females with cubs. He also found that sows with first-year cubs were more likely to defend their cubs than were sows with older cubs.

Interestingly, females with young didn't appear to be more involved than did any other age/sex class in incidents related to foraging for human food or garbage. During 1970-73 Herrero found that about one-third of 23 injuries inflicted by grizzly bears were attributable to garbage or food mismanagement. Prior to this in an earlier study ("Human Injury Inflicted by Grizzly Bears") he found that about two-thirds of 77 injuries from 1872-1969 were related to garbage or food mismanagement. It appears that parks and people are learning to manage their food and garbage better.

Herrero found that aged bears may be more dangerous than other bears due to their poorer condition. He also found that "running can trigger attacks and that a calm walking backward increases chances of charges not leading to contact."

Should you pack a firearm in a national park? That decision could reduce an attack/mauling and/or land you in the hoosegow; but it is a decision you need to consider carefully.

It is critical to your safety to have a weapon that will stop a bear. For years experts have discussed the most effective weapon for stopping a brown bear charge, and the controversy continues. Bear men generally recommend a rifle of the .30 caliber or larger variety and a bullet of at least 200 grains. They suggest iron or open sights since man is so close to a charging bear.

Kodiak guide Alf Madsen wrote in *The ALASKA SPORTSMAN®* in September 1957: "For an inexperienced hunter attempting a trip into grizzly or brown bear country, my advice is to carry a rifle no smaller than a .30-'06. To get the maximum in velocity, flat trajectory and shocking power, the .300 Magnum is excellent. These rifles are normally heavy enough, but I know of occasions when a bear disappeared into the brush after having been hit with six shots from a .375 Magnum with a 300 grain load. It is almost impossible to believe the punishment these large bears can take before they succumb, and this is what the hunter should keep in mind. Even though he carries a heavy caliber rifle with a heavy slug, he can still get into trouble.

"The shocking power of the .375 is so great that a bullet placed near a vital organ such as the heart will kill the animal, though it does not actually touch the vital part . . . A shot in the shoulder or the big joints of the legs will completely pulverize the bones — but the bear will keep going unless hit in a vital spot."

Wesley Blair, a guide who researched guns for bears was quoted in the April 1966 *ALASKA SPORTSMAN®*: "Hal Waugh, an excellent guide from Fairbanks area states, 'The .375 Weatherby Magnum is the most efficient killer I have ever seen in action. Probably equal with a proper bullet to my African results with the .458 Winchester.'"

Blair went on to say, "It is interesting to note that the majority of Alaskan guides use the .375, quite often a Weatherby, as a back-up rifle and consider it an excellent weapon for the big bear."

In yet another article in *The ALASKA SPORTSMAN®'s 1970-71 Hunting Annual,* vol. 1, veteran guide Earl Stevens concurred: "Were I a hunter buying a rifle solely for brown bear, however, or a guide buying one for back-up purposes, it would definitely be the .375. It is dependable and hard hitting, and as a brown bear rifle it is second to none."

Wesley Blair said in the April 1966 *ALASKA SPORTSMAN®:* "Even more important than the rifle is the choice of bullet. When hunting big bear it is necessary that the hunter choose a bullet with a heavy jacket that offers the maximum in penetration and still expands properly. Even the very fine .300 Weatherby Magnum is a poor bear gun with the wrong bullet selection. One guide reported that his client scored several hits in the chest area on a big grizzly with a .300 Weatherby and never knocked the animal off its feet. The guide had to stop a charge with a .375 Magnum. When they examined the bear they found the light woodchuck bullets had exploded under the skin of the bear in the fatty tissue.

"Hal Waugh suggests that the best bullet for the big bear in the .375 Magnum caliber is the 270 grain MGS bullet. Many of the guides highly recommend the 180 grain Silvertip bullet and the Remington Bronze Point in commercial loads and the 180 grain Nosler for handloading. However, if you have a favorite company, write them and ask what they would recommend for big bear."

Blair also commented on sights: "The brown bear guides all agreed that the best sight for hunting on Kodiak Island and along the coast of Alaska is the open or receiver sight, depending upon individual preference. The Williams receiver and the Redfield Sourdough seemed to be the top choices."

Even more critical than the caliber and the bullet weight is the placement of the bullet. Alf Madsen *(The ALASKA SPORTSMAN®,* September 1957) wrote, "On a charging bear there isn't much choice. Chest and head shots are good if they hit one of the small vital parts that must be hit to stop an onrushing bear. A shot in the eye, nose or forehead will stop him instantly. Of course, it will ruin the skull, but it may save your life. Either of these shots will enter the brain cavity. Popular belief has it that the bullet will ricochet off the bear's skull, but it won't. The skull isn't that thick. Near misses and grazing shots have brought that popular fallacy into being."

The key to stopping a charging bear is bullet placement, and if you can't hit the animal in the head or spine, it is critical to break him down — to destroy his front legs or shoulders (or back legs) to slow him enough for a killing shot.

In the spring of 1967 prior to my working for the Alaska Department of Fish & Game, I sought advice about an effective weapon in bear country.

A young lady in one of my classes, Karen Young, assured me that her father would advise me about my choice of weapons. I sent him a note with Karen and he wrote back: "Most people, including myself, are not proficient enough with a handgun to shoot one effectively. Most fatal bear attacks occur very suddenly and under the most unfavorable possible conditions. Therefore a weapon that can be 'unlimbered' with the least possible delay and one where great accuracy of aim is not important would be desirable. It would seem that a shotgun would meet these specifications.

"However I have serious doubts that two well placed charges of 'buck' from a shotgun would stop a large, determined grizzly. Have you considered a large caliber rifle — and acquiring a high or reasonably high proficiency with your shooting? A rifle in the bush might come in handy as a means of obtaining food if you ever got lost. I used to carry a .451 Alaskan — and also a gold pan which I beat constantly in bear country, it makes a lovely din and seems effective in discouraging bruin."

A shotgun's effectiveness in stopping a charging bear is a highly controversial subject. I asked Sergeant Bob Brown of the Alaska Department of Public Safety to share some findings of a study he did. After the mauling of Cynthia Dusel-Bacon, his department provided a training program for the U.S. Geological Survey in California. Bob said, "I took skinned (not fleshed) brown bear skulls down there, and I placed these skulls on the firing line. We shot a 12-gauge shotgun at these skulls at varying distances to show penetration of 00 buckshot and slugs.

"Shooting from 50 yards with 10 rounds (nine pellets per round), few, if any pellets, hit the skull. At 25 yards a few more pellets hit the skull, but none penetrated it. At 15 yards there was more penetration of the fleshy tissue, but not the skull material itself (it chipped one tooth and entered the tissue by the cheek).

"If using buckshot or birdshot within 15 yards, it will penetrate a bear's skull. Shot has killed and will kill a bear; but I wouldn't recommend it because of the non-penetrating capabilities.

"We put a slug in at 15 yards; and the slug definitely caved in the upper part of the skull. All the 12-gauge slugs we fired at 25 yards penetrated the skulls.

"The eight-foot bear that was hit by two trucks near Eagle River in 1976 did not die immediately. A passerby had a 20-gauge shotgun, and he shot the bear with two Behrneke slugs from a distance of 20 feet (shooting from behind and above the animal). One slug passed through the neck and the other one hit the top of the skull, but it didn't penetrate (it chipped off a piece of the skull and put a crack in it).

"You start shooting a shotgun at anything exceeding 25 yards with buckshot, and your pattern is so scattered it doesn't have any real effectiveness. We recommend using a slug. Accuracy is good up to a hundred yards with a slug.

"We do not advocate using a shotgun over a rifle that has the power of stopping a bear and in which the user feels competent."

Regarding pistols Bob told me, "We don't have any authenticated reports where any lives have actually been saved from brown bear using a handgun. There have been times where a bear has been killed by a handgun, but the individual was also killed. We do not advocate the use of a handgun because about 80% of the people who use large caliber handguns can't hit with them. Many seldom use or practice with their pistols. I've been told by people that they don't intend to shoot their pistol until they are actually attacked by a bear.

"I am a firearm instructor and an expert shot with handguns but firmly believe the handgun is no match for any bear.

Experts still debate the issue of an adequate firearm. Some say a pistol will work. Others say a shotgun is okay. One guide told me "The best thing to do with a .44 Magnum if a bear charges is to put it in your mouth and pull the trigger, 'cause he'll kill you anyway!"

Your choice of weapons should be based on sufficient research.

One of the keys for the mauling victim's survival is his will to live. Many men whose life blood oozed from them never gave up. They steeled themselves and determined to survive. It is this will to live that makes the difference when the chips are down.

The last area of advice I want to touch on is the spiritual. We can readily see the effects of the physical and mental aspects of our world — if a bear charges us, we experience the physical, and our thought processes come into play. Sometimes we go a step further to the spiritual — many men have uttered a prayer to God.

It is my earnest belief that the God who created us is ultimately concerned for each one of us and that He will honor our prayers for His will.   □

URSULANEOUS

"If you snore too, the bear don't like that. If you're out there in the woods and he hears you snoring, he'll look you up. Bear, he doesn't like any snoring. He must think it's another bear." (Gust Jensen, personal interview, October 1977, Anchorage)

"Yes, I've seen a grizzly forepaw torn off in a trap. The trapper should have made a drag. That is, he should have pointed a log and fastened his trap to that. Instead, he fastened the chain solid and when the bear was caught he pulled his paw off rather than stay there and be killed. Well, when you get an animal like that mad and coming for you, there's only one thing to do and that is give him all you've got and hope for the best. There isn't any use in running unless there's a tree handy. A grizzly can outrun a pony at times and he can run uphill faster than he can come down." (Fred Mansell as told to Ed Green, The ALASKA SPORTSMAN®, August 1938)

Many subjects I researched for this book fall under the heading of miscellaneous. The genus and family name for bears is *Ursus*. Therefore for this section of bear miscellany I've chose to wed the terms, including under it general information, unsubstantiated materials, conclusions and advice.

For the person who has never been in the jungle-like

undergrowth of Southeastern Alaska or the thick alder patches, description almost defies imagination. Jim Allen of Anchorage told me, "If you've been in that country down in Southeastern, you could walk from here to my greenhouse (25 yards) and couldn't see a herd of elephants." The brush and foliage consists of devil's club, mosses and alders.

Alders are small trees of the birch family which grow in clusters or groves (called alder patches frequently) in abundance. The tree begins to grow vertically but it is crushed down by snow and assumes that horizontal position until it is strong enough to maintain its vertical growth, growing parallel to the incline of a slope, usually growing downhill. Each tree assumes a shape much like a letter Z, the long "leg" growing horizontal to the ground. These trees usually average four inches in diameter and 25 feet in length — probably two-thirds of that length is parallel to the ground.

Alders are so close together it is nearly impossible to go through them. Part of the difficulty lies in the fact that in hunting country the hunter usually encounters alders on slopes. The easiest way to go through these trees is by flowing "with the grain," usually either upslope or downhill — it is extremely difficult to work across slope, especially with a pack.

Bears can be found in just about every imaginable kind of terrain and herbage. Their environment includes heavy timber, thick brush and devil's club or high grass and alders or tundra, lichen and willows — depending on which area of the state you find them.

Bears are highway builders. They travel the same trail year after year, generation upon generation (often in the same set of paw prints). This does not mean that bears do not wander elsewhere besides trails.

Interestingly enough, a bear's paw prints are as unique to him as a man's finger prints or a fish's scale print. The "Bear-Man" of Admiralty Island, Allen Hasselborg, often pointed out to visitors, who walked bruin's salmon streams with him, the tracks of different animals and differentiated between them not only by size but also by swirls and whorls of individual prints.

"The peculiar shuffling gait of a bear results from the absence of a clavicle to hold his shoulder bones steadily apart, as in most animals. Thus as his forelegs move his shoulders 'work.'" *(The ALASKA SPORTSMAN®, October 1950)*

Among the other characteristics of bears is their sense of humor and fun. Bears have been observed glissading down the snowfields as a youngster would go sledding in the winter. Enos Mills and Andy Russell both related incidents in their classic bear books where bears played in the snow with absolute relish; and George Bishop wrote in *ALASKA®* magazine in August 1972 about a bear-snow experience he had: "During a spring brown bear hunt at Herendeen Bay on the Alaska Peninsula many years ago, our party spotted a sow bear leisurely feeding on a mountain slope. As we watched, she repeatedly raised her head and looked carefully at something in the distance. Swinging our binoculars in that direction, we found three bear cubs perhaps half a mile from her, entertaining themselves by repeatedly sliding down half a mile of snow-covered slope.

"The game started with all three at the top. One cub would start down the steep slide by sitting on its rear, and balancing there, while it sped down the slope. When it was 100 or more feet from the start, a second cub would start down the slope. When it was 100 or more feet down, the third cub started its slide.

"As each cub neared the end of the snow, which fed onto a rough boulder-strewn slope, it flipped over on its belly and dug its claws in, to stop almost instantly.

"When all three cubs were at the bottom of the half-mile-long slide, together they ran back to the top and repeated the exciting game.

"After an hour and a half of sliding, they tired of the game and started to explore.

"Shortly the mother, which had continued to feed and keep a watchful eye on her playing cubs, walked to the long slide, and after a long and careful look at the surroundings, mimicked her cubs by sitting down and speeding down the fast chute on *her* rear. When she reached bottom, she rolled over, dug her claws in and stopped. Instead of running back to the top as the cubs had, however, she walked in the ponderous fashion of an adult brown bear.

"She slid down the chute three times, then led her family away across the hills."

Frank Dufresne commented on the bears' humorous nature in the December 1963 *ALASKA SPORTSMAN®*: "Andy Simons, a famous Alaskan guide, and I once witnessed one of these 'teenagers' balancing himself like a tightrope walker on the crumbling edge of a snow cornice high over our heads. Below him a melting snow chute sloped steeply down to the green tundra where Andy and I stood. Suddenly, we saw the young bear leap off the rim in a bellywhopper dive and come scooting down the slippery incline like a boy on a bobsled. Accelerating to dizzy speed, he came rolling end over end to a grand finish no more than a few yards away. Without so much as a glance in our direction the youthful Groucho picked himself up and climbed back to do it all over again.

"Andy showed no surprise. 'I've seen 'em do crazier stunts than that,' he insisted. 'I've watched a grizzly swim across a lake, touch shore on the other side and swim right back again.' "

It is quite common to see bear cubs romping and cavorting about, with nary a care in the world. One man witnessed a sow playing a game with her cubs. They were beside a small stream near which a short tree was growing. The mother would pull the tree top over into the water, a cub would mount the limbs, and mom would release her grip, catapulting junior skyward in a shower of spray. The cubs waited their turn and never seemed to tire of this game.

Another common characteristic of *Ursus* is mother's stern code. Junior often needs maternal guidance as Frank Dufresne related (same article as on page 289): "Once I observed . . . a family in the act of crossing a glacial torrent in Alaska's Valley of Ten Thousand Smokes. While the cubs fretted anxiously, the mother picked each one up by the scruff of the neck and ferried it to the other shore. But when they balked at a mere rill a few moments later, the mother spanked her whimpering brats soundly on their rumps and sent them bawling through the shallows. She knew where to draw the line on pampering."

Bears use a multitude of sounds to communicate with other bears and other animals. Whoofs, sniffs, roars, growls, snorts, moans and meows characterize their "speech," depending on the animal's age and condition.

The effect of man's voice on bruin is a subject well worth studying. There are many recorded cases of man "talking down" a bear in a touchy situation. Allen Hasselborg frequently "talked" bears down. He rubbed shoulders with them for so long that he was familiar with every bear in his immediate locale; he probably treated them much the same as if they'd been his children — speaking calmly to some and harshly to others. Usually his "talking" worked as a password for his passage into bear country — he also had tremendous savvy toward bear nature.

Some bears have retreated at the sound of man's voice, and others have given ground when hit with a stick. Several instances tell of man thumping bruin with a stick and living to tell about it. Some men have resorted to other tactics to shoo off a bear. "When

Frank Bobner, logger operating on Admiralty Island, went out one night last summer to get a caterpillar tractor he had left near a creek, he found a brown bear loitering beside it. The bear seemed to have no intention of leaving, so Bobner threw some gravel at it. That was ineffective. The brownie just stood, opening and shutting his mouth in a disconcerting fashion. Bobner picked up a tree branch and shied it at him, and finally swung the Coleman lantern he carried in front of the bear's face. It was fully five minutes before the brownie took the hint and made tracks in the opposite direction. Those tracks were nine inches across! At another time, when six brown bears blocked his trail, Bobner used a stick of dynamite to scatter them. They moved away quickly that time, he says." *(The ALASKA SPORTSMAN®, January 1944)*

A bear's nature is definitely interesting and different — they have their own individuality. No two bears will do the same thing in a given situation; and a bear may not do the same thing twice. Though there will always be exceptions to the last statement, it would serve us well to commit it to memory.

A rule of thumb used by guides and bear hunters-in-the-know is to measure the width of the front track and add one inch to guesstimate the size of the "squared" hide. Interestingly enough, it seems that brown/grizzlies weigh 100-150 pounds per year of growth up to about eight years of age and about 100 pounds per squared foot. Those are not scientific measurements, but offhand generalizations.

A brown bear's power and means of using his paws is phenomenal. "The man came upon a bear, which he shot and badly wounded. Accompanied by a friend, he followed up the blood trail which led into a thick patch of alders. Suddenly he came upon a large unwounded male bear which charged him unprovoked, and at such close quarters that he was unable to defend himself. Before his companion, who was but a short distance away, could reach him, he was killed. The bear frightfully mangled the body, holding it down with his feet and using his teeth to tear it apart." *(Selected Alaska Hunting and Fishing Tales,* Vol. 3, Alaska Northwest Publishing Company, 1974)

Sometimes the bear's power is matched by man's courage. In pre-rifle days many men faced bears with spear, and the story is told of an Eskimo named Takumik who did combat with a polar bear; the man was armed only with a knife, but he killed the bear, earning himself the fame of the greatest of the old-time hunters. *(Hunters of the Northern Ice)*

Guide Clark Engle told me about flying over a grizzly that

stalked and charged a good-sized bull moose. The bear sprang from the brush within a few yards of the moose which fled. Bruin took a couple of jumps, lunged and grabbed the bull's hind quarters with its front paws, lunged again and pulled with its front paws ending up on the moose's back where the bear bit the moose in the neck and killed it.

One day while playing with our little boy I contemplated the comparative strength of a brown bear. I was pretending I was a bear while I wrestled with Benny who was five and weighed 40 pounds. I weighed 180 or 4.5 times as much as Benny. If I multiply my weight by 4.5, it comes out 810. I threw Benny around with ease and wondered what an 810-pound bear would be able to do with me. It is unnerving.

Much of the material I researched was inconclusive or difficult to substantiate. Stories about bears in the Great Land are numerous. Some of them which I was unable to verify follow.

The owner of the Tangle River Inn on the Denali Highway was the proud possessor of an old-timer's hunting knife. The inn's proprietor had taken this knife from a big grizzly bear he'd killed. The knife was lodged between its front shoulders near the spine of the bear, and the hair had grown around the wound sealing it. If this story is true, think of how long the original owner of the knife lived after sticking it into the bear.

Bernie Smith was hunting, camped across Cook Inlet from Anchorage, when one night he had a feeling something was opposite his tent in the inky blackness. He thought about firing a round into the night, but decided against it. Not much sleep that night. Next morning he found huge brown bear paw prints in the sand just outside the reach of his campfire light.

A man and woman encountered a bear along the highway near Palmer. The bear took a swipe at the husband through an open window as the man sat behind the steering wheel of the car, maiming or killing him. His wife developed a speech impediment which she has to this day.

Several years ago in Southeastern Alaska some men were boating up a river when a brown bear ran out on the bank and attacked the boat which was able to stay ahead of the animal. A geologist on board was so frightened his hair turned white.

A grizzly ripped a guy's leg off some years back across the Inlet from Anchorage.

A guy on the Yentna River had a brown bear charge into his cabin, and he beat it over the head with a shotgun, chasing it away.

On the opposite side of Cook Inlet from Anchorage a cheechako took to a tree when a black bear approached his moose kill one afternoon. The hapless guy stayed there the night even though the bear left some time shortly after chasing him to his heavenly perch.

The man took a considerable amount of energy sticks and similar goodies with him and spent the night in a cramped position. It rained off and on all night, and the guy spent two or three very uncomfortable nights in the tree while bears and wolves devoured most of the moose below. He finally descended the tree and shot a bear in defense of life.

Another man was trying to sleep one night when a thieving bear tried to reach his jerky under his pillow. The man scared the animal away.

A hunter and a guide flew over a bear, decided to collect its hide, landed and were both killed. Evidently the bear watched the plane, stalked it, surprised the men and got them both. This may be a somber message for those who like to fly over and harrass bears. (Possibly same story as Pennington-Kendall, pages 92-93.)

Two men were fishing out of Whittier in Prince William Sound. They'd concluded their fishing and were returning to shore when they encountered a black bear between an island and the mainland. They had some rope on board and decided to strangle or drown the critter, made a noose, stuffed it over the animal's head; and the fun began. The bear decided to board. They grabbed a pipe and started whacking the bear on the head. It took several thumps before they could even stun him, but they finally killed him.

Some old-timers used shotguns on bears, and their "shot" consisted of pellets linked by a steel leader or cable. As the shot left the barrel, it followed a chain-like whipping action. At least one account told about a prospector who rounded a drift log on the beach to come face-to-face with a brownie. He immediately shouldered and fired his shotgun from a distance of but a few yards. The blast blew off half the bear's head.

A couple of theories exist regarding brown bear ferocity. Some of the men I spoke with told me they believed the Interior grizzly was more ferocious than the coastal brown bear, probably due to the fact that they have to work harder for their food. Others felt that there was a difference between the bears on Admiralty and Kodiak islands. "Jack Alexander, a Department of Fish & Game biologist who has trapped many bears on Kodiak Island and who also worked on the Admiralty Island project, said that he was impressed by the difference in temperament between the animals from the two islands.

"Trapped Kodiak bears always try to move away when approached. The Admiralty Island bears are much more aggressive and nearly always charge." *(ALASKA®* magazine, January 1974)

One area of contradiction is that of the polar bear's nature. Many people indicate that polar bears view any dark object on the ice as food (perhaps assuming it is a seal); and the bear charges immediately. These people feel that nothing will deter the bear from an outright confrontation.

There are others, however, who feel that a polar bear is as startled as man in a face-to-face encounter and that both will depart the presence of the other with haste. This group feels that it is the polar bear's nature to be inquisitive and want to check out various activities — that if a bear is running towards man, it is only on a curiosity satisfying journey and will turn back once satisfied.

Perhaps there are differences in polar bears in accordance with their locales. Maybe some polar bears have not seen man and "charge" to get a closer look at their two-legged neighbor; maybe they are unafraid of man or maybe there are polar bears in some areas that *are* meaner than in other areas.

Three myths I've encountered could use some study and explanation before acceptance as fact. Probably the most widespread is the belief that a man can outrun a bear downhill because the bear's longer hind legs make it difficult for him to run downhill. I wonder if the bear is aware of this "fact."

Another misunderstood bear activity centers around a "rubbing" tree. Some say the bear stands on hind legs and stretches to full height and rubs his back against the tree to show his size, in an effort to communicate his authority or place in the bear pecking order. Others claim the rubbing tree is just that, a place for bears to rub their backs.

A most unusual idea involves a method of escaping a bear mauling. Several years ago I was told that a sure means of avoiding a bear mauling was to spit in the bear's mouth. I have no knowledge of the success of this action nor do I care to experiment, however, should a bear ever attack me, I'm certain I won't be able to salivate enough to spit into his mouth.

That the bear has a keen sense of hearing and smell is undoubted. Occasionally one stumbles onto a bear that is blind or deaf, but rarely. In his book, *The Grizzly, Our Greatest Wild Animal,* Enos Mills stated the grizzly could hear the stealthy approach of a hunter under favorable conditions a quarter of a mile away and that same bear could smell a man as far away as a mile or more.

During the summer of 1963 in Alaska there was an outbreak of black bear attacks. Of almost a dozen bear attacks where the animals were examined, none was rabid. Several explanations for the bears' actions were given including the lack of blueberries and other feed, but no satisfactory conclusion was ever reached. Interestingly enough, several of these attacks occurred while the victim lay asleep in a sleeping bag, some in tents and others outside.   □

THE BEAR'S FUTURE
IN ALASKA

"*... further protection of these animals is a proper move. Admiralty, Baranof and Chichagof islands should be set aside as sanctuaries for the perpetuation of America's greatest game animals for the enjoyment and edification of coming generations. There should also be established a large sanctuary for the perpetuation of the brownies in the Aleutian Peninsula country for the same purpose.*" (John S. Vincent, The ALASKA SPORTSMAN®, April 1935)

"*On the McNeil River, where a lot of guys go to take pictures of bears fishing, a guy shot a bear with a .44 and killed it. She had a first year cub with her. And he pushed his luck — he got too darn close. He was fortunate he's even alive; but the sad thing of it is, the bear's the one that should be alive because the bear didn't do anything that a wild animal protecting its young wouldn't have done. This guy should have known what he was doing, he was a registered guide. He was stupid!*" (Clark Engle, Master Guide, personal interview and taped story)

"*... driving around Turnagain Arm is more dangerous than bears.*" (Al Thompson, mauling victim/game warden, personal communication)

"*How we value the grizzly will ultimately decide its future.*"

(Dr. Steve Herrero, Professor of Environmental Science and Biology, University of Calgary, personal communication, April 1979)

Just before the turn of the century the Alaskan brown bear was all but exterminated on the Alaska Peninsula by hide hunters. The great beast fell victim to hunters who helped supply the royal families and aristocracy of Russia with skins. Old-time hunters living on the Alaska Peninsula told of the hunter in those days taking an average of 20 bears a year. Fortunately the demand for the hides of this noble beast fell off in 1899, and the hunting all but ceased until the early 1900s.

This giant brown bear of the peninsula was so abundant at one time that his tribe had worn deep trails, three by three feet, in the tundra, and his masses wore steps and paths in the rocks they passed over. In some areas these trails resembled the paths that barnyard Bossy took to the milking parlor. But those days of abundance are gone.

Man may be hunter, developer, photographer, backpacker, prospector or rancher. He wants to protect his interests. However, we must face the question of man's intrusion into bear country. Where do we draw the line?

With the current trend in anti-hunting and conservation, growing numbers want to protect bears. On the other hand, there are those who advocate reduction of these creatures, quite often where "progress" is impaired. Those who wish to reduce the bear population are developers, and those who have had bad experiences with bears. The "protectors" and the "reducers" have strong arguments, it is difficult to argue with them.

Anti-hunters oppose cruelty to animals and condemn those who hunt for an animal that is often hunted only as a trophy (not for food). Conservationists want to protect the species from annihilation. The progress-developer group is more concerned for "progress" than the wildlife. The hunter-sportsman group wishes to utilize the resource or seek a trophy. Those who have had bad experiences regard the bear as a threat.

Knut Peterson, who was mauled in 1949, wrote me, "Alaska is a heavy producer of oil and gas, more and more people moving in all the time and a lot of people will get killed and crippled just to preserve a big game animal for the sportsmen. Every season someone gets hurt or killed."

Even though the bear that mauls or kills is a real threat, it is a rarity. Very few people are injured by bears, considering the large numbers going into the woods. Izembek National Wildlife Range Manager John Sarvis wrote me in February 1979 " . . . bears are not deliberately out to harm people. In nearly every adverse encounter between bears and people, humans have precipitated or aggravated the situation. It is true that bears are normally and naturally afraid of people and will avoid humans unless conditioned otherwise. If bears actually wanted to harm or eat people they could have and would have had a 'field day' already. The surprising thing (but proof that bears are not that 'bad') is how few adverse encounters do occur considering the numbers of people going into bear habitat each year."

Mauling victims share divergent views of the bear's existence. Some feel no animosity for the bear and seek to accept full responsibility for their being in the bear's territory in the first place, while others would just as soon never see another live bear.

After Al Johnson was attacked in Mt. McKinley National Park, he told me, "My bout with the sow hasn't dampened at all my enthusiasm for the enjoyment of Alaska's wilds . . . coming from a man who could easily have resentment for the brown bear, I would indeed be saddened to see them driven from Alaska as they have been from many states."

On the other hand Knut Peterson told me, "After having been badly mauled by a grizzly bear myself, naturally I wouldn't be the best advice giver on how to avoid getting in trouble with them. About the best I know of, which of course would be ignored, would be to put a heavy bounty on them and do away with them. What good are they anyway?"

Almost every year men vanish in the Great Land's mammoth wild country, and it is anybody's guess as to their demise — certainly some of them were killed or eaten by bears, with not a shred of evidence for the survivors. But the truth about these disappearances and other actual maulings is not always revealed. Some men were killed by bears while others died of natural causes and became part of the bear's diet.

It is imperative to reconstruct each mauling to determine if possible where the guilt lies in order to eliminate future such threats *and* to guard against unnecessary action taken against an innocent bear.

Careful management allows man to use this wildlife resource for hunting purposes. The brown/grizzly is the most dangerous big game animal on the North American continent, and a tremendous challenge to the sportsman. As long as bears are in abundance and man does not abuse this resource, he should be permitted the privilege of harvesting them.

Lee Miller of the Alaska Department of Fish & Game shared his expertise in bear management with me. For hunting, the brown/grizzly is a two season bear (spring and fall). Hunting regulations are changed constantly, altering seasons and open and closed areas in the 26 game management units of the state. To ensure proper bear management sportsmen may take only one brown/grizzly every four regulatory years. Hunters seeking information on brown/grizzly regulations can obtain a copy of the Alaska Department of Fish & Game hunting regulations which are available every July at their offices and some retail outlets.

To the question "How many brown/grizzly bears are there in Alaska?" Lee Miller responded, "Since aerial surveys such as the department does every winter on moose are not practical for bears, except in a few isolated cases, no one really knows. To build up its data bank on brown/grizzly and polar bears, the Alaska Department of Fish & Game in 1960 requested the Board of Fish and Game to require that every bear that is killed must be examined and sealed by the Department of Fish & Game. The regulation became effective in 1961. From 1961 through 1979, the department recorded a sport harvest of over 3,500 polar bears and 13,833 brown/grizzly bears.

"This is probably the largest collection of data on these big bears ever gathered. These data include the date and location of kill, sex, length and width of hide, condition of hide, length and width of skull, and since 1969 the age of the bear. These data, when broken down by game management unit or subunit and compared year after year, give some insight into what is happening to a specific segment of a bear population. These things are a primary concern to game managers who are charged with collecting and interpreting data in order to propose seasons and bag limits to the Board of Game.

"Of the 13,833 brown bears taken in the last 19 years, about 43% that were harvested in the state are from two game management units: 8, Kodiak Island group, and 9, the Alaska Peninsula. These two areas are still producing record book bears. About 14% of the total comes from Southeast Alaska and the remaining 43% scattered throughout the rest of the state.

"At this time brown/grizzly bear populations throughout the state are thriving. Proper management of this species and its habitat will ensure healthy bear populations for both the hunter and non-hunter alike."

Revenue from hunting licenses and related fees support the management and scientific research of these animals, allowing not only the sportsman, but also other outdoor enthusiasts to benefit from the wilderness experience with brown/grizzlies.

Man is also permitted to defend his life, family or property from bears under a Defense of Life and Property law. It appears that the current management program ensures the future of these majestic animals, the game managers having profited from the concern expressed in the past.

Fred Mansell stated in *The ALASKA SPORTSMAN®* in August 1938: "I'm afraid there's going to be something serious happen soon if the government doesn't take steps to curb game hogs. Alaska and British Columbia are the last strongholds for the fighting grizzly.

"You see, the North country is our last frontier. We have game that will attract hunters from all over the world, but we'll have to take care of it."

And Frank Dufresne, former director for the U.S Fish & Wildlife in Alaska, stumped for bears in *ALASKA SPORTSMAN®* in December 1963: "Today the grizzly bear's fate hangs in the balance, for he is the continent's number one trophy. He has been pushed from one wilderness pocket to the next until there are presently no more than 20,000 left in Alaska, and perhaps not more than 500 in our other western states. The latter are mostly in the national parks in Montana, Idaho and Wyoming, where tourists can sometimes see the once proud and respected beasts grubbing in garbage heaps. The great Golden Bear of California — the state emblem — is totally extinct.

"If Old Groucho is going to be able to stand the pressures of a growing number of hunters, and a continuing development of new highways and airways from our populated centers to the wilderness, Alaskans are going to have to outlaw all manner of airplane hunting in line with the 'fair chase' ruling of the Boone and Crockett Club against spotting game animals from the air as well as herding. Groucho is going to need more protection under stricter game laws and those laws will have to be enforced."

Since Dufresne's day it is no longer legal for big game hunters to fly and shoot animals the same day.

The bear's current status hinges on game laws regulating his future. Basically, the animal's future depends on these laws being enforced and man's concentrated efforts to try to live in harmony with the animal.

In defending bears John Sarvis of Izembek National Wildlife

Refuge wrote to me, " . . . bears are just another species — which deserve a place on this planet and whose habitat is gradually being reduced or destroyed like many other wildlife species. Partially because of the many ingrained fears people have of bears, it seems that when people live in bear habitat the first request is to eliminate the bears. People don't always feel this way about other species of wildlife. But for some reason perceive bears as an enemy. It is far better to be thankful that there are still areas left where bears can survive and appreciative of the fact that bears still exist as part of the ecosystem. Hopefully people will come to appreciate being able to live in areas that are still functioning naturally. Because of what this signifies (i.e., a healthy environment) they will want to co-exist with bears and other wildlife rather than eliminate certain species of occasional problems."

It is critical to manage the bear resource properly, which it appears the Alaska Department of Fish & Game is doing; but it is even more important to care for his habitat. The bear can adapt more readily to man than he can the elimination of his bear environment. If the bear is to survive as he has in the past, he must have the necessary bear habitat to do it in.

The polar bear is currently thriving. Airplane hunts are now prohibited for the ice bear. Natives hunt him with dogs, and some whites (not in Alaska) pursue Nanook by way of Eskimo or white guided hunts using dogs and dog sleds. The polar bear is on the increase and is temporarily safe from any serious threat.

The black bear enjoys the distinction of being the most numerous Alaskan bear. Regardless of human intrusion, the black will most likely be around forever. He may retreat before man's "progress" and become less obvious, but he will more than likely maintain his high density.

Man has a responsibility to bears. We need to consider the true nature of bears, use precaution in his territory and manage this wildlife resource in such a way that we can utilize it now and yet guarantee our future generations the thrill of sharing its majesty, power and beauty with us.

It is my hope and prayer that I can always take my wife and family into bear country and watch a ponderous hulk of a brown bear wading the riffles of a salmon stream with a shining salmon flopping from his mouth . . . or that they gaze in awe at a mountain grizzly excavating tons of earth in search of a whistler . . . or that they share with each other the rib-splitting laughter of black bear cubs glissading down a snowfield head over tea kettle in the Great Land of Seward's Folly. ☐

Alaskan Bear Harvest Reports

Since 1961 hunters have been required to report to the state every brown/grizzly bear killed in the 26 Game Management Units (GMU) in Alaska. During the years 1961-81, 15,601 brown/grizzlies were reported. About 50% of these were killed in the three most productive GMU's: the Alaska Peninsula (GMU 9), where 24.5% of the statewide kill was made; Kodiak and adjacent islands (GMU 8), 18% of the total; and Southeastern Alaska (GMU 1 and 4), with 11%.

Brown/grizzlies were killed in all parts of the state except for GMU's 2 and 3 (which include islands in the southern half of Southeastern Alaska), and the Aleutian Islands (except for Unimak Island where about five bears a year are killed).

Biggest inland producer of brown/grizzlies was the Nelchina Basin (GMU 13), with about 7% of the statewide total. Next largest was the Kuskokwim valley (GMU 19), with 4.6% of the statewide kill. Another 4.4% were killed in the Yukon and Tanana River valleys (GMU 20). The next largest producer was the west side of Cook Inlet (GMU 16), where 3.9% of the total were harvested. Most other GMU's produced from 1% or less to 2% of the total.

Bibliography

BOOKS

_____, *Alaska Book, The,* J.G. Ferguson Publishing Company, Chicago, 1960.
A comprehensive collection of Alaskana including history, biography, resources, development, recreation, flora and fauna, hunting and fishing.

_____, *Alaska Hunting Annual,* Alaska Northwest Publishing Company, Anchorage, 1970.
Collection of hunting stories.

Beebe, B.F. and Johnson, James Ralph, *American Bears,* D. McKay, New York, 1965.

Berglund-Shore, Evelyn, *Born on Snowshoes,* Houghton Mifflin Company, Boston, 1954.
Autobiographical account tells hardships of growing up in Alaska, trying to subsist with mother, sisters and old trapper.

Burford, Virgil, *North to Danger,* Longmans, Toronto, 1954.

Caras, Roger A., *Monarch of Deadman Bay,* Little, Brown and Company, Boston, Toronto, 1969.
A fictional account of the birth, existence and death of a legendary Kodiak brown bear, portraying bear nature and Kodiak environment graphically.

Chase, Will H., *Alaska's Mammoth Brown bears,* Burton Publishing Company, Kansas City, Missouri, 1947.
Chase describes the brown bear's easy-going nature. First half of book is a biographical sketch of Tyee from cubhood through death from eruption of Katmai. Brown-black bear fight, brown bear hunt, Yukon close call, information about destruction of brown bear in late 1800s, fire power and a plea for conservation/co-existence.

Clark, James, *Man is the Prey,* Stein and Day, New York, 1969.
Creatures that prey upon man — insects through elephants.

Clark, Marvin H., Pinnell and Talifson: *Last of the Great Brown Bear Men,* Great Northwest Publishing and Distributing Company, Spokane, 1980.

Craighead, Frank C., Jr., *Track of the Grizzly,* Sierra Club Books, San Francisco, 1979.
Culmination of Craighead's extensive study of the Yellowstone grizzly and related areas. Objective look at the bear's past, man's relationship to bruin, park service mistakes and some thought provoking questions regarding the bear and man's responsibility to bruin.

Cramond, Mike, *Killer Bears,* Outdoor Life Books, New York, 1981.

DeHart, Don, *All About Bears,* Johnson Publishing Company, Boulder, Colorado, 1971.
> A look at Alaska's bears, hunting and attack stories, tips on hunting bears — including weaponry and field glasses.

Dobie, Frank, *The Ben Lilly Legend,* Little, Brown and Company, Boston, 1950.
> Biography about the legendary Texas outdoorsman.

Douglas, Dick, Jr., *A Boy Scout in Grizzly Country,* G.P. Putnam's Sons, Knickerbocker Press, New York, London, 1929.
> Dick relates various experiences with the Kodiak country and its bears.

Dufresne, Frank, *My Way Was North,* Holt, Rinehart and Winston, New York, Chicago, San Francisco, 1966.
> Dufresne's journey to Alaska and experiences there.

Dufresne, Frank, *No Room For Bears,* Holt, Rinehart and Winston, New York, Chicago, San Francisco, 1965.
> Informative and exciting book about the black, polar and grizzly bear of Alaska. Chapter by chapter unfolds and bruin data, adventure and humor ooze onto the pages. Even more noticeable is Dufresne's stark portrayal of a need to recognize the need to question man's relationship to and responsibility for bruin and his habitat.

East, Ben, *Bears,* Outdoor Life-Crown Publishers, Inc., New York, 1977.
> A comprehensive book portraying the North American bears — denning, birth, eating, mating, nature, size, distribution and observations.

East, Ben, *Survival,* Outdoor Life-E.P. Dutton and Company, Inc., New York, 1967.
> Twenty-three true adventurous close calls people have had with death including bear, lion and moose attacks, snakebite, getting lost and stranded, fishing and water catastrophies.

Eddy, John W., *Hunting the Alaskan Brown Bear,* G.P. Putnam's Sons, New York, London, 1930.
> Detailed account of Andy Simons-guided brown bear hunt via steamship to Alaska Peninsula hunting grounds, then a 30-mile-one-way walk-in month-long three-bear-per-man hunt near Pavlof Volcano.

Flowers, Ralph, *The Education of a Bear Hunter,* Winchester Press, New York, 1975.
> Recounts the start Flowers got in hunting Washington state's nuisance black bears in logging areas on the Olympic Peninsula (tree damage). Relates adventures and close calls as well as information about bears and logging.

Freuchen, Dagmar, *The Peter Freuchen Reader,* Julian Messner, New York, 1965.

Greuning, Ernest (editor), *An Alaskan Reader,* Meredith Press, New York, 1966.
> A collection of Alaskana including history-exploration-statehood, gold rush days, justice, mountaineering, flying, natives, hunting and poetry.

Gubser, Nicholas J., *The Nunamiut Eskimo: Hunters of Caribou,* Yale University Press, New Haven and London, 1965.
> An ethnographic study of the Nunamiut Eskimos and their life style.

Haynes, Bessie Doak and Edgar, *The Grizzly Bear,* University of Oklahoma Press, Norman, 1966.
> Comprehensive collection of stories chronicling the relationship between man and grizzly beginning in the late 1600s — explorers, mountain men, California bears, pets, naturalists, cattlemen, Mexican, Alaskan, Yellowstone, folklore and legend. Superb bibliography included.

Heller, Herbert (editor), *Sourdough Sagas*, Ballantine Books, New York, 1967.
  Collection of background information and stories of the sourdoughs'
  early Alaska.
Helmericks, Constance and Harmon, *Our Alaskan Winter*, Little, Brown and
  Company, Boston, 1951.
  A winter spent among the Eskimos traveling with two hired Eskimos
  over the sea ice of the Arctic Ocean to the Colville River and south into
  caribou country.
Helmericks, Harmon, *The Last of the Bush Pilots*, Alfred A. Knopf, Inc., New
  York, 1969.
  General work about Alaskan bush pilots including most of the
  well-known pilots and incidents which won them their reputations in the
  sourdough skies of the North.
Hittell, Theodore H., *The Adventures of James Capen Adams, Mountaineer and
  Grizzly Bear Hunter of California*, Boston, 1860 (Town and Bacon, San
  Francisco, 1860).
  Biography of James Capen Adams, today's television "Grizzly Adams,"
  recounts his adventures to and in the West, especially catching, taming
  and living with grizzly bears.
Holzworth, John M., *The Wild Grizzlies of Alaska*, G.P. Putnam's Sons,
  Knickerbocker Press, 1930.
  Comprehensive study of the grizzlies of Admiralty Island and includes a
  description of bear country and bear history. Deals with countless
  encounters and many attacks, literary history, classification of species,
  breeding habits, hibernation, food, intelligence, ferocity, conservation,
  photography — methods and values.
Hubbard, W.P., *Notorious Grizzly Bears*, Sage Books, Denver, 1960.
  Comprehensive book covering grizzly nature, characteristics and habits.
  Several man-grizzly encounters are recorded. Bear incidents in several
  western states also.
Huntington, James, *On the Edge of Nowhere*, Crown Publishers, Inc., New York,
  1966.
  Autobiography about an Athabascan half-breed boy who grew up to be
  North American dog sled champion — tragic childhood experiences as
  well as close calls on the hunting and trapping trails.
Jackson, W.H., *Handloggers*, Alaska Northwest Publishing Company,
  Anchorage, 1974.
  An adventurous account of a passing way of life, logging by hand in
  Southeastern Alaska. Jackson shares his adventures subsisting with his
  wife as they enjoyed the outdoors of the Great Land — marriage,
  logging, hunting and fishing.
Keim, Charles J., *Alaska Game Trails with a Master Guide*, Alaska Northwest
  Publishing Company, Anchorage, 1977.
  Collection of memorabilia about Alaska's early master guide, Hal Waugh.
Martin, Martha, *Home on the Bear's Domain*, MacMillan Company, New York,
  1954.
  Sequel to *O Rugged Land of Gold*. Martha Martin and her husband
  experience a multitude of privations and challenges while living in
  Southeast Alaska, trapping and making ends meet.
Martin, Martha, *O Rugged Land of Gold*, MacMillan Company, New York, 1953.
McCracken, Harold, *The Beast That Walks Like Man*, Oldbourne Press, London,
  1957.

McCracken traces the grizzly from the time of the explorers and Indians
to the present, covering adventures encountered along the way by both
man and bear. Included are birth and nature, tales of yesteryear, bear's
relation to man as revealed in legend (Indian and mountain man), sports
the bear became part of, distribution and classification.

Miller, Joaquin, *True Bear Stories*, Rand McNally and Company, Publishers,
Chicago and New York, 1900.
Various bear stories told by Miller.

Mills, Enos A., *The Grizzly, Our Greatest Wild Animal*, Houghton Mifflin
Company, Riversdale Press, Boston and New York, 1919.
A plea for man to consider the character of the grizzly and preserve this
stately creature. Mills covers the bear's nature and habits.

Morenus, Richard, *Alaska Sourdough*, Rand McNally and Company, New York,
Chicago, San Francisco, 1956.
Biography tracing adventures of Slim Williams, Alaskan. From his
coming into the country by way of Valdez and his many adventures.

Murie, Adolph, *A Naturalist in Alaska*, Devin-Adair, Company, New York, 1961.
Naturalist Murie's commentary about lynx, grizzlies, moose, wolverine,
fox, mice, wolves, sheep, caribou and cranes.

Nelson, Richard K., *Hunters of the Northern Ice*, University of Chicago Press,
Chicago and London, 1969.
The setting is the Arctic, the characters are its inhabitants, and the
theme is survival — survival of the Eskimo way of life, a culture which
may soon be gone forever. Nelson describes the Arctic environment and
the animals therein concentrating on birds, fox, polar bear, whale, seal
and wolves.

Oliver, Simeon, *Son of the Smoky Sea*, Messner, New York, 1941
Eskimo boy grows up in orphanage at Dutch Harbor and becomes world-
famous pianist. Marries, has two girls, wife dies, he returns to Alaska to
defend home during World War II, remarries.

Olsen, Jack, *Night of the Grizzlies*, Signet Book, New York, 1969.
Compelling story about several bear incidents in Glacier National Park in
summer of 1967 which led to the attack and deaths of two 19-year-old
college girls, one of whom was partially devoured, on the same night.
Author-reporter castigates park officials for apathetic and inefficient
means of dealing with the man-bear problem that summer and proposes
better methods in the future.

Olson, B.G. and Miller, Mike (editors), *Blood on the Arctic Snow*, Superior
Publishing Company, Seattle, 1956.
Eighteen true tales of the Last Frontier from *The ALASKA
SPORTSMAN*® — bears, aviation, wolves, hardships and mystery.

Ormond, Clyde, *Bear!*, Stackpole Publishing Company, Harrisburg,
Pennsylvania, 1961.
General information about the four North American bears and how to
hunt them.

Pearson, Grant H., *My Life of High Adventure*, Ballantine Books, New York, 1962.
Pearson's introduction to Mt. McKinley as park ranger and his many
experiences, covering his evolution from cheechako to sourdough,
animals, dog mushing and mountain climbing.

Potter, Jean, *Flying Frontiersmen*, MacMillan Company, New York, 1956.
Explorers of the northern skies.

Pryde, Duncan, *Nunaga*, Walker and Company, New York, 1971.

One man's venture from "civilized" life in Scotland to the rugged life and harsh climate of northern Canada as a fur trader, for more than 10 years living among the Eskimos.

Rae, William E. (editor), *A Treasury of Outdoor Life*, Outdoor Life-Harper and Row, Inc., New York, 1975.
Compilation of adventures from the pages of *Outdoor Life* dating back to 1898. Nearly 70 stories of hunting, fishing and outdoor adventure.

Rodahl, Kaare, *The Last of the Few*, Harper and Row, Inc., New York, 1963.
Dr. Kaare Rodahl and his wife went to Alaska in 1950 to develop a Department of Physiology at the Arctic Aeromedical Laboratory in Fairbanks. From there they studied, lived and worked with Eskimos in Alaska and engaged in other scientific research.

Russell, Andy, *Grizzly Country*, Alfred A. Knopf, Inc., New York, 1967.
Russell describes the grizzly of western Canada and briefly depicts the bear of Mt. McKinley National Park in Alaska. Description of bear habitat, the grizzly's character, habits and nature, social life, the animal as an adversary, history and camera hunting.

Schneider, Bill, *Where the Grizzly Walks*, Mountain Press Publishing Company, Missoula, 1977.
Schneider concentrates on the grizzly as an animal to be appreciated in our ecosystem and traces man's disregard for the bear's future since the time of Lewis and Clark. Covers Craighead's battle with mismanagement issue in Yellowstone and outlines plan for beast's salvation.

_____, *Selected Alaska Hunting and Fishing Tales*, vol. 2, Alaska Northwest Publishing Company, Anchorage, 1972.
Nearly 40 tales of hunters and fishermen in the Land of the Midnight Sun.

Sheldon, Charles, *The Wilderness of Denali*, Scribner, New York, 1960.
Comprehensive volume written as a journal and chronicling Sheldon's three years of Alaskan hunting and exploring from 1906-1908. Campfire resumes capture his ecstasies near Mt. Denali and nerve tingling escapades pursuing inhabitants — grizzly, sheep, caribou and moose — in what today is known as Denali National Park and Preserve.

Short, Wayne, *The Cheechakos*, Random House, New York, 1962.
Story about the Short family as they moved to Admiralty Island just after World War II, how they lived and fished commercially.

Storer, Tracy I. and Tevis, Lloyd P., *California Grizzly*, University of Nebraska Press, Lincoln, London, 1955.
Historical look at California's grizzly and the men it confronted —Indians, Spaniards, frontiersmen and Grizzly Adams. Interesting appendixes and thorough bibliography.

Thomas, Lowell, *Kabluk of the Eskimo*, Little, Brown and Company, Boston, 1932.
Thomas portrays life among the Eskimos.

Trefzger, Hardy, *My Fifty Years in Alaska*, Exposition Press, New York, 1963.
Author loses love, goes West then to Alaska, discusses the Yakutat Indians and Tlingits, tells of ships and wrecks along the Gulf of Alaska, relates grizzly/brown bear fight, tells of suicide victim and his experiences trapping, prospecting, finding oil seepages, fox farming and getting chewed on by bruin.

Walker, Dr. Theodore J., *Red Salmon, Brown Bear*, World Publishing Company, New York, 1971.

Walker studies life forms — primarily salmon and bear — at Lake Eva on Baranof Island from April through October 1970, recording his findings, thoughts and questions.

Wickersham, Hon. James, *Old Yukon Tales, Trails and Trials,* West Publishing Company, St. Paul, 1938.
Comments on Alaska history, description, travels, mining, natives and justice.

Williams, Slim, *Alaskan Adventure,* Stackpole Company, Harrisburg, Pennsylvania, 1952.
J.P. Williams relates his experiences in Alaska while surveying. He includes the country and animals concluding with a couple of appendixes on camping and equipment.

Woodworth, Jim, *The Kodiak Bear,* Stackpole Company, Harrisburg, Pennsylvania, 1958.
Primarily book of guided hunting experiences for the big brown bear. Included are chapters on bear facts, Dall sheep hunt, photography and browns, rifles, trophy preparation and the sportsman's Alaska.

Wright, Billie, *Four Seasons North,* Harper and Row, New York, 1973.
Author tells of spending winter in a 12- by 12-foot cabin in the Brooks Range with her husband. Covers reaction to new environment and suggests a return to nature and conservation.

Wright. W.W., *The Grizzly Bear,* University of Nebraska Press, Lincoln and London, 1977 (reprint of 1909 edition).
Classic study of the grizzly covering history, personal experiences, bear nature and distribution.

Young, F.M., *Man Meets Grizzly,* Houghton Mifflin Company, Boston, 1980.

Young, Ralph W., *Grizzlies Don't Come Easy,* Winchester Press, Tulsa, 1981.

MAGAZINES

————, "Alaskan Brown Bear, The," *Alaskan Bowman,* vol. 2, issue 1, pp. 32-34, fall-winter 1979-80.

Barkdull, Calvin H., "The Killers," *The ALASKA SPORTSMAN®,* pg. 36+, June 1954.

Bayou, Katherine, "Brownie in the Dark," *The ALASKA SPORTSMAN®,* pg. 30+, January 1946.

Bayou, Katherine, "The Forty-ninth Bear," *The ALASKA SPORTSMAN®,* pp. 14-15, 31-33, September 1945.

Blair, Wesley, "The Guides, On Guns and Targets," *ALASKA SPORTSMAN®,* pp. 45-46, April 1966.

Brandley, Kent, "Black Bear Rampage," *ALASKA SPORTSMAN®,* pp. 14, 18, November 1963.

Branham, Bud, "The Most Savage Animal on Earth," *Sports Afield,* vol. 169, no. 6, pp. 33-35, 86, 88, 90, June 1973.

Clarke, Tom E., "Indestructible Walker," *The ALASKA SPORTSMAN®,* December 1948.

Cole, Darci, "You Can't Panic," *ALASKA®* magazine, pp. 24, 58, June 1976.

Cole, Ron, "I Was Dying But Not Dead," *ALASKA®* magazine, pp. 22-24, June 1976.

Dufresne, Frank, "Groucho of the Wilds," *Reader's Digest* (condensed from *ALASKA SPORTSMAN®,* December 1963), pp. 121-125, December 1963.

Dufresne, Frank, "North America's Grouchiest Bear," *ALASKA SPORTSMAN®*, pp. 24, 45, December 1963.
Elwell, Niska, "At Your Peril," *The ALASKA SPORTSMAN®*, pp. 16-19, August 1951.
Elwell, Niska, "Freak Hits and Misses," *The ALASKA SPORTSMAN®*, pg. 13, July 1952.
Elwell, Niska, "Rogue," *The ALASKA SPORTSMAN®*, pp. 44-45, August 1958.
Elwell, Niska, "Stone Deaf Discard," *The ALASKA SPORTSMAN®*, April 1953.
Elwell, Niska, "Suddenly It Charged," *The ALASKA SPORTSMAN®*, pp. 6-9, 26-28, November 1952.
Elwell, Niska, "We've Known Some Interesting Bears," *ALASKA SPORTSMAN®*, pp. 10-11, 57-58, 60, March 1960.
Fales, E.D., Jr., "Glacier Park's Great Grizzly Bear Mystery," *Popular Mechanics*, pp. 82-88, 220, November 1968.
Ferguson, Val, "Killer Grizzly," *ALASKA SPORTSMAN®*, pp. 6-7, 45, November 1967.
Gabler, F.W., "Old Groaner," *The ALASKA SPORTSMAN®*, pp. 16-19, 28, February 1936.
Gorsline, Ted, "Man-Eating Black Bear," *Outdoor Life*, pp. 88, 100, 102, 104, 196, August 1978.
Harris, Lucille M., "Dick Jensen and the Bear," *The American Hunter*, pp. 63-66, August 1976.
Harris, Velma, "The Killing Ground," *Outdoor Life*, vol. 162, no. 5, pp. 62-67, November 1978.
Hess, Don, "We Weren't Afraid of Bears," *ALASKA®* magazine, pp. 18-19, August 1970.
Hillborn, John, "Chignik Trapper," *The ALASKA SPORTSMAN®*, pg. 13+, December 1937.
Hunter, Kathy, "Burch and the Bear," *ALASKA®* magazine, pg. A30, October 1977.
Huser, Vern, "Don't Feed the Bear," *Defenders of Wildlife News*, vol. 44, no. 3, pp. 302-307, July, August, September 1969.
Jackson, W.H., "Take a Snozzle Stick," *The ALASKA SPORTSMAN®*, October 1957.
Ludington, Dan, "My Last Grizzly," *Outdoor Life*, November 1959.
Madsen, Alf, "The Unpredictable Kodiak," *The ALASKA SPORTSMAN®*, pp. 6-9, 34-36, October 1955.
Madsen, Alf, "What Caliber for the Kodiak?" *The ALASKA SPORTSMAN®*, pp. 8-11, September 1957.
Mansell, Fred, "The Unknown Quantity," *The ALASKA SPORTSMAN®*, August 1938.
May, Joseph J., "The Toklat," *ALASKA®* magazine, pp. 38-39, April 1977.
McCully, Robert E., "A Brownie Had Me Up a Tree," *The ALASKA SPORTSMAN®*, December 1941.
McPhee, J.M., "Gregg's Meat," *The ALASKA SPORTSMAN®*, August 1949.
Moment, Gairdner B., "Bears: The Need for a New Sanity in Wildlife Conservation," *Bio Science*, vol. 18, no. 12, pp. 1105-1108, December 1968.
O'Neil, George, "Trials and Tribulations," *The ALASKA SPORTSMAN®*, pp. 10-11, 29-30, August 1937.
Pomeroy, E.H., "A Bear's Ambush," *The ALASKA SPORTSMAN®*, April 1939.
Popowski, Bert, "Bears and Bear Rifles," *The American Rifleman*, pp. 22-25, August 1966.

Prechter, Hans, "Bear on the Tracks," *ALASKA SPORTSMAN®,* February 1964.
Puhr, Conrad, "He Grappled With a Bear," *The ALASKA SPORTSMAN®,* March 1940.
Rearden, Jim, "Big Bear with a Bright Future," *Sports Afield,* vol. 165, no. 2, pp. 37-44, 107-110, February 1971.
Rearden, Jim, "Caribou: Hardy Nomads of the North," *National Geographic,* vol. 146, no. 6, pp. 858-878, December 1974.
Rearden, Jim, "The Kodiak Bear War," *Outdoor Life,* vol. 134, no. 2, pp. 17-19, 70-75, August 1964.
Reed, E. Stoy, "Man Meets Bear," *The ALASKA SPORTSMAN®,* January 1939.
Richey, David, "My God, I've Gotten Too Close!" *Outdoor Life,* vol. 161, no. 1, pp. 58-59, 134-136, January 1978.
Ross, Roland Case, "Sanity for Bears and People," *Defenders of Wildlife News,* vol. 44, no. 2, pp. 168-178, April, May, June 1969.
Sarber, Hosea, "Keep That Bolt Down," *The ALASKA SPORTSMAN®,* pp. 15-17, October 1936.
Saunders, Dan, "Hunt For A Man-killer Grizzly," *Sports Afield Hunting Annual,* pp. 26-29, 1976.
Schneider, Bill, "The Grizzly: Is He Villain or Victim?," *Outdoor Life,* vol. 156, no. 1, pp. 53-55, 128-129, January 1977.
Schneider, Bill, "Last Fight for the Grizzly," *Outdoor Life,* pp. 55-58, 137-140, January 1978.
Shankle, Perry, Jr., "Surprise Grizzly," *ALASKA®* magazine, pp. 54-55, 93, May 1977.
Smith, Harold E., "Jack Thayer Was Killed by a Bear," *ALASKA®* magazine, pp. 23, 62, August 1971.
Snow, C.R., "Bears of Southeastern Alaska," *The ALASKA SPORTSMAN®,* pp. 6-8, 21, 25-26, August 1936.
Speer, Otis H.,"Big Bears are Bold," *The ALASKA SPORTSMAN®,* December 1943.
Waugh, Hal, "More About Bears," *ALASKA SPORTSMAN®,* March 1964.
Williams, Carl, "My 40 Years With Bears," *Outdoor Life,* vol. 165, no. 2, pp. 82-85, 134-137, February 1980.
Young, Ralph W., "Brown Bears Do Attack," *Outdoor Life,* August 1959.

REPORTS
Bell, Sgt. William H., official report re: Robert MacGregor fatality, Alaska Department of Public Safety, July 23, 1976.
Bratlie, Art, memorandum re: bear attacks-human beings, Alaska Department of Fish & Game, Juneau, November 10, 1965.
Buskirk, Steve, "Chronology of Human Injury Inflicted by Grizzly Bears (in Mt. McKinley National Park)," 1976.
Herrero, Stephen, "Conflicts between Man and Grizzly Bears in the National Parks of North America," pg. 12, Third International Conference on Bears — Their Biology and Management, pp. 121-144, Binghamton, New York, Moscow, U.S.S.R., June 1974.
Herrero, Stephen, "Human Injury Inflicted by Grizzly Bears," *Science,* vol. 170, pp. 593-598, November 6, 1970.
Herrero, Stephen, "People and Grizzly Bears: The Challenge of Co-existence," paper delivered to John S. Wright Conference on "Wildlife and People," Purdue University, Lafayette, Indiana, February 1978.

Jones, Robert D., memorandum/official report re: extermination of bear (Jay B.L. Reeves), Izembek National Wildlife Range, Cold Bay, Alaska, August 7, 1974.

Jordan, Lt. Terry, memorandum/official report re: Cynthia Dusel-Bacon mauling, Alaska Department of Public Safety (Fish and Wildlife Protection), Fairbanks, Alaska, August 23, 1977.

Lancaster, Michael, official statement re: Robert MacGregor fatality, Alaska Department of Public Safety, July 23, 1976.

Sarvis, John E., official report re: Jay B.L. Reeves fatality, Izembek National Wildlife Range, Cold Bay, Alaska, August 3, 1974.

NEWSPAPERS

_____, "Bear attack case returns for retrial," *Anchorage Times*, May 9, 1980.

_____, "Bear attacks sleeping camper," *Anchorage Daily News*, July 23, 1975.

_____, "Bear Mauls Man," *Anchorage Times*, September 18, 1975.

_____, "Bear Mauls Sleeping Man," *Anchorage Times*, July 23, 1975.

Freeman, Nancy, "Fifty Years," *The Kodiak Fish Wrapper*, vol. 2, no. 5, May 1976.

_____, "Grizzly Bear Kills Photographer," *Anchorage Times*, August 5, 1974.

_____, "Grizzly Bear Mauls Hiker," *Anchorage Times*, August 8, 1979.

_____, "Hunter mauled by bear," *Anchorage Daily News*, September 18, 1975.

Janson, Lone E., "The Hazards of outhouses in Alaska," *Ruralite*, pg. 12, Portland, Oregon, March 1976.

Johnson, Harry A., "Sourdough Gave Grizzly Nine Bites," *Great Lander*, July 18, 1973.

_____, "Juneau Man OK After Mauling," *Anchorage Times*, October 31, 1978.

Hunter, Don, "Grizzly Is Shot After Chewing Pig, 'Scarfing' Duck," pg. 1, *Anchorage Times*, July 25, 1978.

Massey, Jay, "The Bear Problems," *Anchorage Times* (E-section, pg. 2), June 18, 1978.

_____, "Report Relates Attack By Bear," *Anchorage Times*, September 19, 1975.

Rogers, Barbara, "Woman Is Mauled By Bear," *Anchorage Times*, August 15, 1976.

_____, "State Can Be Responsible For Injuries Caused By Bears," *Anchorage Times*, August 25, 1979.

Index